ENABLING AND INSPIRING

ENABLING AND INSPIRING

A Tribute to Martha Harris

Edited by Meg Harris Williams

in consultation with
Maria Rhode, Margaret Rustin, and Gianna Polacco Williams

Published for
The Harris Meltzer Trust

by

KARNAC

Published in 2012 for The Harris Meltzer Trust
by Karnac Books Ltd.
118 Finchley Road, London NW3 5HT

Copyright © 2012 individual authors of chapters
Copyright © 2012 Meg Harris Williams for editorial matter

The rights of the authors have been asserted in accordance with
§§ 77 and 78 of the Copyright Design and Patent Act 1988.

All rights reserved. No part of this publication may be reproduced, stored in a retrieval system, or transmitted, in any form or by any means, electronic, mechanical, photocopying, recording, or otherwise, without the prior written permission of the publisher.

British Library Cataloguing in Publication Data
A C.I.P. for this book is available from the British Library

ISBN 978 1 78049 106 6

Edited, designed and produced by The Bourne Studios
www.bournestudios.co.uk

www.harris-meltzer-trust.org.uk
www.karnacbooks.com

CONTENTS

About Martha Harris ix
About the authors xi
Preface by Meg Harris Williams xxiii

PART I
In England and abroad

1 *Mattie at work*
    Gianna Polacco Williams   1

2 *Mattie as an educator*
    Margaret Rustin   11

3 *Mattie's teaching methods*
    Ann Cebon   19

4 *Mattie's contribution to the study of infant observation*
    Janine Sternberg   25

5	*A psychoanalytic revolution from a speculative to an empirical point of view* Didier Houzel	33
6	*The role of Martha Harris from the beginning of the GERPEN* James Gammill	39
7	*Martha Harris: an indelible creative memory* Carlo Brutti and Rita Parlani Brutti	45
8	*Made in Hampstead and exported throughout the world: Germany and Austria* Ross A. Lazar	53
9	*Mattie in Bombay* Sarosh Forbes	63
10	*Turning points enabled by Martha Harris* Marja Schulman	67
11	*Growing points and the role of observation* Meg Harris Williams	77

PART II
Clinical work and supervision

12	*The experience of supervision* Catrin Bradley	85
13	*Mattie as "maternal container" for a trainee* Evanthe Blandy	99
14	*A glimpse of prenatal life* Romana Negri	109
15	*Assessment of a little girl and her parents* Simona Nissim	125

16 *Supervision of a five year old boy*
    Andrea Watson   141

17 *Revisiting some lessons learned from Martha Harris*
    Dina Vallino   153

18 *Reminiscences of an infant observation with Martha Harris*
    Angela Goyena   163

19 *Family consultations in the footsteps of Martha Harris with toddlers at risk of autism*
    Maria Rhode   197

PART III
Personal recollections

20 *Shorter recollections*
    Gabrielle Crockatt, Hélène Dubinsky, Ellen Jaffe, Judy Shuttleworth, Brian Truckle, Eleanor Wigglesworth, Ricky Emanuel, Katherine Arnold, Herbert Chaim Hahn, Carlo Papuzza, Maria Pozzi, Renata Li Causi, Torhild Leira, Eve Steel   211

21 *Memories of Mattie*
    Valerie Sinason   231

22 *Mattie's legacy*
    Asha Phillips   241

23 *Mattie on maternal containment*
    Anne Alvarez   249

24 *Baptism under fire: finding my feet as a child psychotherapist*
    Caroline Gluckman   255

25	*On becoming a psychotherapist* Margot Waddell	265
26	*Remembering Mattie* Alessandra Piontelli	271
27	*Personal recollections of learning from Mattie Harris* Pamela Sorensen	279
28	*Mattie's house: a memoir* Selina Sella Marsoni	285
29	*A tribute to Mattie* Patricia Kenwood	309
	Postscript: among schoolchildren Meg Harris Williams	313
	Appendix: Portrait of Mattie Donald Meltzer	325
	References	329
	Name index	337
	Subject index	340

ABOUT MARTHA HARRIS

Martha Harris (1919-1987) was born Martha Gemmell Dunlop in Beith, Ayrshire. She read English at University College London, and then Psychology at Oxford. She worked for some years as a schoolteacher, specializing in history, and taught in a Froebel Teacher Training College. She trained as a psychologist at Guy's Hospital, then as a psychoanalyst at the British Institute of Psychoanalysis, where she was a training analyst; her own supervisors were Melanie Klein and Wilfred Bion and her analyst Herbert Rosenfeld. She worked very closely with Esther Bick and in 1960 became responsible for the Child Psychotherapy training which Bick had established at the Tavistock. She developed this in many innovative ways, making use of both her Kleinian and her teacher-training experience. This course came to attract a very international range of candidates and to become a model for psychoanalytically-oriented clinic work with children and families in many countries (the "Tavi Model").

Together with her husband Roland Harris, poet and teacher, Martha Harris started a pioneering schools' counselling service. Roland Harris died in 1969 and she subsequently married

Donald Meltzer (psychoanalyst). They taught widely throughout Europe, Scandinavia, North and South America, and India; and established the Roland Harris Educational Trust, which published for thirty years as the Clunie Press. This activity has continued as the Harris Meltzer Trust.

Martha Harris wrote newspaper articles on child development and the family (the first in 1964), and organized a series of books for parents, written by Tavistock therapists, published as Corgi Mini-books in 1969. *Understanding Infants and Young Children* was also published in 1969, followed by an expanded edition entitled *Thinking about Infants and Young Children* (1975) which has been published in many languages (new edition 2011). Her books on older children (*Your Eleven Year Old*, *Your Twelve to Fourteen Year Old* and *Your Teenager*) have since been reprinted in one volume as *Your Teenager* (Harris Meltzer Trust, 2007).

In 1976, at the request of the UN Organization for Economic and Cultural Development, she collaborated with Donald Meltzer on *A Psychoanalytical Model of the Child-in-the-Family-in-the-Community*, written for multidisciplinary use in schools and therapeutic units. Her many papers on psychoanalytic training, clinical work, and child development, were first collected (though not completely) in *Collected Papers of Martha Harris and Esther Bick* (Clunie Press, 1987) and have since been republished in two volumes: *The Tavistock Model: Papers on Child Development and Psychoanalytic Training by Martha Harris and Esther Bick* and *Adolescence: Talks and Papers by Donald Meltzer and Martha Harris* (edited by M. H. Williams, Harris Meltzer Trust, 2011).

For a full list of Martha Harris' publications see http://www.harris-meltzer-trust.org.uk/MarthaHarris.html.

ABOUT THE AUTHORS

Anne Alvarez is a Consultant Child and Adolescent Psychotherapist and is retired co-Chair for the Autism Service at the Tavistock Clinic, London. She is currently a visiting teacher and lecturer for the Tavistock, and a lecturer on the San Francisco Psychoanalytic Society Child Programme.

Katherine Arnold originally trained as an anthropologist. She trained at the Tavistock as a Child Psychotherapist and then also in work with adults. She teaches on the M16 course in Psychoanalytic Studies at the Tavistock and on various other psychoanalytic trainings. She struggles, in various family contexts and with variable success, with the systems of care we have for vulnerable people: in which she is sustained by family, friends and psychoanalytic thinking.

Evanthe Blandy (née Piper) is a Cambridge graduate in Philosophy and Fine Art. She became a primary school teacher with a view to becoming a child therapist. Mattie accepted her for the training in 1974 and she remained there under her tutelage until qualifying in 1983. Since then she has been in private practice in London, providing therapy for children and adults, consultation, and supervision. In 1995 she became a member of the Guild of Psychotherapists and from 1998 helped to set up and maintain a low fee psychotherapy clinic for disadvantaged people in the London borough of Southwark.

Catrin Bradley (née Hunter) trained as a child psychotherapist at the Tavistock in the early 1980s and worked in inner London Child and Adolescent Mental Health Services in Hackney and in Camden before taking up a post at the Tavistock in 2004. She is currently head of the Tavistock Child Psychotherapy Clinical Training.

Carlo Brutti (medical doctor) and **Rita Parlani Brutti** (therapist) are both psychoanalysts. Together with Marcella Balconi they inaugurated a series of seminars with Donald Meltzer and Martha Harris that for many years took place in Perugia. Here they founded the Aberastury Institute (*Istituto di Ricerca Clinica in Psicosomatica Psicoanalitica A. Aberastury*), which includes the Chiozza School of Psychoanalytic Psychotherapy (*Scuola di Specializzazione in Psicoterapia Psicoanalitica Secondo lo Sviluppo di Luis Chiozza*). They edit the journal *La Psicoanalisi che Viene* (Eidon, Perugia). Website: istitutoaberastury.com.

Ann Cebon studied Sociology and Psychology at the University of California, Berkeley, and is a Registered Psychologist. She trained as a child psychotherapist at the Tavistock Clinic and worked in London from 1966 to 1975, when she moved to Melbourne, Australia. She is a psychoanalytic psychotherapist, and continues to practise, supervise, teach and write. One of her special interests is in the uses of the observational method both in training and in emotional understanding.

Gabrielle Crockatt worked as a child psychotherapist in the NHS, with breaks when she had children, from 1972 until 2009. She is now retired from the NHS, but is senior tutor on the Child Psychotherapy training at the Scottish Institute of Human Relations.

Hélène Dubinsky is a child and adolescent psychotherapist and an adult psychotherapist. She is co-editor and contributing author to *Psychotic States in Children* (1997), co-author of *Understanding Your 15-17 Year Old*, and has contributed chapters to *Exploring Eating Disorders* edited by Gianna Williams (2003), and to several books on adolescents.

Ricky Emanuel is a Consultant Child, Adolescent and Adult Psychotherapist trained at the Tavistock. He works at the Royal Free Hospital in London and teaches at the Tavistock Clinic and for the Trust for Psychoanalytic Psychotherapy in Birmingham. He teaches regularly in Florence at the Centro Studi Martha Harris and is a founding member of the Centro Studi Martha Harris in Palermo.

Sarosh Forbes is a training analyst and child psychotherapist (trained at the Tavistock). He is also a founder member of the Psychoanalytic Therapy and Research Centre, and the founder and organizer of the biannual India-Australia-Israel Psychoanalytic Conference. He is actively involved in teaching and supervising psychoanalytic work in Mumbai, India. His main interests are in psychoanalytic technique, particularly in following the experiences of the analyst closely while with his patient. He is also the author of several publications which include "The study of a defense system in a two year baby observation" and "A clinical study of the unconscious – Freud to Klein to the present day".

James Gammill trained as a medical doctor at Cornell and as an adult and child psychoanalyst with the British Psychoanalytical Society where in the 1950s he was a co-supervisee of Mrs Klein's with Martha Harris, and also worked with Donald Meltzer at the US Air Force hospital in Ruislip. After a period practising psychiatry in Nashville, Tennessee, he returned to Europe and became a training analyst in the Paris Psychoanalytical Society. In 1974 he set up the GERPEN (*Groupe d'Études et de Recherches Psychanalytiques pour le Développement de l'Enfant et du Nourrisson*) which began with regular visits to France by Harris and Meltzer. Dr Gammill is retired but still teaches and supervises child analysts and psychotherapists.

Caroline Gluckman is a graduate of both the Tavistock child and adult trainings. She has worked as a Consultant Child and Adolescent Psychotherapist for Berkshire NHS Healthcare Trust for over 20 years, and is now working mainly in private practice with adults and children, and supervising. She runs a baby observation seminar for the Tavistock M7 Observation Course.

Angela Goyena is a psychoanalyst in private practice in Paris, where she sees adults and adolescents. She is a *membre adhérent* of the Paris Psychoanalytical Society and an associate member of the International Psychoanalytical Association.

Herbert Chaim Hahn trained as child psychotherapist with Mattie in the 1960s while working as a clinical psychologist at the Cassel Hospital and occupational psychologist at the Tavistock Institute. He subsequently also trained at the London Institute of Psychoanalysis; and in group analysis, group relations and social dreaming matrices; and became Principal Child Psychotherapist and Chair of staff at the London Child Guidance Training Centre, and Head of Human Resources in the European School of Management Studies. He then moved to Bristol where he co-founded the Severnside Institute psychoanalytic adult training and membership society, and now lives in Australia, where he works as a supervisor, consultant and facilitator with individuals, groups and organizations.

Didier Houzel is *Professeur Émérite* of Child and Adolescent Psychiatry at the University of Caen, and full member of the French Psychoanalytic Association. He was the winner of the Frances Tustin Memorial Prize in 2002. He has worked with several Kleinian psychoanalysts: James Gammill in Paris, Donald Meltzer in London, Frances Tustin in Amersham.

Ellen S. Jaffe trained at the Tavi from 1974-78; she moved to Ontario, Canada in 1979 where she still works as a therapist and also as a writer and teacher of creative writing. In addition to poetry in many journals, she has published three books, *Writing Your Way: Creating a Personal Journal; Water Children* (poetry), and *Feast of Lights*, a young-adult novel. Marja Schulman (who trained at the Tavi during the same years as Ellen) edited a Finnish-English collection of some of her poems, *Syntymalauluja/Birth Songs*, published in 2005 by the Therapeia Foundation in Helsinki; these poems were influenced by Mattie's approach to infants and parents.

Patricia Kenwood did the Tavistock Child Psychotherapy Training after two years of clinical and psychology research experience following her BA in Psychology at Melbourne. She worked in the Department of Children and Parents, then returned to Australia, where she established and ran infant observation and clinical seminars for staff doing child psychotherapy at the Royal Children's Hospital. She also helped to set up the training programme in psychoanalytic psychotherapy for the Victorian Association of Psychotherapists. She became a member of the Australian Psychoanalytical Society, the International Psychoanalytic Association, and, subsequently, a training analyst. Pat has taught and supervised child and adult psychotherapists, psychiatrists, psychoanalysts and psychoanalytic candidates. She is a past Chair of the Melbourne branch of the Australian Society and of the Society's education co-ordinating committee. Pat worked with Harold Bridger on several Group Relations conferences in France and the UK. She also worked as a Senior Lecturer in the Master's course in Psychoanalytical Studies at Monash University. Now retired from clinical practice, she continues with some committee work for the Australian Psychoanalytical Society and with consultations to colleagues, and as a member of the advisory committees for child analysis and the appointment of training analysts.

Ross A. Lazar took a BA in the History of Art at the University of Michigan, then an MA in Teaching at the Harvard University Graduate School of Education. In the 1970s he trained as a psychoanalytic child and adolescent psychotherapist at the Tavistock Clinic under the auspices of Mattie Harris, qualifying in 1976. He then moved to Munich where he worked at the Biederstein Zentrum for Child and Adolescent Psychotherapy in the medical faculty of the Technical University of Munich. Since 1982 he has been in private practice as a psychoanalytic psychotherapist with adults, couples and families, and supervises clinical work. He is guest professor at the Institute for Research and Further Education in Vienna and Klagenfur, and at the University of Vienna, and a supervisor and coach at INSEAD, Fontainebleau.

Torhild Leira is an child analyst in Oslo; she had supervision with Martha Harris and Donald Meltzer over many years, with other psychoanalytic trainees in Norway, from the early 1970s onwards.

Renata Li Causi is a child and adult psychoanalyst in full time private psychoanalytic practice. Formerly she worked for several years at Paddington Green Child Psychiatry Department, as Senior Child Psychotherapist.

Selina Sella Marsoni began her training under Marcella Balconi in Novara. She then trained as a child psychotherapist at the Tavistock in the early 1970s, under the tutelage of Martha Harris, Frances Tustin and Isca Wittenberg. She trained with adult patients at the BAP under the guidance of Donald Meltzer, Roger Money-Kyrle and Arthur Hyatt Williams. From 1971 she worked at the Child Guidance in Barnet, London, and in private practice. From 1980 she taught regularly in Genoa and Palermo, and in 1985 returned to her home town of Biella in northern Italy, where she set up the *Gruppo Studi Martha Harris*. She retired from private practice in 2008 but continues to teach and supervise, and also conducts courses at the Tempia Foundation.

Romana Negri graduated in Medicine and trained as a child neuropsychiatrist at the Child Neuropsychiatry Institute of Milan University. From 1970 on she attended the seminars of Martha Harris and Donald Meltzer and commenced work projects inspired by them, meanwhile training as psychotherapist. From 1976 to 2004 she was a consultant in the Special Care Baby Unit at the Treviglio-Caravaggio Hospital, publishing some of her research findings in *The Newborn in the Intensive Care Unit* (Clunie Press, 1994; also published in Italy, 1994, 1998 and 2012, and Greece, 2002). She has published an account of supervisions with Martha Harris, *The Story of Infant Development* (Harris Meltzer Trust, 2007), also in Italian (*Andare Osservando un Bambino: La Lezione di Martha Harris*, Borla, 2008). Since 1982 she has been a professor at Milan University teaching in the paediatric department of the School of Psychiatry and Psychology.

Simona Nissim is a child neuropsychiatrist, psychoanalyst (SPA, IPA), psychoanalytic psychotherapist for children, adolescents and families, Tavistock model (CSMH Florence). She works in Pisa. She is Director of the School of Specialization, and is a training teacher and supervisor of the clinical and observation courses of the Centro Studi Martha Harris in Florence and in Venice. Since 2009, she has been European Coordinator of the child and adolescent section within the EFPP Executive. She is on the M7 Masters exams board (Tavistock/ UEL), and has been a visiting teacher at the Tavistock's summer course on disruptive adolescents. Her main areas of interest are autism, the mother-infant relationship, and infant-observation, in both clinical training and research.

Carlo Papuzza is a psychotherapist for children and adolescents and adults, trained by analysts of the SPI (Italian Psychoanalytic Society). He has also worked as a teacher: first of literary subjects at the State School, then psychological disciplines at the Universities of Padua (1974-1980) and Palermo (1980-2009). From 1984 to 1986 he followed a Tavistock model course in Italy.

Alessandra Piontelli, MD, is a psychiatrist, neurologist, and psychoanalyst. She qualified as a child psychotherapist at the Tavistock Clinic. Dr Piontelli is the author of many publications and of five books: *Backwards in Time* (Clunie Press, 1985), *From Fetus to Child* (Routledge, London 1992), *Twins: from Fetus to Child* (Routledge, London 2002), *Twins in the World* (Macmillan, New York, 2008), *Development of Normal Human Fetal Movements* (Springer-Verlag, Heidelberg/Milano 2010).

Asha Phillips (née Bhownagary) is a child, adolescent and family psychotherapist trained at the Tavistock Centre in London. She has worked in social services and educational settings as well as in a hospital paediatric department, including their Special Care Baby Unit. At present she works privately, seeing children, families and couples. She specializes in work during the perinatal period and with children under five. She has been teaching since 1985 on various courses and training programmes for psychotherapists. She is a visiting lecturer at the

Tavistock Centre and lectures both in the UK and abroad. She has published in the *Journal of Child Psychotherapy* and edited issues of the *International Journal of Infant Observation* and is the author of *Saying No: Why it's Important for You and Your Child* (Faber, 1999) which has been translated into 12 languages.

Maria Pozzi is a child and adolescent therapist in CAMHS and an adult psychotherapist privately. She has special interests in treating children with autism, Asperger's syndrome, mental handicap, and in brief work with infants and children under five and their families. She is a visiting tutor at the Tavistock and for the BAP, and teaches and lectures in Italy and Switzerland. She has a doctorate in psychoanalytic research into the process of change in brief work with families of children under five. Her publications include the book *Psychic Hooks and Bolts* (Karnac, 2003), *I Disagi dei Bambini* (Mondadori, 2004), and *Innovations in Parent-Infant Psychotherapy* (Karnac, 2007), as well as papers and book chapters on various topics. She was the winner of the Frances Tustin Memorial Prize in 1990.

Maria Rhode is Emeritus Professor of Child Psychotherapy at the Tavistock Clinic/University of East London, member of the Association of Child Psychotherapists and the Tavistock Society of Psychotherapists and Associate of the British Psychoanalytical Society. She works as honorary consultant child and adolescent psychotherapist at the Tavistock, where she formerly co-convened the Autism Workshop. She has published widely on autism, childhood psychosis, language development and infant observation. Mattie Harris supervised her first training case.

Margaret Rustin is Consultant Child and Adolescent Psychotherapist at the Tavistock. She was Head of Child Psychotherapy from 1986 – 2007, and also served as Dean and later Chair of the Professional Committee of the Trust. She has had a career-long interest in the growth of child psychotherapy practice and training both in the UK and beyond and taught in many parts of the world. Her publications are rooted in a belief in the wide relevance of psychoanalytic thinking. Her most recent book, co-edited with Jonathan Bradley, is *Work*

Discussion (Tavistock Series, Karnac, 2008). She is also a qualified adult psychotherapist and has a child and adult private practice in London.

Marja Schulman has an MA in Psychology and trained as a child, adolescent and adult psychotherapist at the Tavistock between 1973 and 1981. She has a private practice in Espoo, Finland, and has been a training supervisor and teacher of the Child Psychotherapy course at the Therapeia Foundation since 1987. She was organizing tutor for the Child Psychotherapy Training from 1990-2012, and since 2009, has been Chair of the Finnish Association of the Child Psychotherapists. She teaches infant observation and is the author of *Baby Observation* (2002), co-author and co-editor of *The Child Psychotherapist* (in Finnish, 2007). With George Crawford she taught and supervised child psychotherapy and infant observation in Estonia from 1995 to 2008.

Judy Shuttleworth, following her training, has worked as a child psychotherapist in the NHS, and in the training of child psychotherapists. Returning to the subject of her first degree, social anthropology, she is currently undertaking a study of a London mosque congregation – the dimension of community in that nesting of "the-child-in-the-family-in-the-community ' of which Mattie wrote.

Valerie Sinason is a poet, writer, child psychotherapist and adult psychoanalyst. She is Director of the Clinic for Dissociative Studies and President of the Institute for Psychotherapy and Disability. She is an honorary Consultant Psychotherapist at the Cape Town Child Guidance Clinic, University of Cape Town. Her latest edited book *Trauma, Dissociation and Multiplicity: Working with Identity and Selves* has just been published by Routledge (2012).

Pamela B. Sorensen, PhD, trained as a child psychotherapist at the Tavistock in the 1970s. She was Director of the Under Fives Study Center at the University of Virginia for many years and now provides supervision and consultation from her base in

Charlottesville, Virginia. She has published on a range of topics including infant observation, the concept of containment, and work with parents and children together.

Eve Steel did the child psychotherapy training under Mattie in the 60s and later became a senior member of the CPT staff in the Adolescent Unit, working closely with Arthur Hyatt Williams. She also trained as a psychoanalyst at the London Institute of Psychoanalysis. She has worked in Melbourne, Australia since 1981, as a psychoanalyst, supervisor, teacher and academic; and has presented papers at home and abroad. Currently she works in clinical, supervisory and consultant roles with senior professionals and organizations.

Janine Sternberg is a Consultant Child Psychotherapist at the Portman Clinic, Tavistock and Portman NHS Foundation Trust, having worked for many years at the Tavistock Mulberry Bush Day Unit, a small unit for children with complex difficulties. She trained originally as a child psychotherapist at the Tavistock Clinic and subsequently as an adult psychotherapist at the BAP. She is very involved in training issues and active in the ACP. She has written a book which addresses what capacities and skills are needed for psychotherapeutic work and how these may be enhanced by infant observation (*Infant Observation at the Heart of Training,* 2005). She has been editor of the *Journal of Child Psychotherapy* and editorial coordinator of the *British Journal of Psychotherapy.*

Brian Truckle qualified as a psychiatric social worker and worked in a variety of voluntary and statutory health and social services settings before becoming a member of the senior staff at the Tavistock Clinic where he also trained as a child and adolescent psychotherapist. For 22 years he was Head of Child Psychotherapy and family therapy services at Birmingham Children's Hospital. He currently teaches part-time at the Birmingham School of Child Psychotherapy (BTPP).

Dina Vallino is a training analyst of the Italian Psychoanalytical Society (SPI) and an infant observation teacher. During the years 1991-1999, she was project leader of a training programme for crèche and nursery school educators and teachers in Milan. In 1998, she published *Raccontami una Storia* which was awarded the Gradiva Prize, a prestigious annual prize for the best Italian book on psychoanalysis. After this, she published with Marco Macciò *Essere Neonati: Osservazioni Psicoanalitiche* (Borla, 2004), in which the newborn's relationship with the mother is studied through observations of dozens of children in the family setting. More recently, in *Fare Psicoanalisi con Genitori e Bambini* (Borla, 2009), she updated the approach to children's diagnostic consultations, through her own technique of participant consultation. She is based in Milan, where she works full-time as a psychoanalyst of adults and children.

Margot Waddell is a Fellow of the British Institute of Psychoanalysis and a Consultant Child Psychotherapist in the Adolescent Department of the Tavistock Clinic, London. She has taught and published widely in areas covering the whole lifespan, both literary and clinical. Her most recent books are *Inside Lives: Psychoanalysis and the Growth of the Personality* (Karnac) and *Understanding 12 - 14 Year Olds* (Jessica Kingsley).

Andrea Watson completed the Observational Studies course in both Oxford and London, and then took up a clinical trainee post in Aylesbury, Bucks. She stayed there until her final retirement from the NHS in January 2012. She has been a joint organizing tutor of the Oxford Observational Studies course since its inception and has also taught at the Tavistock Clinic and on observational and clinical courses in Italy. She currently teaches in Bologna and practices privately in Oxford.

Eleanor Wigglesworth worked for many years as a child and adolescent psychotherapist in the NHS, trained more recently as an adult psychotherapist, and now continues in private practice near Henley on Thames, where she sees adults and young people.

Meg Harris Williams, elder daughter of Martha Harris, is a writer and artist. She read English and Cambridge and Oxford. Her books are: *Inspiration in Milton and Keats* (1982), *A Strange Way of Killing: the Poetic Structure of Wuthering Heights (1987),*

The Apprehension of Beauty: the Role of Aesthetic Conflict in Development, Art and Violence (with Donald Meltzer, 1988), *The Chamber of Maiden Thought* (with Margot Waddell, 1991), *Five Tales from Shakespeare* (for children, 1996), *A Trial of Faith: Hamlet in Analysis* (1997), *The Vale of Soulmaking: the PostKleinian Model of the Mind, The Aesthetic Development: the Poetic Spirit of Psychoanalysis* (2010) *and Bion's Dream* (2010). Website: www.artlit.info.

Gianna Polacco Williams started teaching at the Tavistock Clinic in 1970 in the course on the Emotional Aspects of Learning and Teaching initiated by Martha and Roland Harris. She has worked at the Tavistock Clinic as a Consultant Child Psychotherapist and has been responsible for the course in Psychoanalytic Observational Studies for many years. She has developed Courses in Child Psychotherapy and Observational Studies in European and Latin American Countries, and founded a number of *Centri Studi Martha Harris* in Italy. She has published widely and was awarded a honorary doctorate in Education by the Tavistock Clinic and the University of East London. She currently teaches for the Tavistock/UEL professional doctorate and works as a psychoanalyst in private practice.

PREFACE

As the twenty-fifth anniversary of my mother Martha Harris' death approached (November 2011), several of her ex-students expressed the wish to revisit and record their own learning experience with her. "Enabling" and "inspiring" were terms she used herself to convey the educational process that takes place between student and teacher, or the self and its internal objects. As she put it: "Introjection is a mysterious process about which we have almost everything to learn" (1978a, p. 176). She stressed how in psychoanalysis, the child or patient introjects not merely the content of the analyst's thought but also the thinking process, which strengthens his own internal objects' capacity to think. An analogous process can occur in attentive reading, making intimate contact with the mind of the author, whether or not they have been known in life.

The intention of this book therefore was not to build a monument on the lines satirized by Byron in his description of King Cheops' pyramid: "thinking it was just the thing/ To keep his memory whole, and mummy hid" (*Don Juan*, I. 221-22). Nor was it solely to paint a collective portrait of someone who was a much-loved friend and teacher of so many people during her lifetime, consistently experienced as being "unique". Rather, it was to present a model/view of introjective learning that would invite future readers to share in the values embodied by Mattie as internal object. As we know from psychoanalytic theory, mourning as a mental exercise is the foundation of all thinking processes from the earliest experience of the "absent breast". The fact that a particular person no longer exists in the external world is no barrier to the internalization of their mental qualities, as we know well from the very fact that we continue to read the classics, perpetually astonished to discover how accurately some author from a bygone age and culture has understood us – that is to say, can endow our world with meaning.

This does depend of course on some type of written record being available. We hope this book will encourage new readers to explore the complex understanding of human relations that is to be found through the close reading of Martha Harris' own finely crafted books and papers; these are classics of their kind, and unusual amongst psychoanalytic writings in the depth of meaning that underlies their apparent simplicity, their elegance of style, and sensitivity to the reader. In this book of tributes will be found testimony to the practical innovations in clinical settings and in psychoanalytic education that resulted from her personal vision, and from her conviction that psychoanalytic ideas could and would "travel" – both geographically to other countries, and laterally to other professions.

Despite her huge influence on a generation of child psychotherapists and analysts, it has often been found difficult to trace in any formal way the provenance of ideas that undoubtedly originated with her and were a natural feature of her humanitarian vision – her "gardening" attitude to the psychoanalytic world, with the requirement to sow and bear fruit. Sometimes this elusiveness has been put down to excessive modesty on her part; sometimes to gender (she eschewed the traditional "male"-colonial habit of labelling an idea in order to acquire possession of it); sometimes to her democratic-style techniques for developing confidence amongst all the participants of a particular task.

It also however had its roots in a belief that unless ideas did travel and find their own form in other minds and places, they would disappear or fossilize; and therefore it was important not to "fix" them through any too concrete attribution.

Nonetheless the fact remains that the flavour of her personality was in a sense a necessary aspect of her green-fingered approach to making psychoanalytic ideas fertile. So we also hope that the personal intimacy of the "memories" recounted in the book will enable a special kind of identification with the process of coming to knowledge that will add direction to new readers' experience of reading Martha Harris' own writings.

Probably it is only since Bion's theory of thinking that psychoanalysis has had the conceptual framework for investigating how the mind builds itself, through gratitude and introjective processes, as distinct from how it fragments itself through envy and projection. The personal accounts in this book, based on the self-reflection of several decades, model this process of mindbuilding, with the aid of a teacher-become-internal object. As a model, it is universally applicable, since it is dependent on internal objects, not external ones. The many authors here represented chose their own mode of writing about their experience, past and present. These include overviews of Mattie's work both in England and abroad; some cases of clinical work or supervision with her or closely related to her; and personal recollections in the form of essays or of vivid recollections of particular moments that have infused the future development of one-time students who are now, some thirty years later, in a position to review their careers.

Some of these recollections will also testify to the subtlety of Martha Harris' often-misunderstood principle of "assisted self-selection". This did not mean accepting all comers and waiting to see who dropped out. On the contrary, if she felt someone was unsuitable to be a candidate for her course, she adamantly resisted pressure from colleagues to take them on. In her interviews she was looking for something less easily defined than answers to questions – for a capacity to identify with the child within and to enable its growth.

Enabling and Inspiring is therefore, we hope, a gateway not to a closed possessive mausoleum of hidden treasures, but to a spiritual sharing of enriching values, wisdom and educational innovation, much of which is still in advance of our time and not yet really implemented. As Donald Meltzer wrote of the principles that lay behind the teaching method she established at the Tavistock in the 1960s:

> The central conviction, later hallowed in Bion's concept of "learning from experience", was that the kind of learning which transformed a person into a professional worker had to be rooted in the intimate relations with inspired teachers, living and dead, present and in books. (Meltzer, 1988; 2011, pp. 345-46).

This book is about the kind of learning that transforms a person into a professional worker.

Meg Harris Williams, May 2012

CHAPTER ONE

Mattie at work

Gianna Polacco Williams[1]

As you may read in the biography written by Meg Harris Williams (1989), Mattie's grandfather was called Mazzini McClure and it sounds as if he was a man worthy of his revolutionary name. The revolution that took place in the courses Mattie was responsible for in the 60s and 70s is evidence that she was worthy of her grandfather's name.

The four-year course in Child Psychotherapy that Mattie inherited from Esther Bick in 1960 was a course with limited places. Two or three people started every other year, with very rigorous selection. This included a session with a psychiatrist. In the early days, whoever was accepted was, from the start, a student in Child Psychotherapy, although they only started their clinical work after a period of Infant Observation and Theory seminars.

Gradually, Mattie adopted a totally different approach, offering much freer access to a two-year course. It was initially called the Pre-clinical Course, but gradually acquired greater autonomy and became a course in its own right. The first title of the new ourse was Course in Observational Studies and the Application

---

1 Translated and revised from *Quaderni* no 18 (Williams, G. P., 1989).

of Psychoanalytic Concepts to Work with Children, Adolescents and Families.[2] As the title was so long, it was often referred to as the Observation Course or M7 (this was the code used by the training office when referring to the course). The outline of the original course in Child Psychotherapy was radically modified.

It was made very clear that in order to start the Child Psychotherapy training, it was necessary first to have completed the M7 course. It was a prerequisite, just as having a degree was a prerequisite. Whoever applied to the M7 course was generally accepted after just one meeting, so long as: he or she had some experience of working with children, adolescents or families; was currently involved in working with children, adolescents or families; and was prepared to commit himself or herself seriously to the considerable amount of work that the course involved. This meant a minimum of 15 hours per week, spread between observations, writing reports and attending seminars, in addition to the work itself (as teacher, nurse etc).

The number of teachers on the course increased considerably and, by the mid-1970s, it was possible to accept up to 20 full-time students every year. For two years, the students took part in four weekly seminars. The most important seminar, alongside the Infant Observation seminar, was one of Mattie's important inventions: the Work Discussion seminar (see the book by Rustin & Bradley, 2008).

We are so familiar with the structure of the course as it is today, that it is hard to imagine it without this essential component. It is also difficult to realize how original it was to introduce this seminar into a course that was initially called "pre-clinical". It provided an opportunity to apply psychoanalytical concepts to work carried out in very different contexts. At times, a seminar with five members might present five different work contexts, often far removed from a 50-minute clinical session.

It was quite an experience to see Mattie at work in this seminar. One could feel how genuine her respect was for the meaning of therapeutic interactions, such as, for instance, the work of a paediatric nurse with a sick child; how she really believed and managed to put across that psychoanalytic ideas can and must

---

2 See Martha Harris' (1979) description of the course in *The Tavistock Gazette*.

be exported in order to deepen the understanding of interactions in different types of work. This seminar, in particular, began to attract students who had no intention of changing their work, but only wished to improve the way they currently worked.

Increasingly, some people applied for M7 with the intention of training later as a child psychotherapist, but, while taking the course, discovered the potential for therapeutic interaction within their own work. They felt enriched by the psychoanalytic perspective offered by the Work Discussion – as well as the rest of the course – and realized that they had no real motivation to change the work they were doing.

I remember, for instance, the head teacher of a secondary school who had started M7 as a prerequisite for the clinical training, with the intention of changing her profession. During the two years of the course in Observational Studies, she implemented very meaningful changes in the school where she worked. She also realized that she had no wish to abandon her role as head teacher. As far as I know, Mrs M remained for many years as the head teacher of one of the most forward-thinking schools in London, in terms of its development of counselling for students, open attitudes to parents, and helping teachers to understand the emotional problems of the students. At least two or three teachers from this school took part each year in the Tavistock course on the Emotional Aspects of the Learning and Teaching Relationship, a course initiated in the 60s by Martha Harris and her husband Roland Harris.

It seems to me that two factors were central to the climate that Mattie created in her course over the years: she was responsible both for the course in Observational Studies *and* the clinical training. This atmosphere made the choice of students as free and as devoid of basic assumptions as possible. It was easy to enter the course if one really wished to do so and I am sure that this astonished people during their first meeting with Mattie. I saw this astonishment when people had their first meeting with me when I took over the course in 1979.

The second factor was that people really felt that Mattie sincerely valued a psychoanalytic perspective in *all* work contexts. The easy access and the value put on applied psychoanalysis helped to erode the elitist element, which can so easily lead to wrong choices, such as students applying for the clinical training even without strong motivation, just to be amongst the "chosen" ones.

I remember that Mattie was annoyed when some of the teachers continued, in the early days, to call M7 the "pre-clinical" course, as this gave her the feeling that we had really understood nothing of the changes close to her heart. This obviously did not help them to feel that they had completed a meaningful piece of work with the Observational Studies course, which was not supposed to be "pre-" anything. (Now, in fact, M7 has become a PgDip/ MA so even more a course in its own right.)

We used to have tutors' meetings, but Mattie never sat us down to talk about the importance of the change in the course title. Making a pronouncement like that would have been very alien to her.

She had a great deal of patience with people who took time to take in new ideas and to develop a coherence that really came from within – the only kind that she valued. She didn't suffer an adhesive type of conformity gladly. At times I might have wished to find her a little more directive, as I might have avoided some mistakes, but I understand – perhaps only now, years afterwards – the reason for her resistance to establishing a party line. Mrs M, the head teacher, applied to the course when Mattie was still organizing tutor. Mattie was her personal tutor, and she took part in the Work Discussion with Mattie. In her case, the "assisted self-selection", as Mattie called it, was not a difficult process, because it was clear that Mrs M did not perceive her choice to stay as a head teacher in the school, as "giving up" something. It was just part of the discovery of the value of applied psychoanalysis in institutional work.

Mattie was also very capable of helping people who were less clear in their choices than Mrs M. Her golden rule was that the work you do best is the work you enjoy the most. She saw the course in Observational Studies as including an experience of vocational guidance and when two years were not enough for this to be completed, Mattie encouraged people to take time if they were still uncertain, or if their tutor had some doubts about the best direction for them to pursue.

A third year of Work Discussion seminars was offered to many who, for instance, had not yet started an analysis for various reasons (and who certainly wouldn't have made the best use of their analysis if they had started it only in order to get onto the clinical training course). Some students were not at all sure that they wanted to become child psychotherapists, but, at the end of the two years, they had also not yet developed a clear alternative work project. Personal tutors – who were most frequently the teachers of Work Discussion seminars – made themselves available for tutorials to help students become clearer about their career direction.

A further course was established with Mattie's help, when she had left the role of organizing tutor but was still teaching at the Tavistock. This was an Advanced Course in Applied Psychoanalysis that would be open to people who wished to deepen their psychoanalytic understanding of their work, once they finished the course in Observational Studies. This course involved the study of Bion as its main theoretical component and an experience of "group relations" as an option.

The course was in no way meant for students who, for different reasons, may not have been advised to undertake the clinical training at that time. For some it was a time for reflection, a course also for people like the head teacher I mentioned earlier (who was indeed one of the first people to undertake the Advanced Course).

Obviously, it would be absurd to maintain that this new approach completely excluded selection, but it excluded selection from high above. As I said earlier, Mattie referred to the process as "assisted self selection".

The greatest difficulty in helping students to make a really free decision about the future was mainly encountered when he or she had come with the intention of undertaking the clinical training, but without having been able to have a taste of our way of working first. They had no equivalent experience of the long period of dialogue, reflection and vocational guidance that the course in Observational Studies offers to students who are trained in England. Mattie often had long correspondence with people who wished to come from abroad. This was one of the points she discussed extensively with me when, in 1979, I inherited from her the role of organizing tutor of the course in Observational Studies. She told me that people who had already uprooted themselves and left work in their country might find it difficult to keep an open mind and to allow teachers to help them to reflect, to observe, and to look honestly at their motivations in applying for the clinical training. If they had left their country with the idea of taking the clinical training they would have felt defeated returning home without having done so.

When it was possible, Mattie asked people she trusted, who lived in the same town or in the same country as those who had applied to the Tavistock, to meet the prospective students and if possible, to offer them a period of supervision on the work they were already doing – a form of individual work discussion. This was especially relevant when they would otherwise have to travel a long way for an initial meeting with Mattie. Mattie gave me a list of addresses of people who could be delegated this task of individual work discussion, or supervision in a number of countries. These same people, as well as others, have over the years started observation seminars, work discussions, and observational studies courses on the Tavistock model, in Latin America, North America, Asia, Australia and South Africa.

In October 1989, for the first time, a student who had completed her observation course and vocational guidance in Australia began the clinical training in London; her teachers in Australia were all former Tavistock students.

The first foreign pilot project of the Tavistock model course was the Course in Observational Studies in Rome, which started in October 1976. In the April of that year, when Mattie and I started talking about the possibility of starting this course as a full course, entirely in Rome, there were about twelve Italian students at the Tavistock, at different stages of the course, either in Observational Studies or Child Psychotherapy, and there were many applications from Italians who hoped to come in the future.

When we celebrated the 60th anniversary of the Tavistock (in 1980) I remember that some students organized a series of comical sketches, one of them a parody of a television quiz. One of the questions was, "What is the fundamental reading for the seminar on Infant Observation?" After some false responses, the correct answer was "an Italian-English dictionary".

In 1989 there was only one Italian student in the clinical course at the Tavistock. But, in Italy, observational studies courses had already been completed by more than 150 people: 40 attending or having completed the course in Child Psychotherapy and 12 the course in Applied Psychoanalysis. Now, there are about 400 child therapists in Italy trained on the Tavistock model.

To return to 1976: Mattie did not feel that the organizational programme of the Rome course was much to worry about. She had really internalized the advice of Bion that what matters is "not the decrease of inhibition but a decrease of the impulse to inhibit" (Bion, 1970, p. 129).

Mattie was the most facilitating person I have ever met. The discussion of the Rome project gave me a precious opportunity to talk at length with her about its aims and the risks that she had become aware of during the years. She had a very well developed sixth sense – much better than mine – for the inhibiting dynamics that can develop in groups and in institutions. All the practical, organizational aspects were very simplified. Mattie helped me a little with the first timetable. She said that it was just a matter of reproducing a model. Since 1976 a day release option had been introduced for the two-year course in Observational Studies, where people came just for one day a week. This enabled students who were working outside London, and at times very far from London, to get a one-day permit to come to the Tavistock, and take all the seminars of the week in a concentrated group of hours. Some students also called the day-release "the Wednesday marathon".

It was not possible to think of such weekly seminars for students in Rome, because of the cost of the flights for tutors travelling from London. So, if we were thinking about fortnightly seminars, which would be needed to cover the same ground, we just needed to hold a double marathon. Some teachers of the Observational Studies course in London could come to Rome in rotation and work on Friday and Saturday, or on Saturday and Sunday. If one heard Mattie talking about this, it sounded extremely simple – and in effect it was. Her formula was adopted, with some changes, not only in Rome but also in many other Italian cities, including Milan, Turin, Genoa, Bologna, Florence, Palermo. From the autumn of 1988, courses also ran in Naples and Venice.

Mattie had a real talent for avoiding unnecessary red tape. She said that it was not at all necessary to ask the permission of anybody in order to start a *pilot* project. It was just essential to begin the work with people who really felt like working hard.

After the Rome course had been running for 18 months and was going well – was airborne – Mattie advised me to bring a report of the work we were doing to the Professional Committee of the Tavistock, in order to discuss possible official links between the Tavistock and the Rome course. The course in Rome was run under the auspices of the Faculty of Education with Professor La Porta as chair, and we were thinking of a similar link with the Tavistock, also under its auspices. Mattie helped me to prepare the report and we were given a very friendly reception. Robert Gosling, who was also a very facilitating person, was chair of the Professional Committee and was deeply influenced by the thinking of Bion, who had been his analyst. He was very aware of the inhibiting dynamics in institutions. He suggested that the course should be accredited, not affiliated to the Tavistock. He felt the work we did in Rome appeared to be identical to the course in London, the teachers were the same, the content of the curriculum was the same, it was just under a different sky. This accreditation, which is largely due to Mattie, has been maintained to this day for the Rome course, and now for other courses in Italy.

Initially, I did not think we could run a child psychotherapy training in Rome. We thought that people who really wished to take that route could come to London to train for the clinical training in London, like the Australian students who took the course in observational studies in Sydney and then came for the clinical training to London. But it looked as if some of the students who had taken part in the first two Rome intakes were interested in and had aptitude for child psychotherapy. It seemed that it was not very realistic for them to come to England for four or five years. Some had families, some had already started an analysis in Italy and some spoke no English. Only two students completed the two-year course in Rome and then came to do the clinical training in London. So it seemed desirable to investigate the possibility of child psychotherapy training in Rome, but I thought it would be very difficult.

Again, Mattie said she didn't see much of a problem. It was, again, a matter of just adapting a model. And this time it would be easier, because we already had experience of this model with the observation course (i.e. the same curriculum, the same number of seminars held by the same teachers "under a different sky"). We certainly could find some psychoanalysts with experience in child work in Italy who might help us with weekly supervisions of intensive cases that "flying tutors" could not undertake.

Mattie gave me her full support in developing this project and she was right – it was possible. The first course in Child Psychotherapy started in Rome in 1979 and Mattie and Don took part in the teaching in Rome, both in the clinical seminars and the observational studies. (It was fascinating to see them discussing infant observation material together.) They also taught in all the observational studies started between 1979 and 1984 – i.e. in Milan, in Genoa and in Palermo as well as Rome. The students, and those who have been helped by the students, in Italy over the years owe a great deal to Mattie as a teacher and facilitator of new initiatives.

In 1988 we founded the first Centro Studi Martha Harris in Rome, which acted as a container for the Observation Course and helped to offer at least some modules of the course in other Italian towns. (There are now six CSMH in Italy and one in France.)

Most people in Italy took the full course. The course in Observational Studies in London was not however always offered as a full course. For some applicants, it made more sense to take just one seminar or two to begin with, and later take the whole course if they felt like it. In the 80s and 90s, about half of the students in London took the course on the basis of this extended formula, which is much easier for those with full-time jobs or small children. Some who had initially thought they would follow the course in Observational Studies as a whole, then decided they might only be able to take an Infant Observation or Work Discussion seminar. It was felt to be important that whatever was undertaken should be done seriously. Despite being very flexible, Mattie was very intransigent on this point.

Mattie was an incredible worker and expected that others, both colleagues and students, should be prepared to roll up their sleeves as well. For instance, she gradually introduced a great deal of written work into the M7 course – with papers on theory, and on the infant observation and work discussion. She thought, and in my opinion she was right, that the written work could be of great help in the process of "assisted self-selection". It would enable us, the tutors, to discuss with the student what he or she had really taken in, what really interested him or her. But, obviously, the students had to write their papers and the tutors had to read them and discuss them with the students. Mattie was prepared to do this herself and expected her colleagues to do the same. In fact, I don't think that any one of us worked as hard as she did.

She was also prepared to take on commitments that she did not enjoy, when it was necessary. For instance, she devoted a great deal of time to administrative work necessary to achieve recognition of the profession of child psychotherapy in the Health Service and a proper salary structure. She was very active and precise when she attended committee meetings and had all the necessary statistics and information at hand. She did not tend to delegate boring tasks and was anything but what one would call in Italian a "baronessa". Indeed, I think Mattie was one of the least narcissistic, least pleased-with-herself person I have encountered. She wished to share values with her colleagues, but it is interesting that a *very* wide range of people say she had a profound influence on their way of working, or inspired them. Cloning was totally alien to her and she was sharply critical of those who liked to be surrounded by "pale replicas of themselves" (as she put it: Harris, 1975a, p. 44). She was intolerant of flattery and could recognize and strongly discourage projective and adhesive identification.

As for introjective identification with Mattie, I think that this is a long and arduous process but very central in the life of many who have known her, profoundly admired her and loved her.

CHAPTER TWO

Mattie as an educator[1]

Margaret Rustin

Mattie was my most beloved and inspiring teacher. She had a wonderful mind. She could reach deep into herself and use the richness and fluidity of her contact with her own emotional being to understand others. Her students were given a remarkable experience, for they were safely held by her breadth of attentiveness while being brought close to the exhilarating, frightening, exciting, beautiful, astonishing ways in which babies feel and begin to think. Mattie's love and enjoyment of children and life and her devotion to psychoanalytically inspired exploration of the early development of mind came together in a particularly faithful way in her teaching, and shaped a whole generation of child psychotherapists.

Seeing the lovely gardens she could create, a glorious blend of colour in which the relative wildness of herbaceous borders and free-growing shrubs concealed the very hard work and patient

---

1 First published in *Collected Papers of Martha Harris and Esther Bick* (1987), pp. ix-xiii. The final three paragraphs were added in 2010 for the Paris event in her honour organized by the GERPEN (see Chapter 5).

care of the gardener, was for me a source of perceiving how she worked at the Tavistock.

When she first took on the task of organizing the Tavistock Child Psychotherapy Training, she was faced with sustaining a psychoanalytic conception of personality growth which Esther Bick had taught. Mrs Bick followed Melanie Klein's still developing thought closely, and was committed to an uncompromising purity of technique. Mattie had to find a way to continue this teaching in a context of considerable disagreement among senior colleagues over some fundamentals. In order to learn, students needed some protected space for grappling with the Kleinian paradigm but also to engage with the wider currents of child psychiatric practice and the Tavistock community mental health approach. The echoes of this creative tension are recurrent in ongoing thinking about training now, and Mattie's way of integrating relevant knowledge through intense concentration on the particular is a powerful model.

The study of the interaction between babies and their mothers, and indeed other members of the family, through the method of infant observation developed by Mrs Bick, was pivotal in Mattie's conception of a psychoanalytic education. The careful regularity of weekly non-intrusive visits allowed access to the intimate interplay of emotional lives in the family nexus. Seminars for discussion of detailed descriptions of all that had been observed was the first encounter most students had with Mattie's teaching. It was an astounding experience. Students would be bewildered by the wealth of unfamiliar detail and what could seem like shapeless chaos, and by the intensity of their own emotional engagement. Mattie's comments would draw together in a memorably meaningful way the available evidence about the states of mind and feeling of the family members, and would offer a language which sounded quite ordinary and down-to-earth for describing emotional events which most of us had never been able to notice before. The clarity and simplicity of the language reflected Mattie's steady concentration on the essential data. Readers will enjoy the limpid style of her writing about the observation of infants.

She had a capacity to be profoundly interested and to share with the seminar her fascination in the unfolding of a baby's potentialities and with parents' experiences of coming to know their baby and new aspects of themselves too. At the same time, the students' emotional responses, their anxieties and development, would be unobtrusively held in Mattie's mind. We felt ourselves very fully known to her through these seminars but also able to trust her use of this knowledge because it was used with love and concern to facilitate our development as individuals and as potential therapists. So she showed us how to appreciate the privilege of coming close to the intimate interior of family lives, of becoming aware of the conscious and unconscious emotional patterns, of seeing how an infant's personality took shape. Particularly characteristic was her emphasis on the interplay of internal factors – the temperament of mother and baby, their individual capacities for tolerating anxieties, expressing emotions and so on – and the external and contingent factors: who was available to contain and support mother in the vulnerable early weeks; how had the confinement been experienced; what might disturb or help mother and baby in establishing the feeding relationship. The combination for many students of beginning Infant Observation and personal analysis was a watershed over which Mattie presided with personal delicacy and kindness.

In the gradual evolution of the pre-clinical training of child psychotherapists to its present form in the Tavistock observation course, Mattie's other central plank was what she called a "Work Discussion" seminar.[2] A very unpretentious and even mundane name for what turned out to be a hugely creative conception. One of her own experiences which contributed to working out the basis for this sort of seminar is documented in her paper on "Consultation project in a comprehensive school" (1968b). Struck by how useful observation of children in a non-clinical context turned out to be to teachers, she gathered together a group of people wanting to train as child psychotherapists and

---

2 A more extensive discussion of the invention and development of the Work Discussion Seminar can be found in my introductory chapter in Rustin & Bradley (2008).

instituted a seminar to which they were invited to bring recorded observations of their experiences at work. The members were from a variety of professions and settings and had a lot to offer each other. The method was for the member presenting to read aloud the written material and to add thoughts as they occurred. The ensuing dialogue between presenter and seminar members elucidated many further details and allowed for the exploration of the emotional aspects of the work setting, both building a picture of the inner preoccupations of the child or children being studied, and clarifying the conscious and unconscious responses of the worker to the children's communications. The helpfulness of these seminars to people struggling with often very distressed and disturbed children was enormous: finding meaningful links which might render the children's behaviour understandable reduced the degree of confusion, anxiety and persecution and freed the workers' imagination and hopefulness.

The Tavistock course for teachers on Counselling Aspects of the teacher's role grew from this same kernel, and Work Discussion seminars have become a standard component of many other courses. The concept now seems so obvious it is hard to imagine being without it, but it arose from Mattie's conviction that a psychoanalytic attitude was relevant not only in the consulting room but in all settings where the understanding and management of the anxieties and conflicts of adults and children were central to the developmental possibilities inherent in the situation. This starting point made all the relationships open to a growing child at home, at school and in the wider community worthy of close study.

Mattie's own enjoyment of teaching, which made her seminars and supervisions pleasures to be intensely savoured, must have been an important factor in her decision to initiate a large expansion in the Child Psychotherapy Training. In the early 1970s, changes in the organization of the National Health Service, an expanding interest in psychoanalysis and psychotherapy, and an increasing number of suitably qualified and experienced applicants provided the opportunity for mobilizing the resources of the tiny profession to launch a much increased educational programme. A generation of those whose training had been deeply marked by Mattie's influence were gathered together to serve as teachers. The privileges of the teacher in presiding over the personal and intellectual development of her students were particularly appreciated by Mattie. The seminars of the Observation Course offered access to the many-layered possibilities of being able to use psychoanalytic methods and knowledge in a broader context than the individual work of the consulting room. Students, their colleagues, the children they worked with and the children's families were all part of the seminar's experience.

Democratic instincts, personal generosity, a capacity for phenomenal hard work, and a conviction that the unique value of psychoanalytic insight ought to be shared as much as was possible, enabled Mattie to inspire her psychotherapist colleagues to take on this challenge. Her own courage and devotion to and happiness in the work underpinned a colossal determination not to be hampered by a weight of bureaucratized organization, nor to pay too much heed to the cautious and in many ways traditionalistic assumptions of most psychoanalytic educators. In retrospect, this shift of gear still takes one's breath away.

Of course her example, because it was so transparently expressive of a whole grasp on life, was immensely influential. The impact she had on those she taught derived from her being as well as from the power of her presentation of psychoanalytic ideas. Her attitude to her students felicitously combined a depth of interest and a great deal of patience when she sensed that honest learning was taking place, with a firm conviction that anxieties must be faced and tolerated. She did not believe in reassurance, but helped her students to bear the rigours of psychoanalytic learning by her kindness and extraordinary capacity to hold in mind their individual vulnerabilities. One of her favourite theoretical references was to Bion's use of Keats' concept of "negative capability", and her approach to teaching was a beautiful exemplification of Bion's ideas.

Many of her colleagues can bear witness to the subtlety of her judgements of people – and very many students benefited from her sensitive contact with the creative spark inside them which could elude other observers but which Mattie could seek out and nourish.

In the later part of her working life, she began to place more emphasis on the importance of writing, and struggled to make more space for writing work of her own. The value of writing also came to take up a larger place in the Tavistock Clinic psychotherapy training.

Her collected papers (1987, 2011) provide a more formal record of her outstanding contribution to thinking about psychoanalytic education for a wider public as well as a delightful re-encounter with her for old friends and students. Re-reading Mattie's papers is truly pleasurable because the grace of her use of language is truly expressive of the workings of her mind. Complex ideas are conveyed so directly, and the sentences bring alive the lived experience from which the ideas derive.

One very short paper will serve to illustrate this quality. It was written for a general educated readership, and concerns sibling relationships. In the last few years there has been a renewed psychoanalytic interest in siblings and a number of publications, including some suggesting that this was a previously neglected theme in psychoanalysis. Mattie's wise musings of 1967 serve as a corrective to this view! The integration of observations from everyday family life with a psychoanalytically informed understanding of both profound infantile anxieties and the natural developmental rhythms of children's lives is allied to a grasp of the central function of parental containment. The imaginative sympathy she conveys for the feelings of a first child on the arrival of a new baby brings her generous personality immediately to mind. She writes of the child's disappointment (barely to be noticed by the baby at first), sense of rejection, anger and depression, and, while noting the necessary element of ambivalence in all honestly based sibling relationships, she also describes the potential for lifelong intimacy and friendship between brothers and sisters. She ponders, with interest, on the variations across time and place in sibling relationships depending on social and familial structures, drawing on history, anthropology and literature to do so. Her learning and breadth of interest open our minds to the richness of what there is to know and the many relevant discourses to take into account, and here is the genius of Mattie as a teacher.

Her own practice as a psychoanalytic teacher and supervisor in fact created a particularly strong set of quasi sibling ties between her pupils. How lucky we were both to feel individually known, appraised and respected and to be aware of being part of a group of pupils for whose development she took so much responsibility. The intensity of the whole experience certainly included extreme reactions to the new babies who appeared when a new academic year commenced and ongoing rivalries which could have a destructive impact were near the surface, but the greatest thing was the experience of becoming part of a working group which was capable of struggling to sustain Bion's work-group ethic within an emotional context of great warmth and intimacy. This inspiring integration of the personal and the professional was Mattie's version of the feminist theme that "the personal is political" which was part of the wider social background of the 1960s and 70s. Within the Tavistock, her outstanding work set the scene for a significant shift in the balance of status and authority between men and women and for a greater appreciation of the central importance of psychoanalytic work with children and parents and of the responsibility to nurture clinical creativity in our approach to psychoanalytic education.

CHAPTER THREE

Mattie's teaching methods

Ann Cebon

During a most enjoyable meeting (over dinner, of course!) Eve Steel, Pat Kenwood, Herb Hahn and I – Mattie's group from Melbourne, Australia – talked about our recollections of Mattie and her teaching methods. We agreed that we shared with each other the extent to which her methods permeated our lives: not only our professional lives at all levels, but also our relations with each other. We share values, curiosity, a love of honesty and forthrightness. For me, there is a thread linking back to Mattie's mind and Mattie's room at the Tavi, where I still vividly remember the first meeting of my group for our first infant observation seminar, with Mattie, in the autumn of 1967.

My intention, while writing my personal anecdotes and memories of Martha Harris, is to attempt to convey her unique qualities as a person, teacher, and supervisor. Writing this short piece has again put me in touch with her way of teaching, one could say her way of being, which was not by theory but by practice. What she gave was truly both "pure and applied" as the mathematicians say, and we, her students, imbibed. She was a truly thoughtful and an ethical person, with total integrity, and this conveyed itself to us. The impact Mattie had on me began with my first meeting with her. While I have now come to think of her as "Mattie", during my nine years in London, and in my subsequent correspondence with her, I always addressed and thought of her as "Mrs Harris".

My first meeting with Mattie came about the day after I rang the Tavistock Clinic to ask to apply for the Child Psychotherapy training, only to be told that the applications had now closed, and the next course would begin in two years. Then the secretary said, "Oh, Mrs Harris is just walking by, I'll ask her if she'd consider a late application." The result of this fortuitous moment was that I was asked to come along to meet her the next day. I certainly did not have the required two years clinical experience. I was 23 years old. I had come to London to do a one-year MSc course in Sociology at the London School of Economics. But disillusioned with my sixth year of academic study, and exploring other options, I chanced on the brochure of the courses offered at the Tavistock Clinic. The description of the Child Psychotherapy training course reawakened my interest in what I had read of Freud, and evoked the pleasure I had from my voluntary work with children as an undergraduate university student in California.

There were several "Mattie dynamics" operating already in my preliminary interview with her. To say I was psychologically unsophisticated was to put it mildly. Mrs Harris asked me why, as I was an American, I was not seeking to study at the Hampstead Clinic. She explained they followed the teaching of Freud, while at the Tavistock, the training studied the work of Melanie Klein, who at that time was not in favour in the United States. "Melanie who?" I enquired.

Most significantly for me, and characteristically for Mattie, she could see that while I was very naive, I was curious and keen, and she accepted me into the training as a probationary trainee. She did not assume a reassuring voice and suggest I go away for two years, read and live and then re-apply, as someone else in another training course had done. She struck while the iron was hot. With that began my introduction to her unique way of enabling each of us to develop *our* own capacities. This experience with Mattie certainly affected my own way of thinking about applicants when I served for many years on the training committee of our local association.

I had come from a rather militant – even aggressive—environment as an undergraduate at the University of California at Berkeley. It had been five exciting and stimulating years, followed by one turbulent year at the London School of Economics. From this background I thought I knew my "rights" as a student.

After only a few months of the course I felt uneasy about my probationary status. I knocked at Mattie's door. Always generous, she asked me in. I asked her whether she could give me any information about my probationary status. For instance, how long might it continue? Could I know the criteria on which she or they would decide whether I was accepted or not? Forty-three years later I imagine I still remember her thoughtful pause before she replied. Mattie (always "Mrs Harris" to me then) said to me that this work did not suit everyone. It required the capacity to tolerate uncertainty. If I found it difficult to tolerate uncertainty, then perhaps it was not the right work for me. I withdrew from her room, deeply embarrassed, but also deeply affected. I may have been in the first weeks of my personal analysis. With her help, I had begun learning from experience, which continues, thankfully, though not always as dramatically, to this day.

As I began the course with literally no formal clinical experience, in the first months Mattie informed me that I would be looking after the young sibling of a child patient as a pre-clinical introduction. I think Mattie saw the mother. I was assigned a room, opposite Mattie's, and given some toys. Each week while the mother had her session, I spent one hour playing with this little boy. I was told to write up the experience and what I understood of his play, in the form of an observation, and subsequently present it to Mattie. This enabled me to observe, interact, and conceptualize, and also of course enabled Mattie to assess me. I was delighted to be given such an opportunity. I think this was another occasion where I was unaware that it was I who was being observed, as well as being introduced to the model of learning from experience.

Another expression of Mattie's exceptional generosity that I was very grateful for was that she took an interest in each of us and tried to help in any way that she could. I needed to work to finance my training and my analysis. Mrs Harris suggested that I apply to the Education Department to have my undergraduate degree from the University of California at Berkeley recognized. She said I would then be able to teach in a school part-time. This would give me experience with children as well as provide me with funds. I submitted my transcripts only to receive a letter that my five years of undergraduate study at the University of California was "too wide-ranging and variegated" to be equivalent to a British undergraduate degree. When I told her about this unfair assessment of my degree, Mrs Harris' reaction was to send me to speak to her husband, Roland Harris, who was an academic at Brunel University. He took up my case, analysed the transcripts, re-categorized the subjects that I had completed, and demonstrated clearly that my studies were equivalent to a Politics, Philosophy and Economics degree from Oxford or Cambridge, with many extra units as well. My qualifications were then officially recognized. I still have the correspondence between Roland Harris and the London Department of Education.

The most significant aspect of my training and subsequent professional life was my two years of weekly observation of a baby girl and her mother, and the accompanying weekly seminar, led by Mattie. From the beginning Mattie's commitment to observation, first applied to Infant Observation, then in the Young Child Observation seminar, and then as a fundamental tool of our work, excited me. We, the trainees, would gather in her room, taking turns to present our observations. The arrangement was that the presenter provided Mattie and each of us with a copy of the observation. As the observer read through his or her observation, Mattie underlined some words and made occasional notes in the column. She did not interrupt the presenter. I still recall how Mattie invited each of us to contribute, comment, and reflect on what we had heard. She listened to our contributions with interest. She was never impatient, and always respectful. As the seminar drew to an end, there was a time when she paused, took a deep breath and then began with her introductory expression "You see, I think …". Then her understanding unfolded, often bringing together elements of our thoughts and shedding deeper insights about what we had heard, or gently but firmly saying why she saw things differently. For me, after six years in academia, the entire process of these seminars, the manner in which she shared her thoughts with us, enabling us to learn, was a window into a new world. She, and the Child Psychotherapy training, opened a world to me, the emotional world of the infant, the world of relationships, of unconscious fantasy, as well as the emotional world of the mothers – and fathers too – and the permeable membrane between them. That was 1967-1968. I qualified as a child psychotherapist in 1971.

When, in 1973, I decided to marry and this meant a move to Melbourne, it was again Mattie to whom I turned. I knew that I had just over a year left in London. I asked how I might best use the time remaining to prepare myself for my future professional life in Melbourne. I think Mattie knew how much I had valued the two-year Infant Observation Seminar with her. Without hesitation she recommended that the best thing I could do was to have supervision with Esther Bick, which she arranged for me. The case that I subsequently took to Esther Bick has been described elsewhere (Cebon, 2007) and reprinted (2011).

In conclusion, I will recall two applications of observation, which I link with Mattie: one in London and one here in Melbourne. As a newly trained child psychotherapist, I worked at Edgware General Hospital, both in the department of Psychiatry and in the medical wards. I was asked to offer a weekly supervision group to nurses on the paediatric orthopaedic ward, where some children were then long-term patients. The nurses were not keen to attend, and I was uncertain how best to proceed, until I asked them to bring an observation of an interaction with one of the child patients about whom they were concerned, or with whom they were having difficulties. I said I didn't mind what the observation involved. It could be a bath, a meal, a physiotherapy session, or whatever they chose. I asked them to record as much detail as possible about what they observed, including their own feelings about the experience. They began, at first reluctantly, to take turns presenting their observations. Slowly the seminar participation grew and they became enthusiastic as they discovered the pleasure and relief that understanding can bring.

In Melbourne I worked for many years at the Royal Children's Hospital. A new director at Yooralla School, then a residential and day centre for disabled children, understood the distress that many of these children suffered. This led to a flood of referrals to our Department of Psychiatry. The intake committee decided to deal with the demand by offering a consultation to the school. I accompanied a colleague for some initial consultations with the staff about how we might help. We both felt overwhelmed by the staff's wish for answers from us. After some discussion, we decided to try working with them in a reflective and active way, through the use of the observational method. Once a month, we spent half a day at the school. In preparation for our visits, we asked them to present one child, including one or two observations of this child in their interactions with the staff at the school, including nurses, teachers, physiotherapists and occupational therapists. Even the bus driver, who transported children who were living at home, took part on one occasion. It really was a multidisciplinary team, actively working with us to deepen their capacity for reflection and understanding of these troubled children. We used the observations the staff brought to reflect together on the interaction of the children's physical, intellectual and emotional experiences. Through careful discussions of the observations they brought, we uncovered the emotional experiences the children had. The staff came to understand with us that how the children behaved and how they felt had meanings at many levels. When the children felt emotionally understood, it was a great help and relief to both them and their carers.

Many of the staff attended our monthly seminars for a period of several years, and found this way of working interesting and helpful to them. Some years later, one of the staff recognized me and told me that the insights she had gained through our meetings had had a transformational effect on her work.

This work is another example of the relief that understanding underlying emotional meanings may bring. Understanding these processes was a gift from Mattie, which has inspired me at a very deep level, encouraged me to facilitate others' understanding, and has stayed with me.

CHAPTER FOUR

Mattie's contribution to the study of infant observation

Janine Sternberg

It is hard to overestimate the influence of Mattie Harris on Tavistock-trained child psychotherapists of my generation (the mid-1970s). In a way that feels similar to my experience of studying psychoanalysis, having been a student of English literature, and finding that nothing that I subsequently learned about human behaviour had not already been realized and alluded to by Shakespeare, so I found in my later research into infant observation that nothing I was discovering had not already been indicated in Mattie's 1976 paper "The contribution of observation of mother-infant interaction and development to the equipment of a psychoanalyst or psychoanalytic psychotherapist". This chapter revisits that paper in the hope of reintroducing readers, however familiar with it, to the wealth of useful thoughts that it contains.

Readers of Mattie's papers will know her written style: of course lacking the hesitations and idiosyncrasies of her speech patterns, but still delightfully feeling as if the reader is in direct conversation with her, not being lectured at. Defences and manoeuvres, undesirable attributes, are all named, but in a low-key, straightforward way, that never sounds critical. In a later paper also on infant observation ("A baby observation: the absent object") she refers to a baby "putting emotions away because they could not be dealt with" (1980a, p. 167) – a phrase which in my mind has such a depth of humanity contained within it. A compassionate, non-judgmental view suffuses the straightforward narrative. The same fluid, almost conversational style, is also employed in the paper on which I am concentrating.

I think it is typical of Mattie's approach that early on in the paper she asks in what sounds like a properly genuine way, "Why do it?" She comments that conducting an observation takes time and acknowledges the views of some that the analytic candidate could learn "everything he needs to know about the child within the adult and the infant within the child" (1976, p. 118) without observation experience. Additionally she warns against adherence to theories which may be privileged because of "personal loyalty or adherence to analytic pedigrees" (p. 119). She then uses the paper to suggest many different ways in which the experience of infant observation can engender or enhance the capacities needed for working as an adult or child psychoanalyst or psychoanalytic psychotherapist, pointing out that "learning to become a psychoanalyst … [is] a process that continues long after qualification" (p. 120). A few years ago I conducted doctoral research to see if I could find evidence to support or disprove those assertions and those of others in the British psychoanalytic psychotherapy community (Sternberg, 2005), and while the research I carried out did not show enhanced capacities in all the dimensions I looked at, it certainly did in most.

Mattie writes within this paper and elsewhere (1968a, 1975b, 1977) of the importance of attention to detail. However strong her theoretical adherence, she was interested in looking at every interaction afresh – of course she saw it through the lens of her particular theoretical perspective, but she was interested in noticing and using the minutiae of what was there to be seen. We see this same quality in the book by Romana Negri, edited by Meg Harris Williams (Negri & Harris, 2007), when we read transcripts of recordings of Mattie commenting on Romana's observations. We see how carefully she examines all aspects: in commenting on Observation 2 she questions the mother's view that the baby, Simone, is sleeping "happily", pointing out the way that he is "constantly being disturbed by some sort of sensation, in some part of its body" (p. 5). Indeed in her 1976 paper she says that observation of the early months brings home to the observer the reality that emotion is rooted in bodily states (p. 124). Within that book when we also hear Meltzer's responses to the observation material we can notice how he and Mattie have different and separate strengths: Meltzer is much more theoretical, using the specific to take flight into generalized concepts. He is very engaging in what he says, but his contribution, by contrast, highlights Mattie's close attention to detail. Although she does of course put what she sees into a theoretical framework there is a strong sense of her really thinking about Simone and his family. In her 1976 paper she states:

> Attention to the details of the observation presented, and discussion of their possible implications, is also then likely to bring out hitherto unapprehended aspects of the situation which may assist the observer towards recalling further details which he did not realize he had noticed at the time. (p. 121)

Later in the paper she links that with the way that "the infant-observer attitude helps the aspiring analyst take not only words, but also details of the patient's total demeanour and behaviour into account" (p. 122).

Mattie is clear that some of the inability to remember arises from the painful nature of what is observed. She comments on how disturbing it can be to be in the presence of a helpless young infant and helps the observer to see the defences that the mother may put into place to avoid having to see this. One of the aspects of Mattie's approach that I admire so much is her ability to speak compassionately about the need for defences, but still be steely-eyed about the problems that they may cause. When describing the ways in which the experience of infant observation helps the analyst she talks of imitation as a "two-dimensional way of clinging to external objects", but goes on that this leads to "impoverishment or stunting of development which occurs when this becomes a pervasive defence against emotional experience" (p. 124). The use of the word "clinging" for me suggests the driven quality of it, the *need* to hold on that more neutral words, such as "keeping hold", would not have conveyed. Mattie describes the observer as needing to have "uncritical interest'"(p. 120) and I feel that this is what she models for us so well.

This uncritical interest forms a central part of what is often referred to as "the observer stance" – the way an observer has to find a non-intrusive place within the family and simply watch "without doing". Many observers struggle to learn how to do this: dropping one's previously prized professional role can be difficult, especially when what is left is a space in which emotions can be felt acutely. This emphasis on infant observation as an emotional experience is at the heart of Mattie's approach to the topic but typically she separates emotion which can be used from some sort of sentimental wallowing: she specifies "emotional experience which requires mental work if it is to be thought about rather than reacted to" (p. 120). She describes how the observer projects his own (interestingly, throughout the paper the observer is referred to as "he") unconscious infantile desires and dreads into the situation between the mother and baby. In her 1977 paper, describing how infant observation is used within the Tavistock Child Psychotherapy training, she views many of the feelings that the observer experiences as deriving from his past: "most people who undertake this exercise find that the closeness to the infant and mother arouses in them extremely intense feelings deriving from their own infancy" (p. 8).

Mattie states that an observer needs to be close enough to the observed situation for the relationship to have an impact but that he also needs sufficient space for observing what is happening within himself as well as in the mother and baby. Over the years we have come to see how the opportunity to recognise those feelings and then consider where they have come from within oneself is of great benefit to the fledgling psychotherapist, helping us to learn to become aware of our countertransference reactions and thinking about what they tell us about ourselves and the other. Mattie writes that the observer "must allow himself to *feel*, but needs to *think* about his feelings in order to restrain himself from acting them" (p. 122). She links this to the need for emotional receptivity in the consulting room.

Indeed, it is in emphasizing the way that the emotional experience engenders capacities within the observer that are essential for future clinical life that Mattie is both clear and inspiring. She declares:

> The central truth one can learn through one's own experience as an observer, and through observing the development of a mother who is learning to be a mother, is directly applicable to the relationship of the analytic couple. (p. 126)

I am struck by the phrase "a mother who is learning to be a mother" – mothers no more spring fully formed into whatever it may mean to be a mother at the moment of birth (or might that be conception?) than a therapist is the therapist they develop into at the point of their first analytic contact with a patient. Mattie points out how as a baby grows and thrives, and as she learns to understand her baby better, the mother's anxiety lessens. Typically Mattie links the mother's ability to learn from her baby (and she states that some infants are better than others at conveying their needs) with her ability to give herself more space and time for reflection. This benign view of normal development, with its understanding that of course infants will differ in their temperaments and the observer will become aware of that through seminar discussions, also makes clear that development takes time, cannot be rushed.

However Mattie of course does not believe that good development will take place whatever the circumstances. In her 1977 paper on the philosophy of the Tavistock Child Psychotherapy training she refers to the way in which trust, love and the capacity to form object relations grows in the child through recurrent experiences of being understood, while in "Towards learning from experience in infancy and childhood" she states:

> Traumatic events throughout life, from whatever source, test the capacity of the personality to hold new experience with its inevitable pain and uncertainty, and to grow from it. This capacity must always, to some extent, be influenced by the nature of the earliest containing objects and in particular with the primary receptive responsive qualities of the mother.

Receptive parents help an infant to have an experience of himself. His identification with them helps him manage later the conflicting emotions and impulses that arise in the ordinary course of living, if he is *being* what he *is, feeling* what he *feels.* (Harris, 1978a, p. 76).

When we hear her direct responses to Romana Negri's observations (2007) we see her constant, quiet insistence that painful feelings cannot ultimately be avoided. She expresses concerns that Simone's parents' attempts to save him from suffering could lead to him having difficulties in relationships with others. From the careful observations and the incisive yet humane comments on them, Mattie helps us to understand how the parents' unconscious identifications lead them to actually make things *worse* for the little boy. Recognising mother's devotion to her son as arising from her narcissistic identification, "seeing the baby as a child-part of herself" (Negri & Harris, p.83), Mattie links this with mother's reluctance to see "any nasty parts" in the child. In that book we are privileged to read a number of extremely astute statements about the strain on the adults' relationship and the manoeuvres a child may go through to avoid the pain of displacement brought about by the new baby.

We should also note how in the earlier quotation about the usefulness of infant observation for becoming a psychoanalyst Mattie refers to "the analytic couple". Elsewhere in this paper she writes that the "essential intimacy and nakedness of the analyst-patient relationship … is probably more analogous to the mother-baby relationship than to any other" (1976, p. 119). She draws a parallel between the way that an analyst "is exposed to uncertainty, confusion, anxiety when bombarded at close quarters by the emotional experience of another person, as a mother is bombarded by the emotional state of the infant" (p. 119).

She later draws an analogy between the mother who may at times give the breast to the baby because she can think of no other way of helping him with his uncomfortable feelings and the analyst who may give interpretations or even reassurance as a way of stopping certain emotions being "unfolded". She refers to "anxious over-activity":

> It is more painful to wait, to remain receptive and not cut-off, to bear the pain that is being projected, including the pain of one's own uncertainty, than it is to have recourse to precipitate action designed to evacuate that pain and to gain the relief of feeling that one is doing something. (p. 126)

Here we see again both her clear eyed and compassionate approach. We are shown the defensive manoeuvres involved in action but we know that Mattie understands how agonizing it can be not to employ those defences. A similar compassion is shown when in writing of clinical work she describes the patient as behaving in an apparently hostile way because he needs the analyst to feel something "which he cannot as yet tolerate feeling himself, because he has not developed the equipment for thinking about it" (p. 125).

Within this we also see Mattie's view about the usefulness of waiting, not rushing to premature action, whether as an observer, a mother or a therapist. Using terms which have since become axiomatic within the Tavistock child psychotherapy training she reminds us of Bion's adaptation of Keats' term "negative capability" and how essential this is in order to learn from experience. With typical understated humour she adds: "It is also achieved more easily through experience which teaches one humility by revealing the fallibility of one's omniscient preconceptions" (p. 120). Although not stated that explicitly, here and elsewhere we see Mattie's view that, of course, practising as a psychoanalyst or psychoanalytic psychotherapist may not suit everyone: some may prefer to stay within the comforting belief that their preconceptions are infallible. Yet for many who undertake it the experience of infant observation leads to a wish for further growth:

> Such detailed observation has inevitably an emotional impact on the observer which is likely to disturb complacency and to lead to the kind of self-questioning that evokes an interest in personal analysis in those whose desire to get at the truth

of themselves is likely to be stronger than their wish to preserve the status quo. (Harris, 1978a, p. 29)

I am profoundly grateful to Mattie that she was able to see that I might be such a person and to give me the opportunity to embark on a career which has been a source of so much satisfaction in my life.

CHAPTER FIVE

A psychoanalytic revolution from a speculative to an empirical point of view[1]

Didier Houzel

With Donald Meltzer, Martha Harris was one of the architects of the GERPEN. They were invited to Paris by James Gammill, Geneviève Haag, and Jean and Florence Bégoin for the first time during the winter of 1974. The first work session that we had with them was a private one, in the Bégoins' apartment, in which some twenty or so of our colleagues took part. That work session turned out to be so interesting that we decided to invite them several times per year from then on. The number of participants increased steadily, and we came to realize that we needed a more structured organization in order to manage the weekends properly. It was for that reason that the GERPEN was set up in 1983.

Those weekend sessions were highly successful, thanks in no small measure to the teaching and exceptional creativity of Donald Meltzer – and also to the presence by his side of Martha

---

[1] Part of this chapter was written as an introduction to a scientific meeting set up by the GERPEN (*Groupe d'Etudes et de Recherches Psychoanalytiques pour le developpement de l'Enfant et du Nourisson*) in honour of Martha Harris. This part has been translated from French to English by David Alcorn. The remaining part was written directly in English by the author.

Harris, who would always add a personal note to what Meltzer was saying. Sometimes, indeed, she would moderate his standpoint if she felt it to be too cut-and-dried, too indicative of a masculine desire to take a firm stand on things. Don and Mattie, as we called them informally, were a well-balanced and creative couple who gave the impression that they were constantly and deeply in love with each other and shared a real passion for psychoanalysis. We were extremely fortunate to be able to benefit from their joint teaching several times per year, from 1974 until 1983.

One day, Mattie suggested that we should devote part of our seminars to the Infant Observation method that Esther Bick had devised at the Tavistock Clinic. I can remember just how puzzled I felt during the initial sessions when observation material was being presented. My mind, trained as it was in the orthodox French manner, just wasn't getting enough theoretical speculations or metapsychological references! Gradually, all the same, I began to be convinced that she was sharing with us a fundamental way of working – to such an extent, indeed, that I myself embarked upon an infant observation, supervised by Anik Maufras du Chatellier. That experience led to a sea-change in my conception of psychoanalysis. I am now convinced that psychoanalysis is an empirical science based on observation – but a particular form of observation that I would call "psychoanalytic observation". That revolution, which brought me from a speculative point of view to an empirical one, I owe it above all to Martha Harris – and I am sure that many of my colleagues will have had a similar experience.

Martha Harris was one of Esther Bick's first pupils, when in 1948 training in child psychotherapy was initiated in the Tavistock Clinic; it was John Bowlby, at that time the director of that prestigious institution, who asked Esther Bick to take on that task. Martha Harris took over from Mrs Bick in 1960 as head of that training programme, which included Infant Observation as a compulsory subject (nowadays in the first and second year of the programme). It was Martha Harris who had the brilliant idea of broadening infant observation to include professions other than that of psychotherapists; she was convinced that anyone professionally involved with children – teachers, nursery nurses, special needs workers, paediatricians, etc – would be able to benefit from this particular mode of learning. Her activity was not, however, limited to applying Esther Bick's method of observation. She was herself an outstanding child and adolescent analyst. The papers that she wrote – published in French by the *Éditions du Hublot* – bear witness to that.

Infant observation and the psychoanalyst's activity share a common denominator – what I earlier called "psychoanalytic observation". I did not in fact invent the term "psychoanalytic observation" – I am borrowing it from Donald Meltzer. Here is what he has to say:

> Psychiatric diagnosis with children as carried out in most hospitals or child guidance clinics is a rather elaborate and unstandardized process in which history-taking, psychological testing, and play interviews with the child play a variable part in different centres. But the basic method is to amass data and, in conference, to reach a group impression by reviewing the data. My own experience in running a large child guidance clinic as against an extensive experience in private psychiatric consultation convinces me that the psychoanalytic method of observation is far more accurate, both diagnostically and prognostically, if psychotherapy or child analysis is a real possibility. (Meltzer, 1960, pp. 37-38)

This is how Don Meltzer describes "psychoanalytic observation":

> Our source of information is our own relatively analysed mental apparatus, by means of which we can experience a degree of identification with the patient and follow the affective and phantasy processes in ourselves resulting from partial identification. This is not understood, yet it is no different methodologically from the calibration of any scientific instrument as an extension of the human sensorium. And of course it is to the extent to which we have succeeded in what other scientists call standardizing the apparatus that we become accurate psychoanalytic observers. (ibid., p. 41)

Obviously, a personal analysis, one that has been as thorough as possible, is by far the best calibration tool for our mind so as to prepare it for psychoanalytic observation. That said, Esther Bick's method of observation also makes a significant contribution to this, whether simply as part of a one-off training programme or linked to the person's own psychoanalysis and development thereafter. These are two personal experiences in which observers can observe their own mind in the situation in which they find themselves immersed. That is what characterizes psychoanalytic observation and distinguishes it from other kinds (experimental observation, ethological observation, etc) in which observers must leave aside their own subjectivity and focus on an object or a situation external to them. It is what the French anthropologist Georges Devereux (who trained as a psychoanalyst) called "participant observation", in the sense that the observer is part of what he or she is observing. Esther Bick described those who observed infants as a special kind of participant observer.

In 1980, Mattie invited me to visit the Tavistock Clinic and attend some seminars of the course for child psychotherapists. I went to London with my wife and we stayed at Don and Mattie's home for several days. I remember the kind welcome Mattie gave us. I can still see her cutting from her garden some beautiful flowers to decorate the room she had prepared for us.

That visit was decisive for my thinking on child psychoanalysis and child psychotherapy in my own country. At that time there was no official training in child psychoanalysis in France. The French psychoanalytic societies affiliated to the International Psychoanalytic Association were not involved in that field of psychoanalysis. People who wished to be seriously trained in child psychoanalysis or psychoanalytic psychotherapy either asked for sypervision the small number of private psychoanalysts practising with children, or even crossed the Channel and came to London to have an actual training as child psychoanalyst or psychotherapist.

We have in France a long tradition of theoretical speculation which, I think, is quite respectable and which created some brilliant thinkers in several intellectual fields like logic, mathematics, and philosophy; but hindered to some extent not so much the exploration of nature, but the possibility of easily connecting empirical data with thoughts. We remain essentially dualistic as in Descartes' definition: on the one hand a thinking substance – the soul – without extension; on the other a physical substance – the body and the material world, extended and known through the mediation of our sense organs. But there is also another kind of dualism in Descartes' legacy which has influenced French thinkers, including psychoanalysts. This kind of dualism is correlative of the first one, but it deserves to be stressed considering its importance within the psychoanalytic field. I mean the opposition Descartes underlined between thinking, which brings us an absolute certainty about our existence ("I think therefore I am"), and our deceitful senses which never assure us whether what we are perceiving is actual or not, perceived or dreamt. The problem for psychoanalysis is that it is based on the hypothesis that there is a consubstantiality between body and mind, that the thoughts stem from the body through complex transformations, that there are not two substances – body and soul connected by the pineal gland as Descartes hypothesized it – but a psycho-soma as Bion stated, which belongs to both our physical and our spiritual natures. I think the contempt that many French psychoanalysts have for child psychoanalysis is linked with this aspect of Descartes' dualism. Treating a child with psychoanalysis does not permit of ignoring the body and the bodily needs as may be possible with an adult patient.

After my visit to the Tavistock Clinic I had a dream of setting up another Tavistock in France. Unfortunately I never met the patron who wished to give the amount of money that plan required. So, with some colleagues, we found another way. As soon as we could we formed a small group of psychoanalysts to organize a training course for child and adolescent psychotherapist on a background similar to that I had discovered at the Tavistock.[2] This group affiliated itself to the European Federation for Psychoanalytic Psychotherapy in the Public Sector (EFPP) founded in 1991 by Brian Martindale. Shortly after, a second group was formed in Bordeaux, then another one in Paris;

---

[2] The first group set up in Normandy was comprised of Louis Edy, Didier Houzel, Bianca Lechevalier, and Albert Namer.

the Centre d'Études Martha Harris was set up in Brittany in the 1980s by Gianna Williams at Larmor Plage near Lorient; Hélène Dubinsky, Alexandre Dubinsky and Odile Gavériaux wished to join us. In 1999 the different groups combined as the FFPPEA[3] and the federation affiliated itself to the EFPP. Since this date other groups, set up in Lyon, Lille, etc., have joined the Federation.

So now we have a wide network for providing a training in child and adolescent psychoanalytic psychotherapy in the spirit of Martha Harris, which combines a scrupulous respect for what is psychoanalytically observed with a profound empathy and a genuine modesty.

This spirit seems to me beautifully summarized in Mattie's commentary on the therapeutic consultations that she had provided for a little boy who had important relationship problems; she wrote:

> It was important that the parents had come together, jointly responsible for their son, and that they were enabled to express their problem, their feelings of helplessness as parents, to an 'expert' who was supposed to have some experience in dealing with these problems. But not an expert, who from the height of superior knowledge, treated them as helpless children, instructing them in what to do, or in what they should not have done, thereby confirming them their own childish fears of being discovered to be inadequate and fraudulent parents incapable of responsibility and dependent therefore upon some higher authority. The helpful expert in such a situation is the one who can have a role analogous to that of the understanding mother with the distressed baby, who receives the projections of the infant's anxiety, is with it, and enables it to cope better with the pain because it no longer feels alone. (Harris, 1966, p. 300)

---

3 Fédération Française de Psychothérapie Psychanalytique pour l'Enfant et l'Adolescent.

CHAPTER SIX

The role of Martha Harris from the beginning of the GERPEN[1]

James Gammill

Some of those who came in the first years of our seminars centred on the psychoanalytical psychotherapy of children considered that the central role was given to Donald Meltzer, with only an accompanying role to his wife, Martha Harris. For me, however, the true and dynamic dialogue that focussed on case presentation and analytic theory was of central importance, and was transmitted to our audience.

I made the acquaintance of Martha Harris in the autumn of 1958, thanks to Melanie Klein, who was then supervising my analysis of a boy of three. One day Mrs Klein said to me,

> I want you to meet Mrs Martha Harris who is also having supervision with me. She is one of the best people I have ever known for the psychoanalysis of children. With her there is always a veritable discussion of the material of the sessions, an authentic dialogue. And she has *a mind of her own.*

Mrs Klein did not appreciate those who seemed too submissive to her theories or to what she formulated in supervisions about

---

1   This paper was given in Paris in November 2010 at a conference in honour of Martha Harris organized by the GERPEN (see Chapter 5).

technique. At about this time she had spoken to me about reading *Le Temps Retrouvé* of Proust during her summer vacation and had indicated to me a passage in the book in which Proust speaks of the readers of his work: "I would ask of them neither to praise nor to denigrate me, but only to indicate whether the words they read in themselves correspond to that which I have written" (my translation).

The memory of having tea at Mrs Klein's on a Saturday afternoon with Martha Harris (Mattie) and the family of Hans Thorner remains precious for me, and the affectionate friendship with Mattie that day continued over the years until her tragic and untimely death, and within me ever since in my internal world.

In January 1959, Mrs Harris invited me to attend a seminar at the Tavistock, which Mrs Esther Bick gave for the students of child psychotherapy (in fact psychoanalysis) in training there. There I benefited from being in on the animated *dialogue* between Mrs Bick and Mattie. With her pertinent comments and questions about the clinical material, Mattie helped the students often to recall other details and to comment on their own reactions. I was also impressed by her capacity for understanding and sympathy for the parents' suffering and their defences.

Invited to dinner at the Harris's, in addition to benefiting from the excellent cuisine prepared by Mattie, I was able to appreciate the quality of exchange between her and her husband, Roland Harris. Roland was a specialist in the study of children's education, with also a great knowledge of psychoanalysis including the works of Melanie Klein and W. R. Bion. Tragically, his sudden death several years later put an end to his contributions to his field of work. But fortunately, Mattie was able to keep what she had gained from him and develop it in her teaching and writings.

I had met Donald Meltzer in 1953 and we did the analytic training in London at the same time, as well as working together daily at the US Air Force Hospital near London for three years.

Given these links of friendship with Meltzer, I saw him often after my installation in Paris in 1966 (after several years in the USA). On the occasion of a European weekend of the British Psychoanalytical Society (around 1970, I believe), he announced to me that he and Mattie were to marry, asking for my comment. Of course, I was delighted to learn that two of my dear friends and colleagues were to be together, as was Mrs Bick who was so fond of them. On this occasion, Don said to me: "Mattie appreciates enormously the work of Bion, with whom she did a supervision for her training at the Institute. I have considerable reservations myself, for Bion does not seem to accord sufficient place for affects nor for the elaboration of fantasies." I answered: "I do not know Bion's work well, but I think he emphasizes the affects that accompany the L, H and K links, and it seems to me that alpha-function is essential for the elaboration of fantasies." However, very soon afterwards, under the influence and stimulation of Mattie, Don developed a passionate interest in Bion's work, becoming one of the analysts in the world who knew Bion's work best, giving it his own developmental and clinical applications, as seen in *The Kleinian Development* and *Studies in Extended Metapsychology* and other works.

After the International Congress in Paris in 1973, I invited Donald Meltzer and Martha Harris, and I think also Meg and others, for several days in my country house south of Chateaudun. There they shared with me their experience of work with groups of child analysts in Italy, in Norway[2] and other European countries as well as in America. Then I said to myself, "Well, why not in France, also?"

In a group for discussion of child psychoanalytic psychotherapy cases, created by Geneviève Haag with me in 1970, there were many cases of severe psychopathology including autism – a category which very much interested Geneviève but also Anik Maupas du Chatellier and Didier Houzel, who belonged to this

---

2 For many years they did supervision work with therapists at the Mentalhygienisk Rådgivningskontor in Oslo [note from Grete Tangen Andersen].

clinico-theoretical work group. So I felt it would be very useful to create links with Martha Harris, Donald Meltzer, and also separately with Frances Tustin, to further our understanding of autism and other severe problems in children. Also, I had noted the great interest of Florence Guignard and Jean Begoin in a seminar with them.

So, with the support of my colleagues, on the occasion of a visit to the Meltzers in their beautiful country house near Oxford, I extended an invitation to work with a larger group here. This took place the first time in January 1974, and was the beginning of what later became officially the GERPEN. At the third meeting after our discussion of clinical material, Martha Harris emphasized the importance of including baby observation (after the method of Esther Bick) in our programme. Already, Michel and Geneviève Haag had met with Mrs Bick in London and were very interested.

Some people who came regularly to our meetings tended to appreciate Don more than Mattie, underscoring his "genius and charisma", and failed to appreciate the fundamental contribution of Mattie to the discussions, with her own points of view, which were so enriching and stimulating for so many of us. Also, I found that Don's books became more clear, with an improved literary style, after their union. In "Acknowledgements" in *Studies in Extended Metapsychology*, he himself writes: "Many of my vague notions have been given greater precision by Martha Harris."

I tend to think of Martha Harris in an analogy with Nadia Boulanger who had the gift of stimulating creativity in composers of music, or like Marguerite Long, who I feel favoured the development of the works of Ravel and of Debussy during long walks together at the seaside, sending back inspiration through the beauty of her performances as pianist of their creations.

For those of you who did not know Martha Harris directly, it is fortunate that much of her written work exists in French translation. These writings reflect her qualities of warmth, intelligence and her generous spirit. Also in the programme that follows you will have the opportunity of hearing three of Mattie's former students, who became collaborators and then successors as teachers and authors at the Tavistock – Maria Rhode, Margaret Rustin and Gianna Williams. Their writings translated in French are also in the References. But first of all, you will come to know and listen to Meg Harris Williams, Mattie's daughter, who following the inspiration of her mother and that of Don Meltzer has developed her own work linking psychoanalysis with art and literature – "a mind of her own", also.

CHAPTER SEVEN

Martha Harris: an indelible creative memory[1]

Carlo Brutti and Rita Parlani Brutti

> Friendship is a hermeneutic tool which has been neglected in favour of an almost manic preoccupation with scientific objectivity, or an unjustified recourse to subjectivity. Friendship is a hermeneutic tool because it makes the interpreter and the message part of the same structure.
>
> (R. Panikkar, 1990)

What makes the memory of a person indelible? It is when memory depends not only on the shared events of a long time ago, but becomes living and operative in ourselves, as part of our personality and way of being, nourishing our internal world – something which we have constructed together. The relationship with this person does not then consist of sporadic or occasional memories which might remain circumscribed by their circumstances; instead it persists as an ineradicable creative memory. What can one say about such an experience without fossilizing it, unless one is a St Augustine or a Rousseau – a type of spiritual biographer so rarely to be found?

---

1 Translated from the Italian by Meg and Adrian Williams

Martha Harris has a significance for us that we do not regard as past, but rather as continuing in a way that permits an ongoing affectionate internal *convivere* with this friend and teacher. We would like to make explicit this living dimension of a relationship that, as with every true teacher, has become unconscious and inspires our work without our needing to consciously recall it.

Meg's invitation has given us the opportunity to re-engage in just such an explicit dialogue in our minds, with Martha before us as if contemporaneously, listening anew to her words as recorded in her writings. These reveal aspects and themes which we have only now discovered. It does not matter whether words were spoken or written many years ago and in a different chronological era because, as with the classics, we can always discover new meanings that illuminate our current uncertainties.

The psychoanalytic method and the vertex of the observer

In our revisiting of Martha Harris' writings we turned first of all to those little masterpieces that the passionate and competent dedication of Romana Negri made accessible: writing and overseeing the publication of research on infant development that was developed together with Donald Meltzer (Negri 1989, 2007). So we can listen to the story of Martha showing us how the child, from intrauterine life on, learns to cope with emotions, modulating or avoiding them: how it evolves its own identity and character through entering into dialogue with its environment, such that its ambience is not only found but constructed. An authentic psychoanalytic viewpoint permits us to observe the part played by the child in its own evolution, rather than regarding this as solely the result of conditioning (even "psychic"), and as the passive receptor of projections from the mind of its parents. Martha Harris of course does not undervalue the importance of education and training, nor does she go for the idea that everything that happens to the child is provoked by himself – his emotions and constitution. Instead she has always paid keen attention to relationships.

Martha Harris through her style of commentary – without always needing to explain everything – reminds us continually of the importance of the observer's vertex in psychoanalytic work, where observation is intended to reveal psychic reality. We see how in each interpretation there is an underlying choice between two opposing philosophical viewpoints, determinism and free will (logically antagonistic positions). Martha leaves it quite clear that psychoanalytic thinking can only opt for free will – as Freud showed when he found meaning and unconscious intention in the slips and somatic symptoms that arise after abandoning the struggle to make them conscious.

But psychoanalysis' choice of free will should not be confused with making judgements about alleged laws of reality. Every psychoanalyst knows in fact that only from the vertex of free will are we able to observe psychic reality: that is, to become aware of meaning and intentionality. In real life when we observe and think we oscillate between positions of free will and determinism.

In our opinion, when we acknowledge this, we can avoid muddling reality and thinking: recognizing however that it is through thinking that we become who we are. This means that psychoanalysis can interact with other disciplines for mutual enrichment, without needing to validate itself through something else – such as neuroscience or biology, predetermined by organic causes. Martha Harris' work enables us to avoid the naïve idea that we can believe without seeing and see without believing. For in psychoanalysis the observer must remain aware of the vertex from which he observes: psychic reality. If he is not he will find himself oscillating between the psychic and the physical. No comment can be said to be purely objective or subjective; and it is not the middle ground that we are looking for, but an interpretation that is consistent with *both* internal and external reality.

Observation in psychoanalytic research

The work done together by Harris and Negri provides a classic paradigm of how to do psychoanalytic research that is systematic and rigorous. Together with Racker (and Panikkar in philosophy) this helps us to recognize that the eye of the observer always enters into the representation of the observed data.

We think it is a permissible hypothesis that Martha Harris likewise taught and practiced from a non-dualistic philosophical perspective, and did not confuse some "ultimate reality" with the organization of our own consciousness. This we believe is why Martha and Romana do not quibble over the longstanding debates about the emergence of psychic life and the beginnings of a symbolic capacity. They concentrate on observing from life, and in this way have found the psychic reality in situations that even psychoanalysts had hastily dismissed (Brutti & Parlani, 1990, 2003). As a result of this revolutionary research the so-called "automatic" behaviour of the foetus or newborn infant in the whole area of consensuality – previously considered non-psychic – becomes open to the kind of observation that reveals its meaning.

Observation in training: use and abuse

When it comes to the role of observation in psychoanalytic training, Martha Harris uses it as a specific educational strategy. Here we will confine ourselves to considering how, in her comments in response to Romana Negri's observations (2007), she never yields to the temptation to use pre-packaged psychoanalytic (or sociological) formulae. She draws attention to the way that aspects of theory are often specially selected to gloss over the underlying problems and contradictions that are posed by observation. In this way she leads us towards a strong cognitive stance that reinforces our capacity not to succumb to many of the common errors in thinking. She shows how to avoid naively superimposing theory on an observation that appears not to conform. She makes us realize that this goal can only be pursued with an in-depth understanding of the theory of reference, that acknowledges its implicit qualities and the way in which it influences the way we make observations in the first place, so we are never simply observing a "given" fact. She tells us that an analyst should never forget that what he is observing is always the *relation between him and the patient*, as it is articulated at that moment, and that he can understand its meaning not from the outside but only from within himself.

We have focused here on observation as it is used in psychoanalytic training because it reactivates our earliest interest. For many years we have worked with observation in related fields – with psychotherapists, mental health professionals, teachers, social workers, rehabilitation therapists, etc. Gradually we realized that this tool, as it became ever more fashionable, could also be wrongly employed and even be presumed to be a profession in itself ("the observer"), authorized to "diagnose" the situation in schools, children's homes, or mothers with their children, and then to recommend changes in behaviour that was considered erroneous. The misunderstanding concerns the nature of the neutrality of the observer, who can never be totally outside what he is perceiving. In our time we have also seen much confusion arising from the misuse of observation as a type of group analysis (see Brutti and Parlani, 1996).

So this renewed encounter with Martha Harris, who has always demonstrated the great value of psychoanalytic observation without abusing it, urges us to honour the authentic method in our training practice, so that it does not become "copyrighted" by those who abuse it.

In reviewing our relationship with Martha Harris, we found ourselves paying special attention to one particular paper, "The individual in the group: on learning to work with the psychoanalytic method" (Harris, 1978b), that we asked to publish in Italian thirty years ago (1981). At that time we shared with her and with Donald Meltzer our ambition to export psychoanalytic knowledge to the educational and therapeutic fields in which we were involved: in particular, to the new psychiatric services that were developing in Italy in the light of the "antipsychiatry" movement. The psychiatric emphasis on the physical was seen as an improper treatment of the soul by comparison with psychoanalytic psychotherapy. We have written about how in that period, infant neuropsychiatry and paediatrics in Italy (indeed in Europe) tried to enhance their disciplines as a result of recognizing the huge potential in psychoanalytic thought (Brutti & Parlani, 2010). It was an important phenomenon, despite confusions resulting from mimesis and appropriation, and it had a significant impact on the spread of psychoanalysis. But a price was paid in terms of distortion and sometimes a type of subversion of psychoanalytic discoveries.

How do we become psychotherapists? We ask Martha Harris

It was in this context that Martha Harris and Donald Meltzer came to transmit psychoanalytic thinking about child development to those working with young children. Any attempt to convey the knowledge of one discipline to another can only avoid confusion if those teaching it continue to question their own theory and methods. They must be aware of the differences with neighbouring disciplines, of different ways of teaching in educational institutions, and above all of the ethics operating behind them. These are issues with which not everyone is willing to engage.

Martha Harris posed these questions and pursued them, in a continuing dialogue with both Meltzer and Bion, with which (as our writing bears out) we then took part in our turn. Today they underlie the work which we are doing in directing and teaching at the School of Psychoanalytic Psychotherapy at the Aberastury Institute. For us this experience revives these same questions with a new urgency. We try to reformulate them here, in summary, despite the risk of appearing naïve: What does it mean to become a psychoanalyst? How do we ensure a good "training"? Is psychotherapy a profession that can be taught or is it an innate talent? Can only a person with certain given characteristics become a psychotherapist? If so, what would these be – tolerance, sensitivity, desire to help others, an ability to emphasize, intuition, intelligence?

We will try to give some answers to these questions by making deductions from the teaching of Martha Harris. She put us on guard against the tendency to "collude in the idealization of being a psychoanalyst or a psychotherapist" (1978b, p. 34); underlining that psychoanalysis is a profession that requires (as does any other) life-long learning. This is why training institutions should aim to help their students to mature with an honest attitude, enabling them to change their plan if they find they are not able to sustain the demands of the training. She points out that this is not a matter of intelligence; and quotes Bion saying that being a psychoanalyst does not require outstanding intelligence, "but such intelligence as one has must be available for use 'under fire'" (1978b, p. 37). It follows that the training should not try to protect students from difficult or frustrating experiences, nor believe it is possible to remove the inevitable "loneliness in difficult clinical situations".

In short, Martha Harris guides us to the following conclusions: that the profession of the psychoanalyst is one which should be purified of idealizations, since these are an easy cover for feelings of omnipotence, and a breeding ground for those defences through which we try to avoid contact with reality; and that every profession should be "professed" (Chiozza, 2007), that is, be used in structuring personal identity honestly, authentically. The words "honesty" and "authenticity" – that recur throughout Martha Harris's writings – might suggest a moralistic note; but they mean something much more. In them lies the whole meaning of psychoanalytic therapy – the "science of psychoanalysis" and therefore also its "ethics" (Racker, 1961).

This summary sets out our direction as one of aiming to diminish the defences that uphold regressive and irresponsible tendencies. Not to remove the student's contact with frustration, but to guide them in search of the "truth" of their own thoughts and emotions. These guidelines are appropriate not only for analytic training but also for therapy and education. Also, to help them differentiate desire from need, so that they can understand reality not merely as an obstacle to pleasure and childish possessiveness, but also a place where effective "mourning" can be pursued.

One day long ago, Donald Meltzer, talking about the work that he and Martha were doing together in the world, said that he was the sower and Martha the cultivator. No seed can bear fruit unless it is subject in its development to the attention and patience of the farmer. Martha carried out this essential mission; and we continue to experience wonder and gratitude for having met and known a person so extraordinary.

CHAPTER EIGHT

Made in Hampstead and exported throughout the world: Germany and Austria

Ross A. Lazar

Leaving London and the Tavistock after studying and working there so intensively for more than seven years was not an easy thing for me to do. But having qualified as a psychoanalytic child and adolescent psychotherapist under the superb guidance and professional expertise of Mattie Harris as course organizer, mentor and "motherly friend", it was finally time for me to move on. And because of my "previous life" as a student of the History of Art and German Language and Literature in Munich – not to mention the fact that it is my wife's home – Munich was a logical place to look to in order to open the next chapter in our lives. This part of the decision was made easier by the worsening economic conditions in England at the end of the 1970s, the advent of Margaret Thatcher, and the fact that Germany was booming and greatly in need of well-trained child psychotherapists. Through a great stroke of luck, I was offered a job at the Biederstein Zentrum, a newly opened outpatient clinic for child and adolescent psychotherapy which Professor Jochen Stork – a psychiatrist and psychoanalyst trained in Paris – had established the previous year in the medical faculty of the Technical University of Munich.

But how to even *think about* leaving the relatively safe haven of the Tavi, of both orthodox Kleinian and the invigorating developments in "post-Kleinian" thinking and practice (as it was coming to be referred to back then), and go out into a strange world to attempt to practice psychoanalytic psychotherapy in a foreign language with children and adolescents whose backgrounds and life circumstances were so very different from my own? The idea both daunted and terrified me! But the decision had been made: we were going. In my insecurity and anxiety, I turned to Mattie to ask for advice, to gain support, and to assuage my fears that I was making a big mistake.

The conversation which ensued was brief but potent. Its upshot can be distilled into three recommendations which were of enormous consolation and usefulness both then and now. These were: firstly, do not select patients, but try to work with whoever comes your way. I was in fact terrified that I would be challenged to work with severe borderline, autistic and other psychotic patients, and would be overwhelmed and unable to do so. As it turned out, this was not just my fantasy! But somehow I did manage to deal with it, one case and one step at a time. Secondly, I was encouraged to come back for supervision as often as possible. So for several years I came at least once a term for supervision with both Mattie and Don, sometimes even at 7 o'clock on a Saturday morning, amidst breakfast being cooked, dress patterns and material spread out all over the floor and all three of us being engaged in the most exciting conversations about everything from my patient's material to the state of British, American and world politics! And finally, I was advised to remember the universality of the human psyche in its deep and essential sense – a fact which would help me overcome communication problems arising from differences in background, religion, ethnicity, age and life circumstances.

Consoling in a way, but also pretty powerful stuff! Furthermore, attached to it was a sort of legacy. Although there was no sense whatever of being sent out into the world as a kind of missionary to preach the "true belief" of post-Kleinian psychoanalytic thinking, certainly there was a strong sense of mission in another way. Clearly, Mattie strongly believed that through the training which taught us to wield an exceptionally fine and useful tool for helping people everywhere to live their lives better, we had a certain "obligation" (as she put it) to spread the idea, the sense – not through proselytizing, preaching or arguing, but through demonstration: offering and making available to others what we had learned through our own valuable experience of the teachings and methods of our mentors. She wrote:

> If the benefits of psychotherapy as an art-science are to be shared, it must concern itself with society as well as the individual. As analytical psychotherapists we must realize that it is a privilege, as well as a task, to be able to offer or receive an educational resource so rare and so costly in time and money. It is therefore an obligation, if we have so benefited, to continue to consider how the attitudes which we have found to be essentially life-promoting may be encouraged in others, especially those who have a hand in the rearing of children. (1977, p. 20)

Along with these three pieces of sound, indeed inspiring, advice, there were three areas of work that I had learnt at the Tavi and was convinced I wanted to pursue and, if possible, to promulgate in my new surroundings. These were: Infant Observation, Group Relations training, and the Tavistock clinical teaching method which Mattie had developed at the Tavi and which she and Don disseminated over the years in their travels abroad. The first and third of these point directly back to my learning experiences with Mattie; when I spoke to her about the Group Relations training, I found her cautiously critical of it – not entirely sceptical perhaps, but also not entirely convinced of its worth. (When I asked her in the mid-70s what she thought about attending the Leicester conference, she replied laconically: "Yes, I think that is something one might consider doing if one is of a mind to...").

Infant Observation in Munich

In September 1979, the prominent child analyst and student of Margaret Mahler's, Judith Kestenberg, was invited to come from New York to lecture to us at our new centre. Her subject was "baby watching" as it was being practiced and developed in the USA at the time. Coming from the intense background of Infant Observation as taught at the Tavi I found myself rather critical of the methods used for collecting data from mothers and infants; but all the same this event got me going in organizing the first Infant Observation Seminars in German-speaking Europe at that time. For the next few years I ran two seminars weekly in Munich, and also lectured on the method to interested persons who were for the most part child psychotherapists, but also pediatricians and pediatric nurses, child care workers and a smattering of adult psychotherapists and psychoanalysts.

Despite much interest and new study groups springing up, there was one main drawback, which (although less so than previously) hampers the development of Infant Observation in Germany to this day. For, unlike Italy in the 1970s, where virtually no established trainings in analytical child and adolescent psychotherapy existed at all, Germany after World War II had established rather quickly quite a large network of regional institutes for the training of child and adolescent psychotherapists and psychoanalysts, all of whom were bound to follow a rather strict and ponderous curriculum. Laid down centrally, this curriculum left little room for anything new, least of all something as radically different as the Infant Observation model of training. Nonetheless (and without going into all the in's and out's), suffice it to say that now, Infant Observation is more or less well established in practically all of those institutes; that at least one year of Infant Observation has become a required part of the training; and that many dedicated infant observers are constantly working at trying to improve the teaching skills of those who take the seminars, as well as increasing the areas of relevance reached by those skills.

I believe that without Mattie's demonstrating the fortitude, patience and quiet determination that was fed by her conviction of the ultimate usefulness and inspirational benefits of this work, I would probably have given up early on in the face of the considerable doubts, scepticism and outright attacks brought against it as a way of thinking and working. Following Mattie's inspirational model, I did manage to stick to the task, despite the often considerable opposition to it, for I remained convinced of its worth and of its ability to eventually convince others. Two quotes from her essay "The individual in the group: on learning to work with the psycho-analytical method" epitomize this attitude and serve me as guidelines still: "And yet", she wrote, "change and expansion needs to be facilitated so that psycho-analytic ideas and attitudes can travel and take root among workers who are ready to receive them, so that their usefulness may find homes in which to flourish" (1978b, p. 27). And in regard to those who subscribe to different theories, "schools" and/or systems of thought, she wrote: "If one is truly observing configurations which are there and is describing them well enough, unimpeded by theoretical preconceptions, other people with a different theoretical background may, if they can also free themselves from their preconceptions, make similar findings" (p. 30).

Infant Observation in Berlin, Stuttgart, and Vienna

In the 1980s I was invited to present Infant Observation at institutes in Stuttgart, Frankfurt, Cologne, Freiburg, Gottingen, and Berlin. Through the considerable initiative, effort and generous support of a Jungian colleague, Dr Antje Winkelmann, I worked with a group of fifteen trainee infant observers once a month over a two and a half year period during which we held marathon weekend Infant Observation seminars in which *everyone* presented their observation work each time we met! To bridge over the periods between these weekends, we also set up three self-running groups of five observers each of which met weekly to discuss the work amongst themselves. The upshot was that several Berlin institutes then incorporated the method into their curricula and several students from this project became excellent teachers of Infant Observation themselves.

Through Berlin being the unique city that it is, with its singular and unusual fate, it then happened that the political event which shook the world – the fall of the Berlin Wall – also had a direct and indeed, enormous, impact on Infant Observation in Germany, a fact which I imagine would certainly have interested and perhaps even pleased Mattie to know (see Winkler, 1997). In collaboration with my colleague and fellow student of Mattie's, Suzanne Maiello, five further colleagues were introduced to this training, four of them from East Berlin: two child psychiatrists, one pediatrician, one psychologist and one adult psychiatrist enrolled with a view to undertaking the whole curriculum of the Tavistock Observation Course. Owing to Suzanne's patient, thorough and energetic work, and despite considerable difficulties in communication (the fact, for instance, that all of us ostensibly spoke the same German language yet often found it hard to understand one another), most of these colleagues were able to do an infant observation and became convinced of its pedagogical value.

Subsequently, under the auspices of Dr Agathe Israel and her colleagues, a training institute for child and adolescent psychotherapy was established in the eastern part of the city, the first training institute of its kind in what had been the German Democratic Republic. This institute has grown significantly, training clinicians in child and adult psychoanalytic psychotherapy and hosting annual meetings for teachers of Infant Observation who come from all over Germany, Switzerland and Austria.

Among the other German institutes deserving special mention is the Academy for Psychoanalysis and Psychotherapy in Stuttgart. There, under the leadership of Barbara Hirschmueller and her colleagues, Infant Observation has grown and flourished particularly well. It was one of the first German institutes to offer a walk-in service for parents and infants in difficulties, as well as producing a considerable number of first rate observers and teachers of Infant Observation, in which the teachings of Martha Harris and Esther Bick have played an important role. The Academy has celebrated its tenth anniversary, and enabled Stuttgart to become an important regional centre for the development and encouragement of Infant Observation in southern Germany as well as advancing national developments in its clinical applications.

Finally, it would be amiss not to draw attention to the considerable observational work which has been established in Vienna – Esther Bick's *alma mater* – over the past twenty years, under the auspices of Gertraud Diem-Wille and her colleagues, and supported by close contact with the Tavistock. As a result, Infant Observation has gained a significant foothold in two separate university departments in Vienna. Dr Diem-Wille established a Master's programme in Psychoanalytic Pedagogy, modelled on the Tavistock course, at the Institute for Research and Further Education of the Alpen-Adria University of Klagenfurt/Vienna/Graz, which includes not only Infant Observation but also Young Child and Organizational Observation; while Wilfried Datler has incorporated Infant Observation in undergraduate studies in Education, and also recently completed a major research project into the quality of life of patients suffering from dementia and living in nursing homes, employing a modification of the methodology of Infant Observation as one of its main research instruments (see Datler et al, 2009). With these two Viennese developments, psychoanalysis and infant observation have "come home" to where they started: to the university where Esther Bick did her doctoral dissertation, and to where the pioneers of child analysis first started to work on the idea of a psychoanalytically informed approach to education.

Work Discussion seminars

After the initial phase of offering opportunities to do infant and young child observation in both the East Berlin course and the Viennese courses, it became evident from the nature of the work itself that something else was needed for the students of these courses to round out their observational education and skills. At the Tavistock, Mattie had introduced Work Discussion seminars in order to develop further learning skills. I suggested conducting Work Discussion Seminars for the teachers in both types of group so that they could then pass on this valuable additional learning opportunity. Happily this idea took root, and such seminars are now conducted on a regular basis in both the Berlin and the Viennese institutes.

A further attempt to introduce Work Discussion seminars on a larger (national) scale has only recently been completed, and it is as yet unclear what may become of it. The idea was to train a number of experienced child and adolescent psychotherapists in the method, who would then import it into their home settings. This group, made up of five colleagues from different geographic locations in Germany and representing four different training institutes, as well as the central training committee of the VAKJP[1] (the umbrella organization for all German analytic child and adolescent psychotherapists), were considering the possibility of introducing Work Discussion into their training schemes or curricular requirements. Whether this will happen is still undecided but the foundations are there.

Mattie as inspiration in clinical teaching

I would now like to say something about my experience of teaching of clinical psychoanalysis according to the Tavistock model as promulgated by Mattie and Don Meltzer during the course of their travels throughout the world. As with Infant Observation, I was convinced of the benefits of this method of teaching. Starting in the new Biederstein Clinic, and then after beginning my own private practice in 1982, I found that gradually individuals and small groups of colleagues began to come for supervision, for consultation on difficult cases, diagnostic help and generally in search of a forum where they could discuss their work. They were in search of a place where they could share problems with colleagues and get the benefit of their insights and perspectives without having to adhere to the strict institutional, philosophical, theoretical or methodological tenets espoused by their training institutions.

Inevitably, I found myself in conflict with some of these established institutions regarding the training of child psychotherapists. Throughout my various political trials and tribulations in this area surrounding my work, I felt enormously helped and supported by Mattie's words and attitude *vis à vis* psychoanalytical institutions as she so cogently set them out in the sections on "Working in institutions" and "Work groups and establishments" in her essay on "The individual in the group"

---

1 *Verein für analytische Kinder-und Jugendlichenpsychotherapie* (Society for Analytic Child and Adolescent Psychotherapy).

(1978b). Moreover my direct experience of her discrete, non-interventionist position *vis à vis* a scandalous situation in one of the clinics in which I worked during my training, has served me as a model and a sort of compass with whose help I have been able to better navigate my way through other similarly difficult and dangerous institutional waters. She taught me, and my fellow trainees at the same clinic, what it mean to "contain", to tolerate and thus to "make the best of a bad job" as Bion put it, given that neither we nor she were in any position to amend or even influence the situation much.

With this in mind, and especially after beginning my own private practice, I began to establish small circles of interested colleagues for purposes of clinical discussion, not only in Munich but in Berlin and also in Frankfurt, Stuttgart, Graz and Vienna. In these groups, while encouraging people to try to present their material according to the Tavistock clinical teaching method, the main aim is to create as tolerant and unprejudiced an atmosphere as possible. For only in this way, as Mattie taught and showed us, is anything approaching tolerance and curiosity about the Unknown possible. Only in such an atmosphere does anything even remotely approaching an attitude towards "becoming O" become thinkable.

To give an example: some time in the early 1990's, a group of young child psychotherapist trainees from the Munich Academy for Psychotherapy and Psychoanalysis (which had refused to recognize me as one of its supervisors) asked me to talk with them for just three evenings about the work of Melanie Klein and her successors. I was very pleased to have been asked, and did my best to fulfil some of their wishes and needs in this regard. Suffice it to say that this group, far from being over after three sessions, is still running strong after over twenty years! In it we discuss cases, read theoretical texts (for the last several years we have moved on from Klein to Meltzer and Bion) and in addition, discuss a wide range of related topics, from film and literature, politics and economics, to the state of psychoanalysis in Germany and philosophical links with religion, Lacanian and other brands of psychoanalysis and, of late, neuro-psychoanalysis and even quantum physics! Here too, I strongly feel Mattie's open, tolerant, intellectually curious and wide-ranging attitude hovering over our discussions, no matter how far afield we sometimes seem to stray. For somehow, we always end up back with our patients, and through carefully detailed description and reflective thought, we continue to try to get to know them, their meaning and their "becoming" somewhat better.

Indeed several of these groups in different places are still running strong, with older members dropping out and newer ones coming along, both out of curiosity and pure interest and because they are searching for something which they have not found operating in their training institutions. Ironically, over the years, many of those institutions have begun inviting me to demonstrate the clinical teaching method and to help them overcome their inhibitions, fears, prejudices and sheer ignorance about Kleinian, post-Kleinian, Object Relations psychoanalysis – or the "English School" as it is often called. Difficult as it was at the beginning, it is all the more satisfying that things are now developing and that these modes of thinking are becoming valued and sought after, especially in working with the most disturbed, damaged and underprivileged of our patients.

But despite the relative success of these activities, one major dilemma remains unsolved, and I must admit, frustrates me considerably. It is the fact that, as Mattie again so aptly puts it:

> Even if one is quite convinced that a student recurrently fails to comment upon or even see material that is asking for attention, one can be useful only by trying to approach the material again and again – by describing it ever anew from different angles as it occurs in different contexts. (1977, p. 14)

And, as she goes on to explain, "well meant" corrections "*de haut en bas*", and vague and unsubstantiated implications of criticism without offering a creative alternative are not only not helpful, but serve to increase the frustration and possibly the envy, the idealization and/or denigration of the teacher or supervisor, while undermining the possibility of a stance which allows for and encourages "learning from experience" and the "struggle in the dark towards some glimmer of light" in which we are all engaged, like it or not.

CHAPTER NINE

Mattie in Bombay

Sarosh Forbes

I met Mattie first when she and Don came to Bombay to teach the group here. They were the first British analysts to be invited to teach our group. At that time I was already making preparations to go to London as an overseas guest of the British Psychoanalytical Society. I was by then a qualified analyst but I did want to get some more experience in a personal analysis and supervision with adult cases along with seminars at the BPS.

When I arrived in England a big problem facing me, my wife and our two children was how to finance everything. My wife fortunately got a job with Air India in London but this was not enough to sustain us. This is where Mattie came in. Since I knew her from Bombay I met her and conveyed my problem. She was of enormous help in three most important ways.

First, she suggested that I train as a child psychotherapist, which would not only help me financially but also she felt it was essential in analytic work to have experience with children. And she said that since I was already a member of the IPA I could be a trainee immediately through section 5 of the ACP. I had no clue about any of this and her advice enabled me to get two jobs: one in a school for disturbed children and the other in a child guidance clinic. I took a weekly supervision with Mattie, an experience which I treasure and which will always be with me. During this supervision I had a particularly difficult autistic child in therapy. I still remember her words when I thought this child was not helpable – he had no speech apart from his tantrums, etc. She said never stop thinking, never stop trying to think and understand. This child began speaking and his overall improvement was dramatic. And I became a member of the ACP.

And then Mattie helped my development once again. She referred an adult patient for a five times a week analysis. I had no place I could see this patient, so she offered her own consulting room at Swiss Cottage. And her generosity did not stop here; she asked me one day if I would like to be part of a special Infant Observation she had been thinking about for some time. She said she had been thinking of holding a weekly baby observation seminar for two years for postgraduate qualified ACP members and that there would only be one baby under observation. And that baby would be mine. I was delighted and honoured. The experience was unforgettable. I still remember a battle between the mother and baby when the baby started turning blue and breathless. Mattie commented that this baby would probably become asthmatic as she grew older. After some years when I was in London I visited the family – I was told that the baby, now grown, was asthmatic.

Words cannot express my feelings about Mattie and how much I owe her. In the Bombay group we now have a two-year Baby Observation as part of the psychoanalytical training. For years it was conducted by me, and now one of the students in my group who has qualified as a child psychotherapist conducts the seminars.

The Tavistock/Martha Harris course in India

In 1974 the Bombay group of psychoanalysts founded a public charity trust called the Psychoanalytic Therapy and Research Centre (PTRC), whose aim was to promote the growth and development of psychoanalytical work with children and adults. Although adults and children were treated at the clinic none of the analysts had any formal training in Child Psychotherapy.

This changed when I and a couple of other colleagues went to London for the training. One of my most profound experiences in London was at the Tavistock with Martha Harris. Everyone who came into touch with Martha Harris admired her for her lucid and precise way of thinking and loved her for her generous spirit: this included my colleagues Dr Manek Barucha, his wife Aiveen, and Minnie Dastur, all of whom trained at the Tavistock.

Somewhat later in the mid 1990s after I had finally returned to Mumbai, we began the Baby Observation course at the PTRC. Initially and for several years, I led the baby observation seminars. All thanks go to my experience with Mattie in the special intensive baby observation seminars in London.

Interestingly, this resulted in the notable stimulation of the Mumbai (Bombay) psychoanalytic scene, with the introduction of the two-year preclinical observation course based on the Tavistock model in London. This has generated interest every year since we opened the course for new students. It has led to a two-pronged development. One, it has opened up psychoanalysis to more of the public, and begun a growing knowledge and understanding – which had so far been almost non-existent – in the uniqueness of close and detailed observation which only psychoanalytic insights can obtain. And second, it has stirred and motivated some of the students to continue developing this further by undertaking the clinical training in child psychotherapy.

Further, in quite an interesting way a third development has taken place: most of those who have qualified as child psychotherapists wish to train further with adults and qualify as psychoanalysts. Our group in Mumbai is steadily growing. Although the numbers are still modest, one has to compare this with an almost zero stagnation before 1996; and the exciting fact is that it is growing slowly but surely.

Another offshoot of our growth took place in January 2005 when three of our qualified child therapists read clinical papers at our biannual India-Australia-Israel Psychoanalytic Conference in Mumbai. Our foreign colleagues were quite delighted to see new faces and hear child material from Mumbai being discussed for the first time.

In 2002, the PTRC inaugurated the Horniman Circle Therapy Centre and, later, the Bandra clinic in suburban Mumbai. These are the only clinics of this type in Mumbai, offering psychoanalytic psychotherapy and psychoanalysis to families from all income groups. From July 2005 this was offered on a more extensive and wider scale than previously attempted. We now aim to treat and support children, parents and adults with a range of emotional difficulties. A team of psychoanalysts and child psychotherapists provide consultations, assessments, and both brief and intensive treatment.

To date, with the new infusion of recently qualified child therapists and analysts, together with more senior students in the clinical training, we have formed an adequate team striving to help the people who come to the centre. Recently however the demand has been overwhelming, and the amount of work we can do is limited, since the equivalent of the NHS is sorely missed here and we have to struggle with private funding. Also, although we are located in the heart of Mumbai city, the clinic space is still inadequate. Still the future of our work is looking hopeful, and to improve our situation we are exploring various avenues for funding.

Recently two of our programmes – the training in Psychoanalytic Psychotherapy with Children, Parents and Young People, and the course in Psychoanalytical Observational Studies – received recognition from the Tavistock Clinic. This went a long way in attracting students from fields as varied as education, medicine and social work.

As the member strength increased slowly but steadily, our group activities too began expanding to include more services such as the Young People's Counselling Service; community outreach work in three schools (where our child psychotherapists work with school children, parents and teachers); and most recently, a service that provides psychotherapeutic assistance in the area of Infant Mental Health.

It is perhaps the best tribute to Mattie Harris' invaluable support that the fledgling group whose hand she held while it took its first steps in Mumbai, is now taking confident strides ahead.

CHAPTER TEN

Turning points enabled by Martha Harris

Marja Schulman

We arrived in London in the early autumn of 1973, when my husband Gustav started his studies at the Tavistock Clinic in the Adult Department. He chose to do an Infant Observation seminar led by Mrs. Martha Harris. I had never heard about baby observation. When I listened to his accounts of the seminar, I felt an irresistible urge and need to get involved. He managed to convey to Mrs Harris that his wife was passionately eager to join in. I was a newly qualified clinical psychologist. Could she somehow do it? Mattie said it was ok, that I could visit the family with him. He went once a week to a working class family with a baby and the little two and a half year old girl. The mother seemed friendly and said it was fine if I came along.

I remember well our visit to the family. The house was clean and straightforward, no fancy things. I thought Mrs A probably felt it was very natural for Mrs Schulman to come. There was nothing awkward about it – on the contrary. My observations concentrated on the little girl: the big sister who put a little ball under her blouse, pretending she was like Mummy with breasts.

I remembered doing that myself in my childhood. The baby's nappies were changed by the competent mother according to routine. He was not breastfed.

Maybe I visited the family only once, likewise the seminar, but this experience gave me a memorable experience and was the start of my lifelong passionate interest in baby observation.

I joined the seminar on the occasion when it was my husband's turn to present. I think this happened only once. The seminar went on in an ordinary way. Nobody made a deal about there being an (uninvited) visitor. We presented the material together. He had written the notes and I added some observations about little girl Tracey. The seminar burst into laughter when I pronounced her name as they did in the family – in the cockney dialect.

Would I agree if one of my students asked me if their spouse wanted to come along – even if she/he were a professional? I doubt it.

I did not have a clue what to do in England. I knew about the Anna Freud training but had never heard about the child psychotherapy training at the Tavistock. Therefore I could not imagine that some day – quite soon, in fact – later during the same autumn term, I would be accepted onto the course. I heard there was a Child Psychotherapy course at the Tavistock from an Indian psychologist in the Adult Department, H. Gill. I decided to contact the head of the course and soon met Mrs Harris again. I told her I was interested in child psychotherapy even though I had no experience with children. At the end of that interview she said that I could start straight away. It was November. Many of my trainee colleagues have had the same experience. We had not realized that we had had an intake interview, as the occasion was totally informal. There was no sign of standard interview procedure. She created an atmosphere of spontaneity and exploration. Maybe in this way she got a better contact with the person she wanted to get to know.

The first lectures of the course were by Don Meltzer on Kleinian development. It was a language course for me: the contents were mostly beyond my comprehension but left a deep impression on me. He was taping the lectures as he was preparing his future book on *The Kleinian Development* (1978). Although I did not know anything about child psychotherapy and had only a very vague idea of Kleinian psychoanalysis, it turned out that I had learned some important basic concepts in Finland. We had read Isca Wittenberg's book *Psychoanalytic Insight and Relationships: a Kleinian Approach* (1970). I remember that reading about jealousy and envy was followed by intensive dreaming the following nights. I still find the book as fresh and engaging as I did then. It has given me the essence of Kleinian thinking in a most digestible, clear and supporting way. The other book was Bion´s *Experiences in Groups* (1961), which was hard to read.

However, the basic assumptions and different group cultures first became familiar in our group psychotherapy supervision in Finland. We had been working together: Gustav as the group therapist and I as the silent observer! Our supervisor, Dr Henrik Carpelan – then the only Kleinian psychoanalyst in Finland – said once that if he were young he would go to London. He had met Don Meltzer in Geneva during his psychoanalytical training in Switzerland. Our senior colleagues in Finland gave us some good advice, recommendations and warnings before we left for London: remember Anna Freud, beware of the Kleinians and their deep interpretations, the names of prominent analysts, etc. I thought maybe it was better that I go to a Freudian and Gustav to a Kleinian analyst. It soon became clear that we would stay many years in London – eight years altogether by the end.

The Child Psychotherapy training starts

The fact that Mattie let me start the course in the middle of the term, was a measure of most unforeseen flexibility and generosity. It enabled me to get hold of something very meaningful. Very soon I got advice from her where to start working. One possibility was to work as a "play lady" in the Family Department at the Cassel Hospital. I preferred a child guidance setting. Again Mrs Harris listened to my wish and said I could contact a clinic in Hertfordshire. I enjoyed child guidance team work for the next eight years in Hitchin, St Albans and the Tavistock. I was able to work full time as a child psychotherapist, and had good support for my work in the clinical seminars at the Tavistock. In a most casual way Mattie gave me the names of two training analysts.

My very first patient was a defiant five-year-old boy. He was jumping all over in the large therapy room, even on the furniture in a dangerous way. He got increasingly excited and wild and I was increasingly scared that he would hurt himself. He totally ignored my warnings and threatened that if he fell he would tell his mother that I had hit him. I said he knew that it was a lie. Then he fell and he yelled and yelled. The mother had returned to the waiting room. When the time was up, I met an angry and anxious mother who questioned sternly, what had happened? The receptionist had managed to stop her coming into the room. I asked the boy first to tell his mother what had happened. I was shivering inside and saw myself sitting in the court, and feared this was the end of my career which had hardly started. The mother left the clinic with her son and never came back. It was new to me the way this incident and its dynamics were reflected on and digested in great detail in the seminars. I learned about the case, about myself, about violent projective identification, turning the tables upside down, identification with the aggressor, etc. Mrs Harris thought it was important to develop an internal frame of reference for assessing patients for psychotherapy. This was the beginning of that process. I got over my "trauma", but I have always remembered the incident.

Infant Observation during my training

I observed two babies during my training. The first family moved abroad when the baby was just one year old. During that first year they adopted a three year old child. It was eye-opening to observe closely how painfully space was created for a new family member partly at the expense of the baby. The baby was weaned early but he was very brave. Then I started to observe a three month old baby in another family. I realized soon how much I had missed in not observing the baby from birth. I remember the visits very vividly.

In those days the Infant Observation seminars were very crowded. There was no space for me, but instead I had pair supervision with another trainee, with Miriam Garcia as a supervisor. We were fortunate as we could present almost every visit in the weekly supervision. Once Miriam suggested I should go to Mattie's seminar to present my baby observations as there was some concern about the baby. The mother had mentioned without any sign of worry that she could leave the baby in the high chair alone and even go out for a while. The baby was by then eight months. He was just sitting calmly without crying or protest. I was worried about his development and his autistic ways of coping with the absence of the mother. Once when the mother went upstairs and the baby was again sitting in the highchair, I decided to be more active with him. I played a little with his toys in front of him. He pushed them to the floor, but never reached out or looked for them. I picked the toys up, and the same thing happened a few times. I felt we had contact with each other. Mattie commented that the baby needed my or mother's mental attention and ability to think about the missing toy/mother before he could become able to start thinking and looking for it himself. On one visit the elder sister, who was usually with us, was not there. As the mother did not mention her absence I asked her where she was. Mother told that she must be in the next room and that she had been ill. I went there and saw nothing first, but there she was lying on the floor. She was flat and empty as if the air had been puffed out of her. A big contrast as she was usually a busy body, a sturdy muscular little girl. Mattie described how this little girl's muscularity and active motor activity were her second skin, and now being ill without mother's containment had left her vulnerable, internally not supported, flat and empty. A very inspiring comment packed with understanding. I think she combined Bick's and Bion's ideas in her own thinking in a most graspable way.

Later I joined the postgraduate Infant Observation seminar group with Esther Bick. Jeanne Magagna was the observer of an infant over three years (she published a paper about this experience in the *Journal of Child Psychotherapy* [1987]). This was a most fascinating learning experience. Mrs Bick opened our eyes to the moments of holding and of uncontainment and the infant's ways of coping with these.

It was crucial for my future infant observation teaching that I had the chance to observe more than one baby with good supervision, followed by a three year master-class supervision experience with Mrs Bick. Mattie knew I was planning to leave England in a couple of years time. My teaching skills were strengthened by the baby observation teaching experience at the Tavistock. After my graduation in 1978 I led my first infant observation seminar with four talented first year child psychotherapy trainees. I felt sorry for them that they did not have Mrs Harris or someone else more experienced as their teacher. To my big relief and joy they all later made great contributions in their clinical and written work.

I also had another opportunity of teaching baby observation, to the social worker students at Brunel University with Miryana Ivandic-Renton and Anne Alvarez. We had parallel seminars. After the seminars we shared and discussed our experiences. This was a great way to get peer supervision which was very helpful and gave much needed support.

Supervision experience with Mrs Harris with adult patients

I will say a few words about my supervision experiences with Mrs Harris, because it contributed to my professional development as a psychotherapist, to my understanding of the infant in the adult, and gave me the confidence to take on teaching and training responsibilities when back in Finland. Mattie supervised my adolescent training patient, a twenty-one year old woman whose problem was that she was constantly changing jobs, places, houses, countries, therapists. She was my first young adult patient, and I was nervous. The patient phoned me the previous night to check the time. She sounded very confident which made me even more unsure about myself. Mattie explained she was pouring her own anxieties into me, and said that she was likely to be more nervous than me. I have always remembered this helpful comment. After the first session, my patient panicked. She refused to lie down and was uncertain about coming anymore. She was too scared to come, as a dog nearly bit her in the street. She felt that even the dogs sensed how frightened she was. Mattie said that it seemed that her angry feelings were leaking from her mind into the breast without her knowing, and this led to a situation in which she was frightened of the breast biting her. That was why she did not lie down or trust me. I had no choice other than to try to say that in my own words, as otherwise I might lose her. Since then I have seen this situation many times with babies at the breast and children in therapy. She continued her therapy and eventually resumed the couch. She was often very confused and did not know who she was. Her confusion showed in many ways: in her handwriting, mixed styles of dressing, etc. During the course of the therapy I had a constant anxiety that she would leave. I had considered it to be my own personal fear of losing a training patient. When Mattie heard about it she thought my patient was worried that she might not give herself enough time for the help she needed. After I conveyed this to my patient there was a turning point. When she finally left, she had internalized something good and solid which she appreciated and was grateful for. I often felt that Mattie's comments were paving a way to a major change. They contained truthful understanding and gave food for thinking. My other two training supervisors were Mrs Shirley Hoxter and Dr Meltzer.

Mattie also supervised my parent work. I was seeing a woman whose daughter was having intensive therapy. She developed a deep sense of feeling left out and a grievance that she never had the kind of therapy her daughter was having. She had spent many years in a children's home and had an unhappy relationship with both her mother and her daughter. Mattie suggested I take her for intensive therapy and she would give me supervision. The setting was changed to three times a week psychotherapy, lying on the couch. Mattie knew that I had intentions to apply for the psychoanalytical training. I sensed she was not happy about this but understood my wish to work with adults. She had again a practical and quick straightforward solution and I felt ready enough to take on the challenge. She organized an adult psychotherapy training experience for me with two intensive training cases with weekly supervisions. For the second adult case I also had a woman whose child was a training patient of my colleague. Mattie suggested I contact Mrs Bick. The supervisions with Mrs Harris and Mrs Bick helped me to see the emotional turmoil of the uncontained infant in the adult. Both my patients had suffered from an early lack of maternal containment and they were prone to catastrophic anxieties of falling into emptiness and nothingness. They had developed a defensive second skin structure in the psyche and remained very vulnerable. I could link this with my infant observation experiences. I have worked ever since privately with both adults and children.

One day, before I had qualified, Mrs Harris said to me in the corridor in the midst of a busy day: "I think you could apply for membership of the ACP." This was done in the same casual style as the intake interview.

The summer parties at her house at East Mersea with her cooking are very fond memories, and also winter in Oxford. She had "common sense" (that is, used all her senses with intuition). She was enabling and inspiring in many ways: creative, practical and flexible. She had a great capacity to keep many people and their training needs in her mind in a lively way while working hard. She had visions and dreams, but she was not a perfectionist, but always easy to approach. She reminded me of a northern woman, well versed in the seasonal hardships and delights (external and internal), so down to earth and sensible. She was always busy with life and could seize the moment ("carpe diem"); I saw her sometimes enjoying gardening in a brief time slot between supervisions. She had so many important things to do meanwhile – the care of the child psychotherapy students near and far.

Baby observation in Finland

I had wished that I could take with me the baby observation and plant it to Finland. I hoped I could one day teach it as a part of the training. Very soon in the middle of the 1980s, a first opportunity to teach Infant Observation came via my husband. It was a Swedish-speaking adult psychotherapy course. We did the first seminar together as Swedish is not my best language and he did not intend to take on the seminar. Since then I have functioned as the baby observation teacher in many courses. Then a group of senior psychoanalysts at the Therapeia Foundation in Helsinki (not IPA) asked me to arrange a three year seminar for them with a view to their starting a child psychotherapy training in the future. I arranged monthly introductory child psychotherapy seminars starting with baby observation, then clinical and theory seminars. I could freely choose the literature. Martha Harris' *Thinking about Infants and Young Children* (1975) was one of them.

All the participants had worked clinically with children in child psychiatric settings although they were adult psychoanalysts. I took on the challenge as naturally as earlier in London when Mrs Harris had offered me opportunities and advised me to take on new challenges. I was by no means ready for it, but internally I felt that I was faced with a kind of opportunity not offered twice. I felt should take it on and struggle to do the best I could. It enabled me to have a lively internal dialogue with Mrs Harris as a supervisor and mentor – and my other good objects – and to adopt her attitude. She has been a source of inspiration for my work. I know she would have been pleased to hear about the developments in Finland.

In the seminars I could share what I had learned at the Tavistock and elsewhere with these open minded senior colleagues, who did not know me beforehand. I learned from them how they thought about Kleinian ideas and I developed my own thinking further. It was very important and necessary for me to process and integrate my clinical and theoretical thinking in my own language in my own cultural environment. Very soon after the seminars ended in 1990 a new Child Psychotherapy Training was launched at the Therapeia Foundation in Helsinki. It included Baby Observation, Young Child Observation, and Work Discussion seminars with pre-clinical and clinical parts as in the Tavistock model. Later on I became the organizing tutor. I taught the Infant Observation alone for many years; now we also have other teachers. A ninth child psychotherapy training course will start at the end of 2011.

I have had the opportunity to introduce baby observation also to other training organizations, and to arrange private seminars. There is sometimes a dilemma in the adult trainings: baby observation is seen as taking too much time from other topics. However many feel it would be a shame and great loss to reduce baby observation. In 2000 the first infant-parent psychotherapy training was launched at Turku University in Finland. Baby observation was a natural part of the curriculum. Written work on baby observation is required, shared and discussed in the final seminars.

Many colleagues, before they take on the teaching, have sat in my seminars as an observer. They all had their own baby observation experience during their training.

It was important also to write something about baby observation in Finnish. I wanted to protect Esther Bick's method. Eventually my book on baby observation, *Vauvahavainnointioppia Observoimalla,* was published by the Therapeia Foundation in 2002. It has 135 pages. Many people have read it when travelling long distances on trains or buses ("small is beautiful"). I kept in mind also ordinary people who may want to read it. I wrote it in a very down to earth way, the only way I can write. It has found its readers and is widely used in different trainings. Many want to know about baby observation even if they don't have a chance to do it. An English version is being considered.

Chapters dealing with baby observation have also been included in many Finnish textbooks. My most recent paper "Infant observation as part of training and clinical work with infants and parents" is included in *Early Emotional Relationships and Their Protection* edited by Jari Sinkkonen (Helsinki, 2011).

Although I am happy that there are many who are interested in teaching baby observation, I find myself hoping to lead a new seminar once more, to vitalize my other work. It is now thirty years since I left London and almost forty years since I had the unusual introduction to infant observation which was the beginning of my lifelong interest in it.

CHAPTER ELEVEN

Growing points and the role of observation[1]

Meg Harris Williams

The title of this chapter is taken from my mother's last paper, published in 1982: "Growing points in psychoanalysis inspired by the work of Melanie Klein". Here she reflects on the influence of Mrs Klein and selects what she considers to be genuine subsequent "growing points" in the history of psychoanalysis itself; Bion would call these points of "catastrophic change".

What is a growing point? To pursue her botanical metaphor, a growing point is a place where all the essential genetic information for development is concentrated, ready to sprout or branch outward. It is a point at which different influences converge, meet, and create another shoot (a new idea or "baby"), and there is of course an implication of inevitable "growing pains". She uses the term "inspired by", which always implies a sense of responding to a life-force beyond any single person's control – "the force that through the green fuse drives the flower" as Dylan Thomas expresses it (*Fern Hill*). The historical growing points

---

[1] First presented at a meeting of the GERPEN in honour of Martha Harris, November 2010 (see Chapter 5).

since Klein that she lists in her paper are very few: firstly, Bion's idea of the thinking breast that operates through normal projective identification; secondly, Mrs Bick's of normal unintegration and integration; thirdly Meltzer's distinction between three- and two-dimensionality. These are all concepts that enhance our capacity to observe the complexity of normal development, marking the seismic shift in psychoanalytic thinking from its earlier preoccupation with psychopathology and diagnosis.

I believe that Martha Harris's method of teaching psychoanalytic observation by means of a marriage between Bick and Bion is itself a growing point in psychoanalysis, perhaps one that is not yet fully developed. She tied Bion's imaginative conjectures about the internal group and the infant in all of us with Bick's method of observing the mother-infant relationship. My mother was interested in infants not because she doted on babies, but because infants tell us about ourselves, by activating our core identifications and our capacity to learn from experience, in a way that avoids the confines of verbal communication. The prototypal container-contained link between mother and baby is overseen by what Bion calls a "third eye" (Bion 2005, pp. 20, 23). The third, overseeing eye, entails a sense of being observed by a non-persecutory object. In infant observation, Martha Harris writes, a "reliable watching person" helps the mother "recover her ruptured sense of identity but with additional space to accommodate the child" (1982, p. 85). In other words, the presence of an "observer" is therapeutic in a particular way: not through understanding, but rather, through spatial extension. The new infant for whom space is being found in the world is a living embodiment of the new idea that Bion talks about as requiring space in our minds, and that he emphasizes is accompanied by turbulence and discomfort (growing pains) as well as wonder and surprise.

All the great minds in psychoanalysis emphasize the strenuous nature of observation and the psychic discipline involved. They recognise the distinction between explanation and exploration in the psychoanalytic model of the mind. Observation activates our own transference to internal objects; it stimulates a latent turbulence and initiates the growing-point. It is an indication of interest, and therefore of hope – possibly the most essential requirement for any therapeutic outcome. My mother also made use in her seminars of the fact that a focus on observation can afford relief from competition, "anxiety-ridden interpretation" and "therapeutic zeal", as well as other "impediments", including that caricature of observation the "voyeuristic eye" that seeks only to find "psychopathology in everything" (1977, p. 10). In addition, she saw that the threesome of baby, mother and observer replicated the psychic vertices of the analytic situation – in the consulting room and indeed other fields of self-analysis. Like the three actors in a Greek drama, they can tell any human story. The observing aspect of the mind links the other protagonists in a fertile conjunction; they are all necessary ingredients in the nodal growth-point. Learning to observe truly, and to tolerate what we see, is what enables the growth of container-contained to occur.

My mother saw infant observation (as established by Mrs Bick) as an ideal opportunity for the type of educational experience in which self-observation plays a crucial role. Adding this to Bion's theories about groups, she expanded her idea of an educational experience into other contexts, such as the "work discussion group", using Bick, but in a way that Bick herself was not in a position to do. In her model of psychic education, nobody is merely learning "about" another person – whether adult, infant, family member, or school pupils; they are learning through self-observation. For as Bion points out, we can only see anything at all by virtue of the "marks" which the phenomenon makes on oneself. My mother was constantly aware that it is oneself one is observing and analysing, all the time, whatever the context, alone or in a group. In all the areas in which psychoanalytic observation plays a part, she stressed not theory but "self-scrutiny".

Where Bion generally speaks of observation as the key to the idea that "lies beyond" (the "O" or essence of an emotional situation), my mother (like Mrs Bick) stresses the quality of individuality that lies at the heart or core of a situation. These two ways of elaborating the purpose of observation are the same thing, but with a variation in emphasis. Where Bion's theme is that observation leads us to an abstract, untranslateable Idea ("O"), my mother aims to pinpoint the individuality of the baby (or analysand, or mother-baby couple) . So the aim of observation appears different, but in fact, I think it is the same. Discovering the quality of individuality is the same as finding the abstract "O" behind an educational relationship, the sort that results in "becoming" oneself. My mother focussed on the particular in order to define something more abstract and universal – the principle of growth itself. Her students always stress her astonishing focus on the tiny attributes that indicate individuality – this child and no other: a search to perceive the vital growing point that might lie beyond or buried in the sensuous present. As Bion says, we are interested in the psychic equivalent of the physician's "see, hear, touch, smell" (1970, p. 7). Or as Shakespeare put it, "Love sees not with the eyes but with the mind". In their joint search to discover the infant's individuality, both mother and observer are concerned with noticing tiny manifestations of the principle of growth, and therefore, the potential to expand their own horizons of knowledge.

And this individuality can only be captured, by a process of defining and describing at the same time. For as Meltzer puts it, "Which comes first, the seeing or the describing?" (1981, p. 504); or Bick: the observer "finds that he chooses a particular word because observing and thinking are almost inseparable" (1964, p. 112). My mother stressed the importance of writing not because she wanted to turn psychotherapists into creative writers, but because she believed in the potential of writing, however awkward, to be a truthful discipline for the recording of observations. She saw it not as a means of self-publication or display but as a slow and sometimes painful tool for enhancing self-observation, from which it may acquire a value for others.

In her paper "Some notes on maternal containment and good-enough mothering" (1975b), she takes Winnicott's formulation of the "good enough mother" and considers how to "add depth" to this valuable but quantitative concept. She suggests Mrs Bick's method of detailed observation of the "interaction between individual mothers and infants may help us to formulate better the quality that underlies this quantitative differentiation" (p. 140). She saw the mother-baby relationship as a complex interaction of container and contained, not simply one in which the mother provides "enough" containment for the baby's anxieties. In "Growing points" she writes:

> When referring to the epistemophilic instinct, Mrs Klein laid emphasis on the innate urge of the child to learn about the world. Bion gave another slant to this: he regarded it as the basic need to know the truth about oneself, which is fostered by a mother who is able to discard preconceived theories about children, who is able to be continent and cognisant of her own infantile emotions and to respond to the projections and communications of her own particular infant in its particular context. (1982, pp. 69-70)

There are many ways in which a mother can be "good enough" and it is their distinctness which is interesting, not just the judgement – correct in its way – that to be good enough is better than to be perfect. The good-enough mother is both "continent and cognisant" of her own infantile emotions – that is, she goes beyond a containing function to one of self-observation and self-knowledge. This special type of coming-to-knowledge (which is not necessarily conscious or verbalized) is inseparable from a recognition of the uniqueness of the baby and of her own response to its communications. Beyond and behind the idea of "good enough" is the goal of being real, genuine – a true network of growing points in psychic reality for all concerned.

One of my mother's favourite concepts was "realism". It held a wealth of significance for her. Realism means seeing qualitatively not quantitatively: neither compromising nor sitting in judgement. To be in touch with reality is growth-promoting, and it is the result of true observation. Almost invariably it requires a recognition and acknowledgement of envy, and she stressed that it is "undetected" envy that is damaging. Once it has been linked to observation, and thereby able to be felt "on the pulses" (as Keats would say), it can become useful fuel for the vital spirit of aspiration and desire. Envy is part of the complex fusion of stirring love-hate emotionality at the growing point of the mind.

But to a degree, growing points must be defined by their opposite – the times when the personality is not growing. Growth may be static, or latent. Or indeed, it may be suppressed or perverted. My mother honed her picture of "quality" learning against various areas of non-growth, such as Bick's "second skin" and Meltzer's "two-dimensionality" – forms of avoiding the passionate commitment ("aesthetic conflict") that is required by growth, without being fully-fledged narcissism in the classical sense of projective identification with a superior power. She points out that "It seems likely that areas and states of non-containment, of two-dimensionality and mindlessness exist in the development of every infant and are therefore in us all" (1975b, p. 142). Although she allowed for resting-points in development – times and spaces when psychic reality is not engaged – she did not find these of great value or interest; she did not (unlike Winnicott) consider them a necessary service of the mother for her infant. These gaps in psychic reality, when wish-fulfilment types of fantasy predominate, are places where observation is not, and where escapism and irrationality prevail. She uses the evocative term "lacunae" to describe the types of mental absence which are not covered by the traditional Kleinian concept of projective identification (1978a, p. 175), but have a place in the theories of Bick, Bion and Meltzer. And she regarded them as, to some degree or other, ubiquitous phenomena.

Such areas of non-growth and of non-containment are not however the prime enemy. They may be qualitatively distinguished from some more tyrannical states which may appear more respectable yet are more deadly to the vital spirit of psychoanalysis, such as Authority, or sitting in judgement. She writes: "All too often adherence to theories is dictated by personal loyalty or adherence to psychoanalytic pedigrees" (1976, p. 119). My mother found these areas of complacency absolute anathema to the principle of growth, whether in the individual or the group situation – in Shakespeare's words: "Man, proud man, dressed in a little brief authority: most ignorant of what he's most assured" (*Measure for Measure*). The adult relies on his authority, as the teenager relies on drugs, as (she says) a "substitute for self-awareness" (2007, p. 226). They are forms of action rather than of contemplation. Observation, however, has the power to see through narcissistic or second-skin clothing.

In her later talks and papers she shows concern with the likely possessiveness of the acolytes of Klein and Bion, and warned against rigidifying the formulations of struggling pioneers into rigid dogma, and trying to make followers toe the party line (1982, p. 66). Had she lived longer, she would no doubt have included Bick and Meltzer among those whose ideas were vulnerable to being authoritatively "possessed" by their interpreters (on the lines of Bion's "loaded with honours and sunk without trace" which she was fond of citing). She wrote about the dangers of "apostolic succession" in the following terms:

> The dependent group structure so often manifests itself in the reliance upon a crystallized selection of the theories of Freud (the original Messiah), sometimes pitted against a similar extrapolation from Melanie Klein (a latter day saint). Bion is unlikely to escape the same fate. Their theories in such a climate of polarization are suitably selected and presented to eliminate the essential questioning, contradictions and progressions inherent in the formulation of pioneers who are constantly struggling to conceptualize the clinical observations they are making. Bion's postulation about the impossibility of knowing or describing truth ... may help us to try to relinquish the idea of owning our own particular brand of psycho-analysis. (1978b, p. 32)

Fixed systems of belief, political allegiances and institutional credos are all damaging to the exercise of observation. Yet in a way, perhaps this rigidification of Authority has not turned out to be the main danger. It seems more fashionable at present to adopt the other mode of deflecting growth – namely to imply that these pioneering ideas are outdated or rigid in themselves. We are supposed to qualify all our insights with "but other people might see it differently", thereby depriving ourselves of the passionate commitment that might make an observed moment into a growing-point. We may belong to the club but lose the spirit.

Even the most "respectably documented theories", she writes, are of no value by comparison with "attention to the conditions in which [psychoanalytic] observations may be made" (1977, p. 16). Hence the deliberate freedom from jargon in her own writings. Her writing appears easy to read but, unusual amongst psychoanalytic texts, actually requires the same kind of close reading that she demonstrated in the context of teaching infant observation. Careful attention to its elegance of construction and precision of phrase reveals her model of the mind, constructed from observation and learned from experience.

Bion speaks of the need to approach both books and people by "reading with awe" (cited by F. Bion [1985, p. 241]). This is what my mother means too when she emphasizes, in baby observation, "the respectful experience", as in the concluding paragraph of "Growing points":

> The awe with which Mrs E regards her gallant little baby in the dream is, I think, a variant of the respect and wonder with which Melanie Klein and some of her colleagues—notably Mrs Bick in her Infant Observation seminars—have approached the study of children's developing individuality. The theories, so necessary as an aid in trying to bring together and put some order into the wealth of detail we obtain in child analysis and observation, must indeed be seen as an aid but never as a substitute for the respectful experience. (1982, p. 91)

Awe and wonder are due not to theories but to the spirit of development as exemplified by one particular instance of a "gallant little baby". This, not loyalty or pedigree, is what unites Klein, Bick and all those who are likewise committed to the respectful – not the respectable – experience. It is a state in which observation and self-scrutiny are intertwined in a process of "becoming", and the outcome is unknown. This openness to the next growing-point on the horizon is very different from what is often called "open-mindedness" but is really just hedging one's bets.

My mother liked an anecdote that Bion told her about a trainee who worried about being "only a student", to which Bion replied, "What *are* you when you *cease* to be a student?" (1978b, p. 31). Observation ensures we can continue "living in the question" (like Keats' negative capability), and take our place in what she calls "the great social class of the truly educated people, the people who are still learning" (2007, p. 156).

CHAPTER TWELVE

The experience of supervision

Catrin Bradley

I had individual supervision during my training with Mattie for the two terms leading up to the summer of her accident. Mattie was someone I had known all my life as our families were close, and her inspiration certainly played a part for me in deciding on the career change which brought me into this work. In training I attended her Personality Development seminars, Bion seminars and clinical seminars, and her influence in all these contexts joins together in my mind with the experience of the individual supervisions to make a composite presence, at the root of my therapeutic work. In my contribution to this book I want to think about one aspect of my experience of the supervision I had: the way in which my patient's material, initially so unpromising, flourished so that he (and she – I will give two examples) became able to convey their emotional experience movingly, with powerful imagery. How did this happen?

Mattie paid close attention to the write-up of the sessions I brought to her, getting me to repeat or explain things so that she would have it clear in her mind, and usually we thought about two or even three sessions together. What I said (or didn't say) was never the focus, but the child's material: what direction it was going in, what it might mean, and her mind was full of ideas about it. It felt to me that she sometimes anticipated what was going to happen, as if she could see what was coming next, but reading the notes over now I can see that it appeared like that because she was talking about things I had missed! After she talked about them, then I could see it, next time.

The only time she commented on what I said was when she thought it had closed the material down. Having an open mind and an attitude that allowed the material to develop was what one should strive for. It didn't seem to matter if I didn't understand what was going on: the honest effort to do so was enough and far better than trying to shape the material according to a pre-conceived idea. I remember her talking about the concept of "negative capability" (Keats) and quoting "when a man is capable of being in uncertainties, mysteries, doubts, without any irritable reaching after fact and reason", by which she meant the capacity to tolerate not knowing while striving to understand. That is, to let understanding come to you, to let your unconscious mind have the opportunity of making sense of what is going on between you and the child and to try to bear the anxiety of not knowing for long enough to let that happen. I learned about Bion's ideas from her (see Harris, 1980b); once these were linked to the clinical material the concepts I had struggled so hard with in the reading seminar made a different kind of sense.

I also remember her encouraging emotional engagement in the work. To "be prepared to really tangle with the patient" is a phrase I can hear in my mind's ear – though I doubt now that that word can be right. Surely "tangle" has an overlay of the meaning of "entangle": the risk that one could be drawing the child into one's own pathology, which is not what she meant. But I took from her the courage to try to risk to get close in, and trust, since she seemed to trust me in this way, that it would be all right (that is, that my own internal objects could be relied on to be strong enough to manage whatever then came, with her support as supervisor), and hope that we could sort out what was what from there.

I also remember tremendous hopefulness emanating from Mattie – about the child's ability to grow and develop and also about my own ability to learn from the experience. I often felt stuck in the work; I often felt very worried about the child and his external circumstances; Mattie left those completely to my clinic colleagues to worry about, and concentrated with me on what we could do to move things along from inside the therapy. I used to leave the supervisions with my mind stirred up deeply; trying to digest what she had said and my own response to it. And underneath that, usually feeling more hopeful about my young boy patient.

Mattie believed one should struggle, and encouraged me to expect that my patient would struggle. And that the struggle would bear fruit towards development. There was also an aspect of allowing a space in which the struggle could happen, a "Let's see what he can make of that" (on his own) attitude which was a new idea to me.

One of the threads of thinking we followed in the supervisions was about the process of internalizing: how does a child who has not internalized a sustaining inner reliance on a good object, use therapy to manage to do so? Mattie thought my patient was "unintegrated" (see Waddell, 2006.) That is, that there was early deficit in his experience – or at least in the match of his experience and capacities – and that he had never had the opportunity to establish a containing, focussing, inner maternal holding presence. In our first supervision, when I took material from the once a week work I was doing initially to discuss with her the viability of working intensively with this child under supervision from her, she described him as "at sea", desperately trying to link himself up to, or hook onto, anything available. At the end of the session, when I returned him to the waiting room and his father was not there, she noticed that he had no feeling of the time or attention he had just had from me staying with him inside him, or any picture in his mind of the daddy he was waiting for, who is coming for him, to sustain him while he waited. The way she talked about this, and encouraged me to talk to him about it, was with every confidence that, quite soon, he would begin to be able to fill in that gap with a picture of me, or a picture of Daddy in his mind. In this way he was encouraged to struggle.

Alex, a six year old boy

My patient, who I will call Alex, was just six when I first met him. He was a boy who these days would be diagnosed with Aspergers, and probably also ADHD. Then he was said to have autistic features and to be concrete in his thinking. Alex was most often very active, exhausting to be with, and constantly on the go. Mattie said he was "evacuating his disturbance in random action". That was what his parents (and school) found so difficult too – that you couldn't take your eye off him for a moment because of what he would then get up to. Something destructive or dangerous would end up happening. He was also behind in his speech and had had both speech therapy and occupational therapy to no very great effect. A specific task could hold Alex's attention – but would quickly take on an autistic, stuck quality: for example wrapping the sellotape around the ruler which started as an attempt to fix the ruler, got caught up in that way, and Alex got stuck in repetitively wrapping more sellotape over and over, continuing until the roll ran out, or I detached him.

Alex was the fourth of eight children in the family aged nine, eight, seven, six, five, four, three and one when we started, in a family where the parents used manic cheerfulness to avoid being overwhelmed as they juggled the demands of all their children and their family business – a chaotic family "held together with string" was an image which emerged once Alex started to play. Extra help was roped in as required and a lot of help was required: my colleague did an inventory of Alex's week and discovered that in the course of a normal week over 20 people would be involved in looking after him including me, his teacher, and the army of special helpers at school and young nannies and babysitters at home.

The first time he really used this capacity to communicate about his experience in the way referred to earlier it came as a real surprise in the middle session of the eighth week of therapy:

He ran ahead and shut me out of the room, opened the door to ask what I was saying so that for a hopeful moment I thought he was interested, but then shut it again, though I thought he heard me talking about left out, shut out feelings. I went in and for the whole first half of the session he was very scattered in his behaviour generally and nothing I said seemed to help. There was a desperate feeling of wanting something but only a muddle about what it was – a game, a pooh, a cuddle (as he climbed on and off my lap as if I was inanimate), there was a lot of banging of the door, and the cupboard door and all the moments of play that started lasted only briefly before he was up and causing minor havoc again.

Then he was sitting on the floor and showed me the kangaroo in his hand and I gave up talking to listen and he was trying to put the boy kangaroo in the pocket, where only the baby would fit. He chose the daddy kangaroo instead and went to stand as high up as he could and told me that "the kangaroo was in space", holding it up as high as he could – the tractor and cow, each suspended by a loop on sellotape string from the one above, he said were in the sky. He became more settled gradually as I listened to what he was doing. He was talking about what held what up. The tractor is being held up by the cow – but the cow falls down. He slipped the loop off so that the cow and the tractor both fell. But the cow is held up by the kangaroo – but the kangaroo falls down. But the kangaroo is held up by the moon… but the moon falls down… and the moon is held up by the stars… but the stars fall down. But the stars are held up by the darkness… but the darkness falls down.

Alex collected the toys and the strings from the floor where he had made them fall and climbed back up to do it again. As each thing is held up his voice would rise in hope, only to fall again in despair as, inevitably the holding thing itself would fall. Over and over again: "All fall down."

I said everything falls down. What he needed to feel safe is something that wouldn't fall down

Almost obediently he started again, prepared to give it a go: this time he said "and the stars don't fall down", but this did not satisfy and he changed it back so that the next time everything fell down again.

The alternation of hope with despair was particularly poignant – you could not even rely on knowing that the next thing would fall, that it was always hopeless. Nothing could stand firm. I felt desperately sad.

We talked about him feeling he will fall too when I take him to the waiting room. And that if he could feel that he could be remembered by me it might help him feel less like he was falling... He wanted to hold both my hands to "fall" from the chair – and he landed on my foot. It was painful, and painful too to see how we were back to concrete thinking. As we walked back to the waiting room Alex begged "Carry me" – which he knew I would not do although I held his hand, and I felt concerned about how he would cope until the next session two days later.

When I discussed the session with Mattie I noted down her words: "All the holding up things collapse. He feels himself to be collapsed and that's why he needs you to carry him – he has no belief in a carrying object with strength in it – there is *nothing* that can carry without collapsing. It leaves him without anything inside. He wants to have a carrying you inside."

> The next session Alex greeted me by trying to slap me. His father was shocked and told him off. I held his hand firmly and said, "Let's go to the room and you can tell me why you are so cross with me." In the room Alex was ready to talk very seriously. I said he wanted to slap me because he was cross because of the long wait to come back, with the no-session day yesterday. Alex replied "Yes. Is it evening? Is there a yellow sky in evening?" I asked what he was thinking about it. Alex talked in a frightened and serious way: "In the night there was evening and yellow sky. And there was a noise that I didn't know what it was." We established that this had been a dream, a bad dream that was frightening. He dreamt this on Tuesday after daddy put him to bed early because he'd been naughty (he had broken something). I asked if he could tell me more about the noise – what did it sound like? Alex said he didn't know but then made a barking noise "like that and I went to the window and there was a dog in the morning, we used to have a dog, and I had another dream about a wolf." I said he was telling me about being frightened in the

night time but he still looked frightened as he was telling it to me, and he said: "You look funny when you're talking ... you look like a wolf." I said he's not sure if I'm a bad wolf now. He said "No – you're not", then he asked about wolves and what they ate: "Do they eat people?" I said I turned into a big bad wolf in his mind when he was cross with me: that I went away at the end of the session and he had to wait and now he wasn't sure and still felt frightened. He said "No you're not – you're good. And Daddy shooting the wolf-dog in the dream and then it was you and you couldn't 'teach' me anymore and in the morning there was a dog and it wasn't dead." And he had another dream and it was ice cream ... Alex then told me that he and his brother were the only two who were not allowed ice cream because they had been naughty, and he was angry ... I said he was left with a big muddle (and there is a wordplay link in this as well, as "Barker" was the name of my colleague who the brother referred to was seeing for assessment at the time, so she and I were combined as wolf and dog), and he was frightened that I might be bad or dead but here I was and here he was, back together today.

About what Mattie said about the dream I wrote: "It's about a primitive night terror and a muddle of who's what between him and the breast/me."

Perhaps some experience of being terrified by his own noise, his own screaming, perhaps dreadful hunger – a phantasy of the breast eating him up? The yellow sky could be him looking at a light and seeing a wolf/breast coming to eat him up...

She suggested the meaning of "being naughty" as perhaps being incontinent.

It was clear that he had dreamed this after the Tuesday session and remembered it all this time to tell me on Thursday. He had held in mind the idea that he could tell me, and that doing so would help him not to be so frightened, which seemed such an important move forward towards establishing a helpful internal object.

It seems significant that the game developed after I "stopped talking and settled to listen". I had initially had an idea that if only I could say the right thing he would calm down, and probably everything I had said in the session to that point was motivated at least partly by my wish that he would settle. The change in him when I gave that idea up, and instead settled to listen to him was striking, and showed how thirsty he was for that kind of attention.

One could say that the quality of attention which Mattie gave in supervision was akin to reverie, and contact with this was important in enabling me to offer a different quality of attention to Alex.

I will give a second clinical vignette, which particularly links in my mind to Mattie, although this experience was some ten years later.

Liara, a nine year old girl

This was with a nine year old girl Liara who I was seeing weekly. Liara had severe eczema, for which she had been hospitalized many times, and for which she was on strong medication. The creaming and bandaging routines that her mother was following in order to manage the condition took up a lot of time. Liara was of African/Caribbean heritage, and her skin scarred dark black, the raw bits being a different colour again so that her skin had a disfiguring three-toned, mottled look. She wore trousers and long sleeves to hide this no matter how hot the day. Because her hair did not grow through the eczema scars on her scalp she had bald patches which also needed to be hidden so she wore a beanie hat. However this did not spare her from being teased at school.

Liara, her mum, and her half-sister, five years younger were rather isolated (neither dad lived with them, and there was no contact with any wider family). The relationship between Liara and her mum was abrasive and tense. They each constantly felt attacked by the other and were always angry with one another. Liara's mum used to go in for "the silent treatment" to express her anger, turning a cold shoulder to Liara and freezing her out. It seemed the physical attention to Liara's skin provided the only way in which mother and daughter could come close.

In family work with a colleague the relationship between mother and daughter improved, but as that got better Liara developed a phobia about trees, specifically any tree with flaky, peeling or rough bark. Going near trees became something that had to be avoided and this began to be increasingly restrictive on the family: the park became out of bounds and coming past the plane trees outside the clinic to get to the door was a problem. It was when the idea that this was about "trees with eczema skin" had been formulated in the family assessment that it was decided Liara should have individual psychotherapy.

The therapy sessions were very hard going. Liara went in for doodles, usually drawing the kind of looping line that creates lots of bounded areas to colour in, like a map of different countries, which she would painstakingly then colour without going over the lines. Everything had to be nicely and neatly within its bounds. She was capable of being occupied in this way for long periods at a stretch, rarely spoke, and did not like it when I talked. If I moved too close she would hide her doodles. I often experienced a real sense of loneliness in her presence.

To give a flavour of what it was like to be with her:

> Liara and I sat as we usually did on either side of the table and Liara was drawing doodles. I spoke and she jumped out of her skin as though I had given her a real shock. She asked what I had said. I said she seemed a long way away – it had been a shock to hear my voice. She carried on with her doodles, calming everything down again, and I saw that one was a sign: "Please knock before you come in." I said perhaps she'd like warning like that from me when I was going to speak so that she wouldn't get such a shock – perhaps if I went like this (knocking on the table). She smiled.

Very gradually I was allowed to see more, side by side, and I began to have the sense that she enjoyed my attempts to follow her.

As the summer holiday approached I puzzled over how to talk to Liara about it, for how can we make sense of a separation when we can't manage being together? An image came to mind to do with a change of perspective, that I associated with Mattie. She had talked about Bion's image of the tennis net (Bion, 1973,

p. 37), seen in darkness not as a boundary, but as a lot of holes, collected or "netted" together.

In the holiday break Liara went away on her own to stay with another family for three weeks (with a charity respite holiday scheme), and despite my concern that this was a lot to ask of her, it went well. Liara returned having been taken to this family's heart, and looking quite different with her hair in tight plaits, wearing a pretty summer dress and new shoes.

Something different happened on our return. We moved on from the doodles as Liara took the foam ball (the size of a tennis ball) and made it into a head, with paper eyes and mouth fixed with sellotape and pipecleaner sunglasses.

> When we met two weeks later (as she missed a session to be bridesmaid in her holiday family) Liara went straight to the head she made last time, pulled everything off, and started to wrap it all up again in sellotape, this time using rather more than before. She didn't talk to me at all or look at me. I thought out loud about her not having been here last week, and how she seemed to have got straight in as if we hadn't been away. Liara didn't respond at all to what I said but her silence wasn't hostile. Having wrapped it all up she put what looked like earmuffs on top: I could only think of the word "earmuffs" although I knew it was not right, so I described what they seemed to be and she corrected me, providing the right word "headphones".
>
> I thought aloud about "extra-sensitive ears" which would need some protection from all the sounds that would otherwise intrude so painfully. Liara looked at me sharply. She said "I'm going to rip it all off again", and started to do so. First a big bit rip, then little bits were poked at with the scissors – rip. I put words to what was happening, talking about the sellotape bandage coming off but not coming away easily – it was hurting the "skin" underneath, being torn off, ripping little bits of the ball-skin layer away with it, exposing the underneath/inside. She dropped it at my feet and I picked it up and showed her what I meant about the soft inside, underneath the smooth outer skin, which is now exposed in a few little places, as I put it back on the table. She took it back and inspected those places, picking at it with her fingers

as if trying to smooth off the rough edges left exposed. But the picking went on: pick, pick, pick at tiny pieces past the point where this was a smoothing activity, then a big piece came off and I found myself flinching.

It was very hard to sit with this – to "put up with the experience in a state of not knowing". I knew from my colleague that in the family sessions Liara had on occasion made little piles of white, dead, discarded skin she had picked off in the sessions, but it didn't make watching this attack (which I felt to be on me) any easier. It really did not feel as though it was only a ball.

I felt a push inside myself to interpret the destructiveness, and at the same time realized that I would be doing so in order to try to stop it – to protect myself, rather than to understand.

Liara ripped it right apart and then set to, to pull the big pieces into little pieces. I found it almost unbearable to watch, while she seemed to have a sense of purpose about her, almost of enjoyment, but it did not seem sadistic. I commented on her sense of satisfaction as she was pulling and the picking at it, turning the ball – the head – into these tiny bits.

I had a realization, a change of perspective that this may not be primarily about the destruction, but about the bits:

> Liara asked, "How many bits do you think I've got now?" The number is increasing all the time – maybe 50? 100? She looks at them and nods, assessing, and goes on pulling. Finally there is no ball left at all – only bits and flecks. Liara collected them all together and scooped them off the table into her hand and onto her tummy. Still with a handful she put her hand into her trouser pocket and I asked if she was needing a place for the bits there? She said no, she was scratching her leg, which was itching, and explained that the material of the jean legs was too thick to scratch through properly: she could get closer to her leg inside her pocket.
> She asked "Where shall I put them?" I thought, do we need to keep them – are they rubbish now? and said: "Where had you thought?"
> Liara went to her locker and came back with a bottle the shape of a milk bottle but smaller, and poured the bits in, using her hand like a funnel. Any remaining bigger bits were

broken up more so that they would go in too. All the bits fitted in – and the bottle was then filled to the brim with water. The discarded sellotape was thrown in the bin, the materials put away, but the bottle left out on the table for me as the session ended, in a troubled atmosphere, without words, and I felt very heavy with it for a long time afterwards.

I felt that Liara had found a creative and powerful way to communicate about primitive early indigestible experience and the problem about how to process it became mine too. Where did it start – was the breast she was offered always full of bits (beta-elements) or did it only become so following her attacks? It struck me that there was no other drink on offer for Liara, and that having a different and more welcoming time in the summer holiday may also have helped her to transform the experience into this communication. A communication which was not quite able to be thought about yet, but was on the way to being so.

Some 18 months later as we were working towards ending this image was revisited. (These days she was talking to me freely.) The bottle again got filled up: this time with paper that had been coloured, the colours on the paper made to run in order to colour the water. She stoppered the bottle with plasticene and put it in the cupboard, and told me "It's juice – no it's milk". She said she doesn't like milk particularly, these days, though she does have it on cereal. She used to have a bottle, but before that when she was very little she was breastfed. Then she looked at me: "The milk [i.e. breastmilk] is not really meant to be nice you know. It's bitter." I thought she found the very word. With this she put everything away and was ready to go five minutes early.

They were words which had been long in coming and Liara seemed to move on out from the session with a sense of achievement, while I took rather longer to process what was left with me.

Because her mother continued her work at the clinic we heard how Liara got on in the first years at secondary school, where she did well academically and also became a competitive swimmer of whom her mother was really proud, her life no longer restricted by eczema.

Conclusion

I chose these two clinical examples to illustrate something of the way in which supervision with Mattie has had a lasting impact on my work, and this experience described with Liara was one where I was particularly aware of needing to lean actively in my mind specifically on Mattie's teaching about letting the material develop, waiting to see, and bearing the experience of not knowing.

In her supervisions Mattie conveyed her great faith in children's material: in their capacity to develop, in their own time, an ability to symbolize aspects of their inner world experience. That is, provided one works well enough on creating the safe and boundaried space of one's attention to receive it. For both of the children Alex and Liara, discovering in themselves the ability to communicate so powerfully was in itself important though what we understood was so painful, gritty and disturbing. The experience seemed to give a sense of understanding for each of them that they knew more what the sessions were for, and had more of a sense of confidence and purpose in approaching the work of their psychotherapy. (Alex tried to explain to a new minder who picked him up asking "Has he been good?" that "It's not *for* 'being good' – it's for... it's for... playing.")

In the supervisions I had with her, Mattie often commented on the quality of the object which my patient Alex seemed to feel he had found in the therapy on that particular occasion. She frequently made differentiations for me: for instance when talking about a session when Alex tried to climb out of the window she expanded on the difference between feeling "held in" and "shut in". She said: "You see I think here he's feeling claustrophobic because of his intrusiveness: he feels he's intruding into his object so he feels shut in and needs to get straight out again", and later: "Here he feels safe, held, he feels he has a place in your mind, he's found a welcoming, receiving object."

Although the focus was always on Alex, Mattie was also teaching me about the need for active receptivity in the consulting room: to pay attention to the quality of space in one's mind, which is not just there, but has to be worked towards, struggled for, and protected. I had no doubt about the role that her attention and the creativity of her thinking as supervisor played in the flourishing of my patient's ability for meaningful and communicative play.

CHAPTER THIRTEEN

Mattie as "maternal container" for a trainee

Evanthe Blandy

Mattie was there for me at my beginning, but not at my end. In terms of the training, that is. I did not say goodbye to her. After her accident, I thought about visiting her, but could not bear to see her with her spirit dimmed. Also, I did not feel it was my "place". Only in thinking through this piece, which has taken me over a year to produce, have I come to understand what a live person she is in my mind. Perhaps I have had to come to terms with her loss. I am grateful here, though late in the day, to have the chance to acknowledge the debt of gratitude I feel towards Mattie.

I began my training in child psychotherapy in 1974 at the Tavistock Clinic at the age of 27. My first experience of learning about the human psyche from observation was with Martha Harris, known to all who worked at the time at the Tavistock Clinic, as "Mattie". Mattie was the first person I encountered there as she had interviewed me. When she told me, after 20 minutes, that I was accepted onto the course, I felt I had to tell her that I had applied unsuccessfully three times for another training – in effect that the Tavistock was my second choice. Perhaps I could not believe my luck, but this was hardly an appropriate time to be transparent! But she countered my doubts by saying that what mattered was that as many people as possible train in this kind of work, wherever. I subsequently learned that she believed candidates choose themselves, in effect. She understood that people come into this work because it is their vocation. She must have seen it in me at that time, although I did not know it myself. Her lack of ego, in the colloquial sense, struck me forcibly from the start.

Looking back, she had a mystique. She was at the helm of the Children and Parents Department of the pioneering and rapidly expanding Tavistock Clinic, which was funded by the NHS. She was deeply committed to psychoanalytic clinical work and the ongoing development of theory, as well as to nurturing cohorts of trainees under her watch. Mattie was rich in clinical and teaching experience, and yet open to emerging ideas. She chaired a landmark conference given by Bion, arranged talks by John Bowlby on attachment, and included the pioneering Robertson films on separation in the child psychotherapy training.

However, Mattie's style was more professorial than managerial. Her touchstone was the importance of learning from experience; whether in the consulting room, in experiential groups or through detailed observation of the human subject. Mattie shone in the milieu of the Infant Observation seminar, a small group of trainees who meet weekly to present observations of their mother and infant over two years. I gather it was the part of the training which was closest to her heart. It was in one of these groups, at the outset of my training, that I came into close contact with Mattie, and there imbibed her values and way of thinking.

Mattie was also my tutor. She took me on as a tutee, along with a peer of mine on the course, Caroline Gluckman, as we were both pregnant at the same time. This was the foundation of a life-long bond as "tutorial sibs', which continues to sustain us professionally and emotionally. Mattie offered a financial lifeline by appointing me to a paid part-time trainee post at the Tavistock.

During this time, I was also working with therapeutic playgroups at the William Tyndale School in Islington. I wonder if the idea of children getting emotional help in schools was born out of Mattie's idea of "special time" in schools for needy children. The school funded the project but trainees ran it under the auspices of the Tavistock Clinic. As a qualified primary school teacher, the local education authority could pay me for my work. Parents were informed, and occasionally I would meet with them or the teacher to discuss their progress. Small groups comprising one to four children, who were having difficulties in school, would come at regular times to a large hut in the playground to spend an hour "playing" under the supervision of the trainee therapist. The door was locked so they were protected from any intrusion. Each child had his or her box in a cupboard. I soon learnt to put away the sand-tray, as it would get scattered everywhere. It was rewarding to work with these disturbed children and to witness them creating meaning out of chaos. One borderline child of seven years old began his sessions by drawing dark scribbles, filling the page. By the end of the term, he drew a whole house. He seemed to have emerged from an almost psychotic maelstrom and come "home". I brought these "therapeutic groups" to Work Discussion seminars at the Tavistock; one of these I shared with Katherine Arnold, another peer trainee. It is now commonplace for children to receive counselling at schools, but in the 1970s it was groundbreaking work, and quite a challenge in a school setting. How to explain the "lack of discipline" in the playroom as the thuds, crashes and shrieks could be heard from the playground!

For family reasons, my training at the Tavistock Clinic was protracted. I finally qualified in 1983. I found it difficult to leave what was for many years my "psychological home". I even attended a seminar, with Isca Wittenberg, on what it was like to separate. I remember feeling a bit cross that the issue was being treated as an academic study, with reference to the counter-transference, when it was me going through the experience for real. Not knowing what I was feeling. Feeling ready to leave, impatient. But it was lonely, feeling on the cusp, on the way out. To what?

Geographically, I did not go far. I started up a private practice of my own, in consulting rooms round the corner from the Tavistock in College Crescent, seeing both children and adults. As it turned out, the Tavistock was the last institution from which I received a salary. My professional incubation at the Tavistock under Mattie's "watch" has provided me with a professional and moral compass to work by, which has sustained me through years of private practice, and also informs my supervisory work at a low fee Clinic at the Guild of Psychotherapists in Southwark. The Clinic takes on many borderline patients for whom therapy is a lifeline. For some, it may be their first experience of a "maternal container" – someone thinking about them in a psychologically minded way.

Mattie's Infant Observation seminar group

I attended Mattie's Infant Observation seminar with four other trainees for two years. The observation of an infant was a soul-awakening initiation into the world of psychoanalytic thinking and experience; being in the position of both subject and object of observation. Under her guidance, we witnessed the building blocks of an emergent self being formed, both in the baby observed, and in ourselves as fledgling therapists. There was a "parallel process", with Mattie as a warm and disinterested "mother" to the process of our becoming aware of the language and reality of the emotional life we were witnessing in our infants: the transformation of beta-elements into K (Bion), in the context of a loving relationship with a "good enough mother" (Winnicott). With characteristically furrowed brow from the intense effort of bringing forth her ideas to fruition and communicating them, Mattie would strive to understand an observational sequence of what *prima facie* to a novice was chaotic and meaningless. Her constant proviso "as it were" contained a sort of acknowledgement and apology for any shortcomings of her thought processes as she articulated them. In a sense, her metaphors remained working titles; an open invitation to others to join in this enterprise of trying to understand unarticulated experience, and the importance of metaphor to convey the emotional reality of what was being witnessed or experienced. In Infant Observation, this is sharply realized, as the infant, and often the mother, have no words to communicate. The privileged position of the observer – following, reading and giving voice to this primary dialogue between mother and baby in reporting the observations, using his or her own feelings to register theirs like a sounding box – provides a vivid paradigm for what goes on in the transference and countertransference relationship between analyst and analysand, and for the function of the "third position" – the observing part of the self – which helps to understand what is going on within and between the mother and infant, as well as in therapy, within the analytic dyad.

Whilst I took part in Mattie's Infant Observation group, she published an article in the *Journal of Child Psychotherapy* entitled "Some notes on maternal containment in 'good enough' mothering" (1975b). She asked my permission to use material from my observations in her seminars, which I was most gratified to give. The observations at the time of her writing only encompassed five months of the infant's life. I believe these earliest months of development fascinated Mattie. With hindsight, and a few caveats, I would say, arguably, that that article provides a cogent model for thinking metaphorically about the meaning of the therapeutic relationship, and how as therapists we are a whisker away from the infant the patient has brought with them into the room.

My observations

I observed an infant, Charles, for nearly two years and reported my once weekly observations to the seminar group six times. The story, as Mattie interprets it, is about thinking how well the infant is contained by his mother's presence, and how he deals with her absence or absent-mindedness. She notes moments of containment with mother when she holds him, talks to him, and moments when Charles has to hold himself together in her absence, by relying on his senses: fixing his eyes on the light, the wall, the sound of the ticking of the clock. The following sequence was observed within the first two weeks of Charles' life:

> When mother picked up Charles from the cot, his hands spread out like starfish; he seemed startled. She then decided

to change him; laid him on the mat dressed in a baby-grow suit, and warned me that he dos not usually like to be changed. However, this time he is "good" and does not "make a fuss". As his leggings are removed, his legs fly up in a similar manner to his hands earlier, as if they were weightless. After cleaning him, mother poppered his legs back into his leggings. Charles remained quite motionless during this experience, but concentrated entirely with his eyes on mother's movements: hands, popper, hands move up.

Mattie commented on the way Charles felt contained by mother's attention on this occasion, but in many early observations, he seemed to fall apart when in the bath. Without his clothes, his jaw juddering, he needed to hold on to some thing outside himself: sights, sounds and sensations. In one observation, the observer noted that Charles in distress looked like a beetle, holding himself rigidly in his body, as his limbs were actively shaking when mother left the room. Mattie surmised that he was "shaking away his anxiety". Drawing on Esther Bick's seminal paper "The experience of the skin in early object relations" (1968) Mattie summarized that Charles was sensitive, but having to hold himself together with a stiff backbone, or "second skin", relying on objects outside himself. Mattie's theory seemed to be borne out in Charles's subsequent development. By the age of two years he was finally walking by holding on to furniture round the room.

By the third month, Charles was becoming more aware of me as another person. On one occasion, he seemed to find my gaze intrusive whilst mother was giving him a bath. Mother suggested I go downstairs to get a cup of coffee. However, sticking to my role, I continued to observe the bath-time, not understanding the impact I was having on the mother and baby, considering myself the "neutral observer". Thinking now, I wonder how to understand the neutral position the observer is supposed to take.

The family and Charles had their own story about me as observer, especially as my own pregnancy progressed. It became clear as time went on both that he was aware of my gaze, and that he had fantasies about me. For example, he played coyly with a car, moving it back and forth, giving me "flirty" looks, smashed bricks together, keeping an eye on me as my lump became evident. In discussion, Mattie helped the supervision group to see that Charles was thinking of parental intercourse when he was banging toys together.

On another occasion, when Charles was 15 months old, I arrived at the house when he had just woken up:

> He was half asleep, red-cheeked, and looked at me without expression. Mother took us into the living room and placed Charles on her lap. Charles became very coy and demanding of mother, looked at me impassively for a moment, then burrowing his face in her chest or collapsing his whole body into hers, clasping her pullover in front with both hands, and at one point seeming to try to get through to the other side of her, stretching out with both hands behind her head towards the wall. Whilst talking to me, mother commented on his miserable behaviour and explained that he was teething. Although she was talking to Charles in a play-reprimanding voice, she seemed pleased that he was showing his feeling in this way, and patted and rubbed his back whilst he squirmed. At one point he stood up, patted her, and fell back into her body. After a while he seemed to calm, and sat still, his expression cleared and he looked intently from mother to me as we talked as if he was trying to figure something out. He seemed infected by the excited tone of mother as she was telling me something.

In this sequence, Mattie surmised that Charles is reacting to my pregnancy and wanting to get inside mother, under the "skin" of her clothing. Mother seems happy to go along with this phantasy. Also, that he is trying to figure out, as it were, by watching our "intercourse", what goes on between mother and father to make a baby. What was remarkable to witness for the supervision group was that small children are aware of the facts of life and are busily constructing their own theories without having to be "told".

Charles had a difficult birth. I do not know the details, but I wonder if some of the early material was relating to his attempt to come to terms with a trauma, evident in his panic about falling apart at bath times. The starfish hands and legs flying up lasted only a fraction of Charles's life span, in the first weeks, where he seemed to feel lost in outer space and weightless. In writing this piece, I had a reverie about how such a birth might have been experienced by him, based on his post-birth reactions.

And the "therapeutic dyad"?

With Mattie, in those early weeks of infant observation, we learned to see how essential it is for the infant to find a mother who is attuned to him and who will protect him from needless intrusion. A mother who loves him. In relating to infantile feelings in adult therapy, it is essential for the therapist to be attuned but also to set limits. This is necessary in reality. The task is to help the patient, as well as the infant, over time, to come to terms with the necessary frustrations that a real relationship brings, and hopefully benefit from its rewards as well.

Thinking of a patient whom I saw in a low fee clinic, his connection to me as his therapist was tenuous throughout, and he missed many sessions. However, I persevered, weathering the bleakest feelings in my countertransference, containing his despair. The two-year therapy helped the patient move from a psychological position where he had "no front door" and was repeatedly robbed, to a position where he had a new door that was lockable, and he could see that there was now work to do "indoors". Going back to Charles, whom I observed and revisited soon after his second birthday, he was finding his feet by walking round the room holding on to furniture. Holding on to external objects for his sense of safety had enabled him to find his feet. He also internalized an experience of attunement with mother, which enabled him to integrate as a functioning family member, actively engaged and taken up by the ongoing stream of family life.

Studying under Mattie at the outset of my training made me aware of the abiding infantile issues which all patients bring with them into the consulting room. This provides a vital touchstone for understanding clinical data in the consulting room, which would otherwise remain obscure. Not least, the importance of the concept of containment, in understanding both the infant's need, and the need of the infant-in-the-patient.

Postscript

Aside from the training, Mattie would open up her home for social get-togethers for the Child Psychotherapy Department. She and Don hosted summer picnic parties once a year at their cottage in Mersea, to which all were invited. Meg, her daughter, would be there too. I remember them sitting on the low balcony overlooking the garden. They felt like "royalty" to us; graciously welcoming us into this informal and happy occasion at their home. We brought a quiche, and sat on the lawn on rugs; trainees with their families mingling with teachers, admiring the roses, taking the long walk down to the beach, and back.

Being invited to contribute to this book, along with others, feels like a reflection of Mattie's inclusiveness and warmth. I feel I still belong to Mattie's summer party. However, I wonder, does my contribution have enough rigour? Is it sentimental? What would Mattie think? In the infant observation seminars, Mattie was notably rigorous and unsentimental in her thinking – which with hindsight feels a bit strange, given that we were concentrating so much on mothers and babies.

My closing questions reflect the way she is part of an ongoing internal dialogue for me. I suppose it is the tension that has to be managed in therapeutic work, treading the line between feeling and thinking, whilst being there, trying to help the patient realize their "true self".

CHAPTER FOURTEEN

A glimpse of prenatal life

Romana Negri

I met Martha Harris for the first time in 1970, at the Institute of Infant Neuropsychiatry of Milan University, where she gave periodical seminars up to 1973. I was struck by the profundity and subtlety of her comments regarding the supervision of some little girls who were the subject of play observations. Her perceptions enabled her to modify the diagnostic and prognostic evaluations which had been hypothesized. We had also proposed that she supervise some single observation sessions of newborn infants. Although it had not been possible to offer her all the material and there was insufficient continuity with the observations of the infants at home, I was all the same struck by her ability to capture these earliest mental experiences together with the dynamics, intensity, and undertones of the mother's feelings.

Up to then my interest in newborn infants was mainly concerned with the neurological aspects. I had also started counselling sessions in the intensive care unit of Seriate Hospital (Bergamo), aimed at the early detection of cerebral palsy in little patients recently discharged from hospital. My work consisted of making a neurological evaluation of the infant before discharge and then following it up to two years of age.

During my counselling I had been sadly impressed by the dark looks, the corrugated foreheads of the little patients affected by cerebral suffering, who were hospitalized without their parents present. Thanks to the hospitality of Professor Marcella Balconi at Novara Hospital, I started the infant observation of Stefano with the supervision of Martha Harris. It was an exciting experience that enriched me so much and enabled me to perceive how a child's mental development proceeded, in the emotional context of his family environment, providing an ideal setting. I cannot forget even the enthusiasm and the joy that Martha Harris transmitted while commenting on the child's development.

During the same period Professor Federico Bergonzi, the head physician of the intensive care unit at Treviglio Hospital, asked me to work with him, on the early diagnosis of infant cerebral palsy in hospitalized children. I became part of the Unit and thanks to the observational work I was doing with Martha Harris I had the chance of thinking about my function, also because I was working in a hospital environment quite different from my previous one. From that time, thanks to the sensitivity of the head physician, parents were permitted to stay in the ward with their children, but I soon realized that it was really very difficult for those parents to keep in touch with their children and with the nursing staff, who were hard-pressed by too many tasks. The observational work with Martha Harris had made me conscious of a child's exigencies but also of the resources which can enable it to overcome difficulties and so attain the best possible development. I thought then, that if I wanted to make any sort of effective preventive intervention, I must not limit my initiative to neurological examination, and must make interventions not only with the children, but also in terms of working with the parents and nursing personnel.

I spoke about that to Professor Bergonzi, who seemed quite interested and supported me, taking part in the initiative and attending the discussion groups that I had started with the nursing staff. Of course, the observation of a seriously preterm newborn from the first days of hospitalization, applying the principles of Infant Observation, had a significant impact on the different activities going on within the unit. The work enabled the parents and the nursing staff to directly look for and learn to recognize the tiniest movements and initiatives of a baby, even one so small and suffering. During my morning meetings with Martha Harris at the hotel, we spoke a lot about my activity; she gave me very good advice and encouragement to go on. I remember that one day I complained about the fact that in Italy the institutions did not take psychoanalytic types of work into sufficient consideration, unlike the situation in Britain. She answered in a way that really surprised me: she said she had been positively struck by the fact that I had been able to introduce such an innovative initiative into a public hospital so easily.

I have written about my work in the intensive care unit of the Treviglio-Caravaggio Hospital in Bergamo in my book *The Newborn in the Intensive Care Unit* (Clunie Press, 1994), published in Italy by Cortina where it is now in its third edition.

Martha Harris's picture of prenatal life

In 1985 I began to do research into prenatal life, founded on the echographic observation of three non-identical twin couples from the 12th week of pregancy, and continuing after birth. The meetings with Martha Harris were in part what pushed me to do this, though in the main, it was the fact of observing seriously preterm newborns that made me realize it was necessary to expand our knowledge of the experiences lived by a foetus in the uterus, in order to understand their meaning better. And in this context, of understanding prenatal meaning, I have for years been really impressed by the supervisions given by Martha Harris in 1982 about a child I had in therapy named Federico.

Federico's case was of great interest because it reached back to a very significant sequence during his prenatal life and it demonstrated the validity of Martha Harris's intuition about foetal experiences, which have been recognized only recently, as a result of echographic and neurophysiological investigations.

Federico's story

Federico was born on the 1st December 1977, when it was not possible to follow pregnancies through echographic observation. He was the second-born after Filippo, who was two years older. During her pregnancy his mother had been fraught with anxiety owing to the absence of foetal movements from the fifth month, so she thought the baby was dead, despite her obstetrician's reassurances on this point.

The delivery was very traumatic, by emergency caesarean. The baby had the umbilical cord wound all round its neck and body. The doctors told Federico's mother that in order to survive in the womb he could not, and also should not, move. Had he moved he would have strangled himself and died. At birth, then, the baby had a cyanotic asphyxia and the mother a protracted haemorrhage, so Federico was admitted to the special care unit for ten days. His mother looked after him herself and breastfed him. The baby did not suck properly and he often puked; he was breastfed up to eight months.

From the very beginning the mother experienced great difficulty in dealing with him; she also had an intense guilt complex. The baby, when awake, cried quite frequently; he had circulation difficulties, with cyanosis at the extremities; his skin flaked off; he slept a long time and often through meal times. When bathed he became faint, went limp, and looked "as if he was dying". He was not a bright baby, he was always running a temperature, he did not show much interest in his surroundings, he was motionless or moved with difficulty, he looked hypotonic. By the time he was one year old he was not interested in toys, but he seemed to be "mesmerized" by them. His mother thought that Federico was brain-damaged. Instrumental and specialized tests excluded problems of an organic character. His weaning period was particularly difficult; he had difficulty in moving on from one type of food to another, always wanting the same vegetable purées, the same fruitshakes, etc. He frequently puked, especially when he was nervous or distressed. When awake his hands trembled.

When Federico was 18 months old, his little brother Matteo was born. Federico did not show any particular jealousy of him. From then on, he manifest a peculiar mania for cleanliness. He was very fond of cleaning himself, going on and on. His meat always had to be cut up the same way. He liked to fold and cut paper, always the same way. He wanted his days to be perfectly planned. According to his mother he was a very "deep" child and his "manias" didn't do him any good. He used to fill his pockets with tiny objects that he kept for a long time. He played on his own. He was very reserved, then suddenly without warning he would talk about something from the distant past. During a period in hospital due to a urinary infection, he puked so much that the doctors thought he had a brain tumour. His feeding was always a problem: in the morning he had some milk but only in a feeding bottle while touching his favourite blanket.

His sleep was often disturbed; he needed his dummy and blanket to fall asleep; he suffered from day and night enuresis. He did not want his food or his cup to be touched, except in a certain way. He became nauseous at certain smells (the smell of breath, a lady's glove, etc.). He didn't welcome shows of affection from anyone but his mother. He would not eat pasta with tomato sauce, he was terrified by blood or by death. He said he did not want to die and he wanted to know all the details about anything painful. In the school courtyard he saw two dead birds and he said they were mother and child: he wanted to know if the child had died because it wanted to save its mother or vice versa. He wanted to go to the cemetery to his grandfather, because he was there on his own, and he was very upset to see some broken graves.

At the infant school he stayed on his own and was so anxious to go back home straight after lunch that he ate voraciously. He recalled unpleasant facts years after they had happened, and still had the same reactions to them. He had an extremely low pain threshold – a light scratch made him feel bad. He went to bed and would stay there forever. He was afraid of heights, of "falling down".

I started the psychotherapy when Federico was five years old, with two sessions a week. He was a handsome child, with delicate features, dark intelligent eyes, a blond page-boy haircut. He was always very elegant. His relationship with his mother was very close, exclusive, intimate, acting as though he were her "boyfriend" – this was my direct observation. In front of me, Federico wanted to be picked up in her arms; he kissed and cuddled her; he touched her hair, looked at me and laughed, especially before the summer holidays when he went on like that during the whole session. I had the impression that his mother, too, lived that relationship exclusively. Federico opposed the treatment for a long time, he came to the sessions quite unwillingly. He came in with his mother for the first eight months, until the session of 18th November 1982, the one following a supervision with Martha Harris.

Supervision

At the supervision I described three sessions to Martha Harris: those of 15th June, 18th June and 18th November.
On the 15th June:

> Federico came in with his mother and asked for some glue to repair his toy plane. He glued and dirtied his hands, pressed the tube, blotted the table on purpose, but said that it was the glue coming out that dirtied everything – "How disgusting!" – expressing such intense worry that he closed the glue tube, saying: "Luckily I got it back into the box ... I can't do anything any more", and he asked to go and wash his hands.
>
> During the same session, together with the intense feeling of contamination anxiety, some relevant processes of identification concerning his mother took place. He wanted his mother to speak on his behalf – to say how many days they were together on holiday at the seaside, or to tell me about how his uncle's dogs attacked his daddy's animals. His mother had to speak for him because "he is voiceless".

M.H.: I was thinking that projective identification takes place inside the mother; and with no foetal movement, there is a lot of anxiety. There is a problem of his really projecting outside himself and therefore also of introjecting – this is very muted in him.

I was also thinking that his recalling events from long ago is exactly the same kind of mental problem. Storing information in an unconscious way is a matter of depth of experience, of being able to forget something in such a way that it comes out when needed. He just has to remember and to hold on to everything in a kind of "cleaning".

We see the contamination anxiety: he cleans everything. The crying shows that he has difficulty organizing his body and his feelings about himself and really opening his eyes to experience – to something more immediate than the past. He has difficulty in beginning to have any present feeling of himself. This complex about dirtiness is a feeling that everything is contaminated by him and he's being contaminated by everything. Again this is a problem of not having some body organization – where the dirt comes out from the bottom and the food goes in at the top. He is disturbed about his body and the functions of its different parts.

I suppose the trembling all the time is very like, for instance, what all little babies do when they are taken out of the bath, shaking all over; it's a primitive sort of shaking before becoming more integrated.

He seems to be a very intelligent child. So he has two brothers: Filippo, who is older, and the little one Matteo, after him.

Martha Harris's comment takes us back to the experience of a baby in its prenatal period. From the seventh week we can see the gradual appearance of motor activity in a foetus, which integrates with sensorial activity according to a sequence which begins with the skin of the oral region and facial block; after the vestibular function, smell and taste develop, followed by the acoustic and visual functions. A foetus from the tenth or eleventh week brings its hands to its mouth, to its face, to its head; it swallows the amniotic fluid; it kicks out; it touches the surface of the placenta, the walls of the amniotic sac; it rolls on the horizontal and on the vertical plane; in this way it establishes relations with itself and with the environment, demonstrating from the 16th week a true "foetal personality", in which interest in the placenta with its many sensorial qualities plays an important role. Owing to the early maturation of the amygdala, there is a correlation between motility, sensorial experience and emotionality; and experiences that affect its physical activity can be perceived emotionally by the foetus as extremely dangerous.

Federico was deprived of these developmental experiences. The mother's description of the baby's first period of life is very suggestive as it is the expression of Federico's foetal memory, recapitulating what he experienced during his prenatal life – the painful experience of feeling constrained by the umbilical cord and also feeling any possible movement as extremely dangerous.

What Martha Harris recognizes as Federico's difficulties in body organization makes us think that such a process begins with a foetus' motor sensorial experience. As Bobath has shown, "the movements of a newborn are a continuum of those existing in intrauterine life" (Bobath 1979, p. 75). This seems to underline how the memory of the experience lived in utero is fundamental to improving body organization during postnatal life.

But this is not all. Martha Harris also sees a new connection between Federico's immobility and motor inactivity during his foetal life, and the passive permeability of the experiences which lead Federico to remember very remote events: because he is not able to store information unconsciously, he has to "hold on to everything in a kind of cleaning". So we can understand why his pockets are a kind of "store house in the bottom", which enables him to keep and carry his fantasy world around. The very intense anxiety about of death experienced by the child can also be identified in the significantly reduced vitality of the postnatal period, which became acute again after the birth of his little brother. It goes back to how Federico felt in the womb, when the slightest movement was associated with the threat of death.

On the session of the 15th June:

> Federico came in with his mother, went to his drawer, and started playing with the animals as he had done the previous session. He said: "One of these may be the wolf. He put the toy house on the table, placed the animals inside, and mimed

a fight among them; he made them go out of the house, then he spoke as if he were the wolf, but he said that the cow was pretending to be the wolf. He added that the child was playing a trick on his father and he was hiding up on the top of the roof. I made comments on his game aloud. A moment later he wanted to go to the bathroom and for his mother to go with him. I went with him to show where the bathroom was, then I came back. His mother was waiting and she whispered something about the infant school. Federico called from the bathroom: "Mummy!" His mother went to wipe his bottom then they both came back. Federico carried on with his game, a fight started and the daddy was killed by the child; Federico told me that the child would not come out of the house any longer. Then he picked up a little sow with its piglets. I made the comment that there were four piglets. He said "How do you know they are four ... eh ... when shall we finish? Can you tell me?" I answered that I understood he was sorry that was the last session before the holidays; we would meet again in September for our sessions.

He went to the drawer and complained that the roof of a toy house was missing. I told him he thought that other children rummaged into his drawer, so some toys had disappeared. He asked me to look for the little roof with him. I told him that looking in his drawer together was an chance to see many things to do with his work with me. He seemed happy about this and thanked me when I gave him the cowshed roof. He contradicted me: "No, this is the pirates' house, the pirates are inside." He went to the drawer and took another baby doll (there are two baby dolls) and put it to sleep inside the house. He played with the house of the pirates who "wanted to find the treasure", together with the pirates who had the baby doll inside "that does nothing". He played very quickly, and I thought he didn't want to be seen by me.

Federico took a multitude of tiny beads out of his pocket. He explained they were bombs and he put them inside the toy house. He giggled: "This is a torpedo... let's put the bombs inside, all of them ... they explode at 33°." I said he was showing me Federico's wolf-part and pirate-part biting, throwing bombs, blowing up the house. He took the toy cars and took the roof off a small digger and emptied the house of all the bombs (in my opinion they looked like small children coming out of their mother, wounded), then he put the bombs inside the ambulance which exploded, and the police car and fire-engine exploded too. He said he had played a trick on the animals because the house was full of bombs. He turned to his mother and said: "Did you tell Romana we've got a cat?" He added they had had it for some days and the mother specified for a week. He went on playing with the beads/bombs. Some fell to the ground and he said, "They've fallen, can you pick them up?" He mimed the sound of the ambulance and made the diggers and the ambulance full of bombs crash. He alternated the sound of sirens with the sound of collisions. He said: "Let's put them into my pocket" – referring to the beads/bombs – and added: "How much time have we got?" I answered: "Five minutes." He went on causing crashes, then said: "Uncouple!" and all of a sudden he stopped playing. On my asking he said that he had stopped playing because he was thinking of his boat; he talked to his mother about it, describing it. Towards the end of the session he asked me why there were two drawers. He peeped inside the one that was not his, glimpsed a toy bear that was not his, and told me he liked that better.

M. H.: In this session, when he says the cow is a wolf, he is saying that he feels he has a mummy cow and because of the holidays he is becoming a wolf: he is projecting into the cow his own kind of wolfish anger. It is as if during the holidays he does not want to be the parents' child – instead mummy should look on him as a little husband and be preoccupied with his bottom. So it seems that he goes to the toilet in order to ask his mother to wipe his bottom, as if to show you that he's married to mummy, and you should feel the little child has moved out. As soon as he sees his mother talking to you, he sees you and mummy forming a couple, and he doesn't want to have that at all. You both have to be, I think, quite exclusively interested and caught up in him.

When he puts the child up on the roof, he feels that he's the big one who's on top and taller than daddy; and when there is this battle and the daddy is killed, daddy is somehow an enemy who is taking you away from him. The child has killed the father and the child will not come out anymore; he has been injured in the fight and then he can live inside, really inside the mummy all the time. I think the child that has killed daddy and now stays inside, is trying to deny the separation of "going out".

Then he says: "The roof of the little house is missing." This would seem to be a conscious suspicion of other children that must be related to the little baby, Matteo. He must have been no more than two when Matteo was born, and he was breastfed too; and the house with the roof gone means that some other baby has taken mummy's breast away from him. I think he has the feeling that the little baby also takes your thought away from him: you don't think about him all the time, just as he has the suspicion that other children get in and take things out of his drawer. I don't know whether his mother has said anything, but I imagine he does feel very persecuted by his little brother touching and playing with his toys. The bomb is also linked to a contamination anxiety. I wonder whether these contamination anxieties increased around the birth of the little brother; I would suspect so, and I would suspect also that his fears about death and dying increased about the same time.

R. N.: When he walks with his brother he is very obedient and protective, but he is also very possessive and jealous; he plays the victim.

M. H.: I think his attacks are probably very secret in a sense that he doesn't dare to be openly aggressive.

R. N.: During a party at school for Filippo's birthday, he went to Filippo's teacher and told her that Filippo was not nice to his brother when the parents were away. The mother was told this by the teacher.

M. H.: That would look as if he does have a kind of secret romantic relation with his mother split off from the family.

R. N.: This is the situation I saw in the sessions. His pockets were always full of things and in some sessions he took them out, not always, and the mother found these things when she washed his clothes.

M. H.: I would think I could take this as if the pockets were a kind of store-house in the bottom where he puts things that could have the meaning of babies, but they could also have the meaning of bombs; I think it may be connected with the kind of little world that he carries roundabout with him, a fantasy world in which he is not the son of his mother, but somehow married to her and in fantasy he actually is the mummy: he has all these sorts of things in his pocket and brings them out.

When you are representing the mummy and the mummy's bottom, he gets secretly into you and bombs all these children that you keep inside – he's very jealous about that. And there are the fire-engine and the police car. And when he says that he and his mother have got a cat, and it means that mummy has got a baby and you are meant to feel left out.

It is interesting when he says: "Uncouple". It is very expressive as if, literally, what he's doing is really blowing up the couple relationship, the parental relationship. And then this boat: the boat is something you get into; he is breaking up the parental relationship and then gets into and remains inside the mummy. I would think that is absolutely connected to the explosive, aggressive fantasies about the holiday.

And then at the end he says: "I can't understand the reason for these two drawers" at the end. That is very funny. Maybe the baby means: "You don't need two drawers – you need only one for me." There are two drawers, and you keep one for some other child, and he is very suspicious you're giving him something better. I think this is very nice; I mean he is very engaged with you, and I'm surprised he has now got to the point when he can let his mother go.

> On the session of November 18th, Federico came in with his mother. H was holding a large robot and tried to launch its "atomic fists" and spears against me. I told him he was angry with me because I had missed the previous Tuesday session and I had informed Filippo by phone instead of speaking directly to him. He went on playing; he made the robot launch its atomic fists against the toy house and cars, then he

took the baby doll out of his drawer, put it on my table, and there hit it with the robot spear. He impaled it at the umbilicus and then at its foot; then he undressed it. He laughed and showed it to his mother: "It is naked!" And with the spear he hit it again at the umbilicus, he stripped its legs, its head; he couldn't strip its arms; he took the atomic fists and put them inside the trunk of the doll through the holes created by the stripped legs and head. In the meantime he said: "The baby girl can't do anything like this." Then he emptied the doll, put its trunk and pieces back into the drawer, threw himself on the air mattress. Then he got up, went to his mother and whispered in her ear that he was naked. He hitched up his sweater and made her rearrange his disordered underwear. He made the robot dance, then he fetched the emptied doll with just its head and trunk and made it dance. Next to it was the robot. He took the robot again and sang softly: "Where is it… where is it", then added: "My brother says I must put the gold inside the tummy" (he explained to me that the head of the robot is a person and the tummy is his brother, another person). He took out of his pocket some little pieces of wood and some tiny gold metal balls, as small as a pin head, and said: "Where shall I put them? In the tummy … no", but then he patiently put them inside the robot, which could be partly opened through two small flaps. The session was over and I realized that he was not so willing to go. I told him about my impression that he would like to stay there. He confirmed it, and at the following session he came in alone, leaving his mother in the corridor.

M. H.: It is the umbilicus: he had this problem during the pregnancy. It is as if he is deprived of the use of his limbs, immobilized. After he has immobilized the doll like this, he goes and lies down; he is identified with this immobilized baby inside the mummy. I was thinking about his preoccupation with death and looking at some of his bad fears about death. I suspect they probably became more evident with the mother's next pregnancy and after the birth of the next child, as if his fears of death have much to do with identifying with this attack against the baby inside the mummy, because I think he is very jealous and has very strong emotions. He copes with this jealousy of the brother by forming a kind of couple with the mother and then trying to protect the baby from himself. He does look as if his head is another person.

R. N.: The head and the tummy are the two brothers in the robot. He said the head was one person and his brother was the tummy.

M. H.: He uses his head to be able to project into the brother all the nasty things about himself that he doesn't want to know: so "the big brother" is the naughty one, and then he can feel that he is a good boy, that he is blameless. I would think that is connected with attacks on the baby: as if that was "the big brother" – a big brother who contains all these bad fears – that's not him. And these little dummies that he keeps in his pocket as bombs …. Yes, it is as if he projects his bombing, explosive attacks into "the big brother".

I would suggest in this way you're dealing with his jealousy about the little brother, his jealousy about any possible other babies, his kind of secret bomb-throwing; but the big brother becomes the receptacle for all the bad and naughty things that happen in the family. In this way he does keep his very special position and his tyrannical hold on the mother. I suspect that is why he couldn't separate from his mother. I would think this has to do with his wanting to keep an eye on her, a tyrannical eye on her – she shouldn't be free to go and do anything else. I would suspect he does tyrannize over her a lot: she's not supposed to be with daddy, she's not supposed to be with the other children, she's only supposed to be in attendance on him.

Conclusion

As Martha Harris underlined during the supervision of these sessions, the child started showing a sort of attachment to me. As the therapy went on he showed he was aware of the link and the help he got from the treatment. It was in fact a good link but it also kept him tight, close, and it prevented him from growing, from being autonomous. It would take a long time for Federico to be able to face the problem of separation, to consider all the aspects linking him to me and to his mother. He realized that when he did face the problem, he would find something missing – he would have to experience the feeling of solitude. For a long time he couldn't face the experience of sorrow for a loss; he had to deny it through omnipotence: it was me, it was his mother dependent on him; it was Federico who did me a favour coming to the sessions, it was he who went away, it was he who, through a process of projective identification, became the father who looked after the mother.

The treatment went on for eight years, throughout primary and secondary school. When he was 13, in accordance with his mother's musical ambition, he went to the Academy of Music in Milan, where he took the diploma as piano player when he was 22 and as a harpsichord player when 25. During all that period he commuted to and from Milan and lived quite on his own. He showed a late adolescent crisis when he was twenty-seven and he started playing with a group of African musicians. He went to Africa with them, where he rented a big house which accommodated the musicians and their relatives. He lived there for a year, being convinced that the group and the African music would realize his ambitions. He came back to Italy with the idea of selling all his properties and return to Africa forever. He went around wearing a turban and African dress. His parents were hopeless and asked Federico to meet me together with them. During our meeting he was more and more convinced of the validity of his decision. In the meantime it was not so easy to sell his house in Bergamo; he wanted to meet his harpsichord teacher and he struck up with her again; also he had a girlfriend. He started going to concerts of classical music again and playing his instruments. When he was offered some concerts, he prepared himself with great care, played successfull, and was much appreciated. He no longer spoke of his African projects and his parents, following my advice, didn't speak about them either.

Two years ago he linked up with a boy of the same age, a very good friend and also a musician. Since they they have worked together in a recording studio. There he meets successful musicians and he has increasing opportunities to play in concerts and be appreciated. A wellknown Italian music label, Amadeus, has published a CD of his. He didn't sell his house to go to Africa, but he has bought a house with a garden in the country, where he can play the harpsichord more freely.

He hasn't shaken off his habit of keeping a lot of tiny objects in his pockets.

CHAPTER FIFTEEN

Assessment of a little girl and her parents

Simona Nissim

Coming back to this case that I presented many years ago to Martha and Donald Meltzer, has given me the pleasure of thinking that I am leaving live, fresh, enjoyable memories to students and younger readers. Mattie and Don are no longer with us, but their ateliers – gathered *viva voce* by craftsmen-students who had the privilege of sharing their experience with them – are precious material to be handed on.

I am going to present two consultation-assessments of a little girl, Serena, 16 months old, and her parents (mostly her mother); and one can see how clinical material through its nuances may merge into infant observation. The special interest of this work lies in the interaction between Mattie and Don, both very close to the emotions of the baby and her parents – often in a synergistic confirmation of common thinking, rich and complementary; at other times in a sort of counterpoint, with reflections coming from a different vertex. In their free, cultured and never compliant mix of thoughts and hypotheses, I was moved to find a demonstration of the dual characteristics that Meltzer loved to emphasize were an inherent feature of the technique of interpretation: the "hunting" aspect fulfilled by himself, while the "gardening" qualities belonged to Mattie.

In a fertile supervision situation such as this (with a small group of participants meeting with Mrs Harris and Dr Meltzer three times a year over four years in Florence), the two attitudes of mind seem to be composed and integrated into a meaningful narrative. In the material presented, we can see a way of thinking that finds it way towards a gradual, patient, wide exploration of the material itself, in search of a new mental space that can accomodate fully the particular therapist-patient relationship.

First assessment session

Serena was a little girl of 16 months who had been admitted to the paediatric unit of the hospital owing to severe dehydration, resulting from her active refusal to eat. My colleagues in the department called me for a consultation because "the baby cries and cries almost without interruption, and the mother seems strange too." This is my account of the first assessment session:

> On my way to the paediatric unit to visit the child, I hear a cry and a heavy noise of heels coming from the entrance of my department. I see a woman of uncertain age (I learn later she is in her late twenties): haggard-faced, tall, skinny, pale, with black, uncombed hair falling straight down her face. She wears dull-coloured, old fashioned clothes, and purple shoes with thin high heels. Her eyes are large, dark and restless eyes, with a frightened look, sometimes indecipherable. She has a tiny screaming baby in her arms. She introduces herself by her first name, Sabina; I invite her into my room and she whispers that she has come from the paediatric unit and begs me "to do something immediately or my child will die." She refuses to sit down, believing that rocking her child while standing may calm her. Hearing my voice, the child initially cries louder. She is dressed in long, wide pajamas and has a scarf on her head. She is huddled in her mother's arms, her head bent over her right shoulder, her legs also bent: I think to myself, she is finding a position that allows her to take up as little space as possible. Her cry is intense, piercing,

and increases when she turns her head toward me, rubbing against her mother. Serena looks at me for a while and I glimpse two bright, dark, frightened eyes that she immediately shuts, with her little hands clenched into fists. Her face is a little wrinkled, her skin transparent. This little girl dismays me. Her balance is precarious in this position.

The mother continues to stand, shaken by her child's crying. The voice she directs to her child is sweet but the tone is mechanical, using phrases that have been repeated a thousand times: "Serena, stay calm, the doctor is good, get well and we'll go home…". She turns to me saying: "They make us ill – there are so many medical investigations, so many tubes…She will die if things go on like this. Two days in hospital transformed her. At home she was laughing, nearly walking, and now – this. She screams, cries, doesn't speak, doesn't seem to recognize me or her father. It's the hospital's fault; only if I walk back and forth does she sometimes calm down." Then she turns to Serena, who has meanwhile removed her fists from her eyes but continues to cry piercingly, huddled closely against her mother. She says: "Serena, calm down, the doctor is here to listen."

I had made some attempts to "hold" her with my glance, smiling when she looked at me; but my speaking to her in a calm voice in response to her fear, and placing a small soft, musical toy on the table between us, were ignored: Serena' cry went on uninterruptedly. I wondered that there was no mucus or tears, while the crying seemed endless. At times it seemed to come out from her skin, becoming just "the scream"; at other times I had the impression she would concretely enter her mother's body. The direct attention of her mother or me seems to terrorize her, so I decide to latch onto her mother's phrase "the doctor is here to listen" and, aloud, I say that Serena will not let me listen to her mum; then directly addressing the mother, I comment that perhaps it is too painful and difficult to allow that desperate and penetrating cry inside oneself, inside one's ear: but now we're listening together.

The mother looks at me carefully, opens her arms, and for a moment seems to "forget" the baby; she finally sits down and – in the sudden silence of the room – whispers: "Look, on the day I entered the hospital with Serena, I stopped breastfeeding her... I used give her my milk in the morning and evening and these meals were the only ones she would accept after she started to refuse food. " Then she mentioned the reason for hospitalization – her refusal to eat – and I ask if she can tell me how it started. Meanwhile Serena, who has stopped crying, is shaken by a loud, deep breath and, suddenly, falls asleep in a foetal position inside her mother's arms. Cradling her daughter a little mechanically, with care, as if she is afraid to interrupt this "sleep-spell", the mother tells me a bit about herself. She is 27 years old; she was married to a young man from whom she soon separated, and has been living for three years with a 38 year old partner 38, the father of Serena, who has a serious illness (glaucoma) which is making him go blind.

My attempt to gather Sabina's story was immediately assimilated into that of Serena: "Serena was fine till she was five months, a marvel, while she had only my milk in her diet." The child's birth had gone well, after a threatened miscarriage at five months' pregnancy with one week of hospitalization. Breastfeeding was started immediately. The problems began on weaning, with the first solid meal at five months. The mother describes the first emotional crisis, when she tried to feed her soup with a spoon: "Serena was crying so much that she went black, seemed suffocated, indeed, about to die." There is fear in the mother's voice and more than just the evocation of a memory – the event seems to newly materialize at that very moment. Serena's development was very slow, on the lower lines of the graph.

The mother said:"The hospital has changed our baby" and that they wanted to bring her home. "It's true she has put on a few ounces, but she will die here."

Serena knew little of the world outside the walls of the house; she was always with her mother. The parents have no friends, no relatives, no other children; it is clearly a story of loneliness, of greyness, without colours or sounds. Mother says: "The child is happy with me and I with her; she is attached to me, even if we are silent, we understand each other… there is the problem of eating, but we will overcome it at home." Asking me if Serena is seriously ill, she does not wait for my reply, but just asks me to give her, please, another appointment "to return and continue to talk."

When they go out, the mother keeps Serena curled up in her arms; the child alternately opens her lips slowly and makes sucking movements. The mother says she cannot shake hands in case Serena wakes up, but she wants to say thank you.

A moment later, announced by a cry from Serena, the mother returns followed by her husband, returned from work and eager to make his contribtion to the consultation. He appears worried and depressed; he wears thick heavy-rimmed black glasses. He confirms Serena has changed enormously since being in hospital, and that the regression and constant crying scare him even more than her refusal to feed. Serena just needs to return home. While her parents talk to me, Serena falls asleep again in her mother's arms, a light sleep marked by shivering and jerking. The couple appear united in their desire to leave the hospital, but are otherwise emotionally distance: mother and daughter silent on the one hand, father full of anxiety when he describes how his daughter does not seem to know him: "as if she did not see me". After a pause filled with bitterness, he mentions there is no hope for his glaucoma.

They leave with a date for another appointment.

M.H.: Everybody appears very anxious and worried about this child. These anxieties are communicated to the mother, who in turn communicates them to the child. Unfortunately, this is a common situation when a small child is admitted to hospital. The mother is worried about many things: her husband has glaucoma, and it appears she has no-one else supporting her. I'm not quite sure if this is a coincidence, but the first crisis was when Serena was five months old, and it was about this time that she started eating solids. Does the beginning of weaning coincide with the crisis?

S.N.: The solids were started in the fifth month. The child has never accepted the bottle, only the spoon. I also wanted to add that there have been crises like the one I've just described, with vomiting and refusing to eat, although there has never been such a drastic refusal to take either solids or liquids as happened in the days just prior to her admission. I remember the mother kept breastfeeding up to the date of admission: two feeds, in the morning and to help the child go to sleep in the evening. Breastfeeding was stopped very abruptly at the time of admission: this was done on the advice of the doctors.

M.H.: My impression is that the mother has never really weaned the baby, and that the dramatic weaning took place very concretely in the hospital. I would like to return to the meeting with the father. The baby is sleeping when she goes out with the mother; and when she comes back she is screaming The father says she appears not to see him. It is possible that this has something to do with his own difficulty in seeing because of his glaucoma. Do you, Simona, think that there is something in the father's appearance that would make you think about problems in his vision? Would you have guessed that he had difficulties even if you had not known about his glaucoma?

S.N.: I was struck by his very dark, thick glasses – smoky dark. He appeared to be nearly blind.

M.H.: How long has he been wearing these glasses"

S.N.: For the past year.

Mrs Harris remarks that this coincides with the time the child was first fed from a spoon. Dr Meltzer agrees with the possibility that there may be a coincidence between these two.

M.H.: There could be an overlap with the moment when they realize that the father has a serious problem with his eyes, and this has been a source of worry and tension between the couple. So probably, whatever goes wrong in their relationship with the child is experienced in a very special way. When babies are six months old they are intensely aware of very small physical changes in their parents. There are cases where children only a few months old have reacted with anxiety simply because their mother has changed her hairstyle.

Dr Meltzer looks back over the script and considers the point where the child is looking in fear at the therapist, and then covers her eyes with her little fists:

D.M.: I think that the child might be having hallucinations. This is because she cries without any effort. As if, with her crying, Serena is expelling something and this returns as an hallucination.

M.H.: I agree, and I would add more. The crying appears not to be the expression of an emotion, but the expulsion of an object which then transforms itself into an hallucination. It appears this is something to do with the father's change in appearance, the change in his eyes. The worst aspect of the hospital admission was that Serena was weaned from the breast. This was probably the only familiar object she could hold on to in a world that had become alien. For when she entered the hospital it was all totally alien.

D.M.: I would also like to draw attention to how the mother and the little girl presented themselves on their first appearance – the way they were dressed. I got the impression of two refugees who retain a touch of antique elegance but everything else is ruined.

S.N.: I agree, I had the same impression. They were like refugees fleeing, wearing clothes offered by the Red Cross or some charity.

M.H.: I would emphasize the mother's words: "We *must* go home; going home will solve everything." She has the sense that they are refugees in a very hostile world that does not help them: only shutting themselves away can save them. Besides the problem of anxiety about the child, there is the enormous burden of her husband's blindness. She feels bitter about it.

Dr Meltzer says his view is that the bitterness of the father is just a trait of his personality. He asks for more details about the parents. I explain that the father has been a local authority clerk since he finished high school. The mother was born in a simple family; her father was employed by a telephone company. She has never worked, except for a very short period when she was 16 years old, in a family business. They have no economic difficulties.

I recall how the mother could not wait for the appointment with the therapist; she preceded it, going herself to the Child Psychiatric Unit, probably in desperate need of help.

Mrs Harris wonders about the atmosphere of empty closure in the family home – a sort of grey cocoon.

Serena and her parents back at home

I was very worried about this mother and child; and when three days later, they came to tell me they were taking the child home, I confirmed the appointment we had already arranged, but I also asked them if they would welcome a visit at home from our social worker. I felt that, as Mattie said, there was a terrible loneliness.

The social worker's report showed a very sad situation. The father was not at home. What struck the worker was the very close relationship between mother and child in a house totally devoid of life, warmth, comfort. It was hard to describe *what* did not work: there was normal furniture, modern accessories – but signs of pleasure or enjoyment were missing. The child had no toys; there were no ornaments or superfluous items that might just add a note of life or colour. Just the bare essentials, basic but good quality. A ghost house. Another uncomfortable thing was the total, strange absence of noise. The house is located in a suburban area, in a courtyard, so street noise does not penetrate. The social worker could hear only the crying of Serena, which began when her mother tried to give her food. The description of this meal was painful to listen to: the mother would talk to her child in a low voice, using tender nicknames, waiting for the moment when she opened her mouth to scream and then quickly slip in the spoon. This went on for 30 minutes, eating and crying.

After a week they came back to me. This meeting was very brief, because the family arrived at virtually the end of the hour – a delay owing to the father's work. The baby was not crying and initially she ignored me. Then she began to cry very feebly, listening to my voice. Gradually it happened that if I smiled, Serena stopped crying, and at the end of our meeting (during which the mother thanked me very much for arranging the social worker's visit), Serena made contact and accepted playing a game with me: a game with a rag doll, with which I gently touched first the child's hair, then the mother's face, and then the child's face.

M.H.: Like a kiss.

S.N.: Both parents said that Serena was quieter now, and was standing, and sitting. It seemed to me their voices conveyed a desire to cancel what I saw in the first session.

M.H.: As if to show you the baby's good parts, she expressed her gratitude to you.

Third assessment session

I read out my observation of the third session:

> The mother enters my room. Serena is in her arms, upright, a little tense. The little girl is pale but her face is less wrinkled; she appears clumsy, in woollen clothes too big for her. Her eyes are calm. She looks at me; I smile without moving, and I have the impression that she accepts my look and smile. The mother sits, leaning back with Serena against her breast and her face toward me, and tells me that she had been uncertain about coming: "Last night, Serena felt bad again, she would not eat anything, went blue in the face, vomiting and choking. I couldn't bear to look at her like that – but this morning she slept, I had to wake up her to come here. Does that seem too quiet? Serena was really scared, not knowing the people out there – she was terrified by the hospital, she was worried … "
>
> I say that she, Sabina, was very worried too, and we could talk together about her concerns. She replied: "You see I'm afraid - so afraid, for example, if she eats more willingly, that she will not continue and stop completely." She describes Serena's meals as a monumental struggle: she puts the child between her legs, "slowly but firmly," then pushes the spoon full of food to Serena's lips, waiting for her to open her mouth. Serena screams, "as if I was poisoning her", and the mother quickly pushes the spoon into her wide open mouth. With crying, coughing and vomiting, it looks like a war scenario. After the meal, Serena would immediately stop crying. The mother says: "Breastfeeding was different: no difficulty, as long as it was the only food."
>
> Now the mother's voice is soothing. Serena looks up and moves her lips; she has a dreamy expression and a relaxed posture. The mother looks at her daughter and says: "Poor thing, she will have the same unhappy childhood as me." She

tells me she was the second of three children, and often ran away from home: " I was in the middle, I was like a extra, unwanted." After the eighth grade, she left school, and as a teenager described herself as "depressed, sad, angry, hyperactive". When she gave birth to Serena, she felt liberated: "Serena's birth changed me: I felt better, peaceful, resigned."

Serena shuts her eyes and yawns, after a tremor that has shaken her. The mother continues to talk about herself: "I never wanted to adopt a child, I wanted my own child, mine, mine, to give her the love I didn't get, to be friends, to have company. I would never want to make Serena understand things by slapping her, as my parents did to me. I was 16 years old and worked in a small factory." [Serena looks at me and holds her hands joined together.] "I was like my daughter, I did not want to do what I was forced to do: I ran away, to see if I was loved. I married a young man, I did not understand him, I suffered, I was neglected. He was sexually frozen - we did not want children then, I wanted to live and have fun. Then we separated, I don't know where he is now."

Serena slowly shrivels, as if trying to disappear, becoming very small; she makes a chewing movement, turns her head and mouth to the mother's breast, with sucking movements. Sabina turns, asking her if "she is tired", and Serena puts her left arm on her left ear and looks at her mother and then at me, with a serious and a slightly rejecting look. I think she does not want to let the painful words and the resentment of the mother get in to her, and her mother says: "Serena, do you want to unplug your ear?" I mention the pain of listening to sad things and the need to protect oneself (thinking also of the mother's ambivalence). Sabina, looking at me, says: "It's true, I feel pain, I just feel painful things, too much for me alone."

Serena is lively, she picks up a soft toy that I had laid ready on the table, brings it to her mouth, then drops it (without looking for it at all) and puts a finger in her mouth, turning it round her gums ("she has eight teeth", the mother points out); then stands up, serious and static. The mother looks at her, then whispers that seeing her child calm frightens her. I talk about this fear of seeing and hearing her calm. "Yes, I'm used to hearing her going hyperactive." I hint that she also described herself as a hyperactive little girl. "Yes, it's true – maybe Serena is different?" I speak of being calm as a state of uneasiness; she spoke of herself as resigned. Serena meanwhile, leans forward, I feel that she is looking for the toy that had fallen, I offer it to her again; she smiles, then holds her sweater with her teeth, as if clinging to herself. The mother continues her story, saying that no one trusts her, apart from Serena. I wonder if Sabina can trust me and can hope to feel understood.

She says: "I'll explain everything to Serena, explain the sexual behaviour of men - no one has ever talked to me about men, about the facts of life, and learning by ourselves too soon, we get burnt." She was 24 when she met Serena's father "but he was more a father than a husband, I still don't know if he is in love with me or not." Serena, who had stopped holding the sweater with her teeth, raises herself and seizes her mother's hair. The mother smiles and talks about her daughter's autonomy. However, in that gesture she seemed like a newborn baby trying to cling on to her mother. Serena puts a finger in her mouth, again shrivels up and takes on a faraway abstract look, like someone who is not contained. Her mother seems scared, shakes her, indicates the pencils inside a container on the table, pulls out two, beats rhythmically and remarks that Serena likes music.

I try to think out loud what the child might be imagining, and Sabina remembers that she, Sabina, was excited when Serena sucked at the breast, and liked it better when the baby was no longer newborn because she felt she "had more pleasure". It is painful to hear the utter confusion of this mother with her baby and the projection of sexual and erotic experiences on the little child.

I mention weaning. The mother immediately associates it with an episode that took place shortly before the crisis and the refusal to eat: "It was evening, we were all three at home, Serena was cheerful and noisy, and when I went away to prepare for the night, Serena said 'mum' for the first time – I couldn't believe it!"

We have come to the end of the consultation. We agree to see each other for some more sessions, and then decide on a more stable and regular setting. While Serena, still in her mother's arms, looks at me, I wave good-bye with my hand and smile. The little girl, partially bringing out her hand out from where it was tucked into her mother's body, produces a small movement similar to my goodbye. The mother is surprised and tells me that Serena has not yet learned to wave bye-bye. Then, dressing her child ready to go out, the mother addresses Serena in baby talk: "We weady!" (In Italian, "siamo ponti" instead of "siamo pronti".)

M.H.: It is sad that the mother does not see this baby in any other way as a person in her own right. Something is idealized and projected into the child. She wants the child to have everything she didn't have from her own mother. There is no space in this mother. She doesn't manage to respond to the anxiety and pain of this child, who is called Serena but is far from serene.

D.M.: It is difficult to say who is the mother and who is the child in this case.

M.H.: It appears that there is a very fragile line between the child being in a peaceful state of mind, and being dead. When the mother says she is used to seeing her daughter hyperactive, it is as if this behaviour in the child reassures her. Because it tells her that the child is alive.

D.M.: The child has probably been projected into by the growing paranoia of the father due to his loss of sight, and also by the mother's anxiety about the child's survival. [*Looking back over the observation*] Serena puts her hands over her face, then she looks at her mother, then at the therapist with a serious expression... Gradually, as the therapist begins to talk, the child becomes more lively and interested in a soft toy, and she reaches out towards it.

M.H.: It is important that at the end of this observation the therapist waves "bye-bye" to Serena, but the mother says she doesn't know how to wave bye-bye, when in fact she is doing it. Simona felt there was a hint of tenderness in this gesture. I don't feel this child is so ill. It is the mother who is very ill, and the child could really die if the mother is not helped. As if the despair and the bitterness of these two parents would be too much for this child to take in. There is also something of a bitterness related to sexuality in the mother. In fact the breastfeeding may have been a form of compensation.

D.M.: The mother misunderstands the child's needs. Maybe she imposes her own fantasies on the child's behaviour. At one point the child turns to the mother in an excited state and the mother asks, "Are you hungry? Do you want a wee-wee?" Then the mother says to her, "You are tired." The child puts her arm over her ear and shortly afterwards responds to the therapist, who is beginning a game.

M.H.: There is a sequence on the following page, which begins when the mother says that Serena is "very trusting". Then she says "One cannot trust other people", and that she will tell Serena "what men are really like." The sequence continues with the child clinging onto her mother's hair. The mother is talking about Serena's autonomy, while the therapist has a sense of the "clinging behaviour of a newborn baby". Serena has a very adequate reaction. She puts a finger in her mouth and withdraws completely.

D.M.: This is so terrible and paradoxical, that one almost detects some malevolence in the mother, some rage against the daughter, as if she sees her as a little sister, feeling towards her that "You won't have anything that I haven't had.

M.H.: On the other hand, in this part one could read a message in the transference. The mother asks the therapist to be the good mother, the serene mother, the quiet mother for her. Maybe there is a rather desperate request to be helped. As if she was asking for regular sessions, and would like to be followed up.

S.N.: I also sensed this request at the end of the session. When the mother said "We're ready", I felt I was in contact with the child-part of herself, who was turning to me with a sort of baby-talk. As if she was acting out.

Dr Meltzer agrees absolutely with this.

D.M.: Do you know who is the youngest in the mother's family?"

S.N.: The firstborn is a boy, the third is a girl. Serena's mother was the second, only one year older than her sister."

Mrs Harris turns to the place where the mother says she was alone when she had Serena and her own mother didn't come:

M.H.: The fact that she presents herself in such a desperate and anxious way makes me think there is a request here to be helped. There is a request in this sentence which gives a little bit of hope that things could get better.

D.M.: There is already a change taking place.

M.H.: Probably the mother's first description is accurate as she gives an idyllic description of the nursing during the first few months, when mother and daughter were merged together. Then, when the mother was forced to recognize that the child was separate from her, she felt crushed by difficulties, and was not able to receive her baby's projections of anxiety.

S.N.: In the attempt to get an impression of what could have happened before those two days when Serena totally refused to be fed, I was struck by the coincidence told by the mother, namely that on that occasion Serena had said "mummy" for the first time.

D.M.: One has the impression that the mother was close to her mother-in-law who died two years before.

S.N.: I don't know… but it is possible, because she was the only person who used to go and see her at home. She couldn't have any contact with the relatives who lived in the apartment above theirs – her husband forbade her to talk to them as they had quarrelled in the past. Serena's maternal grandmother stopped talking to her daughter in the past and never met Serena.

M.H.: When Simona said that the mother would perhaps like to have her mother near her, she looked at her bewildered and then said that she was "upset and felt terrible", as if she could not manage to think about her pain. The relation to her mother seems to touch an intensely painful area that goes well beyond the standard pathology of the mother-daughter relationship. It can often happen that there is a break in the mother-daughter relationship. But in this case, it is as if there were something locked inside her that continued to cause her harm. This must be very terrifying for the little girl who then becomes the receptacle of the mother's fear.

D.M.: The mother, as a girl, ran away and was not rejected. She ran away many times. The little girl would run away too if she could. The only thing Serena could do was to close the orifices and expel, by screaming, the projections that were directed onto her. That is the type of scream depicted in Munch's painting, *The Scream*. It shows a woman on a bridge plugging her ears and screaming. Serena's scream has something similar to a psychotic withdrawal and probably the girl is delusional. Perhaps you may remember the film *Hiroshima Mon Amour*, where there was a sort of temporary psychotic withdrawal with the main character locked up in the shelter and screaming.

This passage was read again, then also the place, noted by Mrs Harris, when Serena "seemed to become increasingly small".

M.H.: When the mother was speaking to the therapist and Serena made sucking movements with her mouth, she did not understand, and asked the child if she was tired. The fact that Serena perceived her mother's anxiety was contained by the therapist made the misunderstanding less painful, and the little girl could make some direct demands to her mother.

S.N.: I had this feeling even during the first observation. The child by the end was able to relax when the mother was in touch with me.

D.M.: Yes, of course. Again the mother said, "Do you want to pull your ear off?" and the therapist mentioned the pain of hearing; mother commented that she could hear only painful things. Mother spoke about herself and the child became more lively. Then Serena dropped the toy, put her finger in her mouth, and then mother made a remark about her teeth. She then observed that Serena was calm and it scared her when her child was calm. It is paradoxical that she named her Serena as when she is calm, mother thinks she is dead.

M.H.: The mother is terribly ambivalent, as in her mind she mixes up the child with her own little sister. It seems it was the relationship with her younger sister that made her become "hyperactive". When the mother says she had been wild as a girl, one may postulate that becoming wild aroused the desire to have a child of her own, so that she could give it what she did had not had herself as a child. She ran away in the end, she said, "in order to see whether they really wanted me."

Conclusion and farewell

Around Christmas 1975, after a break due to my pregnancy, I started to attend again the seminars held in Novara by Martha Harris and Donald Meltzer. I cherish the memory of a stimulating and passionate scientific curiosity, with a sincere and containing working atmosphere. What I would specially like to bring out is the genuine freedom with which Mattie could speak, reminding me of a dodecaphonic scale.

I remember her lighthearted enthusiasm when the Novara colleagues gave her a gift of a brightly-coloured bag in bright colors, which she received with her communicative laugh. On a personal level, I remember her empathic smile and my emotion when, during lunch, I told her that I had phoned home and my daughter of almost nine months (whom I'd left overnight for the first time), said "Mum" for the first time, in the telephone receiver held by my mother. "See", she said, "You are helping your baby to separate from you (and you from her) without too much guilt, in order to continue growing."

Around 1980, Mattie and Don bought a house in Gromignana, surrounded by chestnut and fir trees, where I used to go with a group of colleagues for summer supervisions; the first time we went there, it was still a little bare, but Mattie had prepared fruit, tart and fresh water for everyone, on the terrace overlooking the woods. The Florentine workshop of December 1983 was the last in which I presented to Martha Harris; these are precious memories, because there were no such events the following year.

My, and all our efforts, following the experience shared with Martha Harris and Donald Meltzer, are directed increasingly towards encouraging others to find their own way forwards. Slowly introjecting their legacy, we try to help trainees to be passionate about ideals, without idealizing others or ourselves: to avoid merely imitating their teachers, and most of all (as Gianna Polacco Williams reports in her [1989] paper in the "Homage to Martha Harris" in *Quaderni di Psicoterapia Infantile*), to refrain from being content with producing "pale replicas of oneself".[1]

---

1 Harris 1975a, p. 44; see below, p. 10.

CHAPTER SIXTEEN

Supervision of a five year old boy

Andrea Watson

The decision of Dr Meltzer and Mrs Harris in 1977 to split their analytic practice and to work half-time teaching and analysing in Oxford was one that had a transforming effect both professionally and personally on many people's lives, including mine. I was able, as a psychiatric social worker working in the Child Guidance Clinic in Oxford to attend the clinical seminars that Dr Meltzer began leading. It was the experience of these that convinced me that I both wanted and needed to undertake an analysis for myself. Dr Meltzer referred me to Doreen Weddell and I began my analysis with her in July 1979.

At this point I had absolutely no thought of training as a child psychotherapist, but this began to change gradually under her influence and encouragement. Looking back, I believe that she anticipated that she probably would not live long enough to complete my analysis and she wanted to leave me in safe analytic hands before she died. She had already suffered a number of strokes that had left her with physical though not mental impairment. She died after I had been in analysis with her for 18 months, but within that time she insisted – and I think that is not too strong a word – that I undertake an Infant Observation with Mrs Harris and also that I entered supervision with her for the work with children that I was beginning to do.

The paper that follows, with some alterations and additions, is the one I finally presented for the Work Discussion module of the Psychoanalytic Observational Studies course organized at the Tavistock Clinic. What strikes me most strongly on the rereading of this paper is the incredible richness of Peter's material and my almost complete lack of understanding of this at the time! I want to be clear in saying that although the material is from Peter and myself, the interpretations and the psychoanalytic insights are really pure Mrs Harris. This paper, I think makes apparent the debt of gratitude that I owe her.

A friend of mine whom I met through the Infant Observation seminar pointed out that a characteristic phrase of Mrs Harris was "You see I think" – which appears on the surface to be merely a linguistic tick. If you punctuate it, however – "You see, I think" – then it becomes abundantly clear what Mrs Harris was able to do. We brought our eyes to see, she brought her extraordinary mind to think, and the combination is, as always, more than the sum of the parts.

"A patient, incapable of abstraction, strives to exist with a mental apparatus engaged in introjection and projection of beta-elements" (Bion 1962, p. 60). This I feel was Peter when I first knew him on referral in October 1979. He came to the clinic with his mother on two occasions, without his father or his elder sister, having been referred by the school medical officer because he was "distant" and difficult to teach, slow to learn, unusually aggressive towards other children and was given to sudden twitches and flinging of the arms. In these two sessions spent the first sitting under his mother's chair, playing, from time to time, a very frightened peek-a-boo and in the next he tried literally to climb the wall. He scrabbled frantically at it with hands and feet, making animal-like sounds of distress or machine-gun noises. He was five and a half years old.

His mother maintained throughout the sessions that she did not think there was much wrong with Peter and that she felt that this kind of behaviour, which was apparently very common was normal and to be expected of boys. The only area of concern for her was his day and night time wetting, which she felt quite hopeless and helpless about, and admitted that she had given up trying to train him but just changed him without comment.

She was unwilling (or unable) to try any new approaches. She did not relate to Peter – or he to her – during the sessions. What struck most forcibly about his mother was a deadening flatness in her demeanour. It was impossible to imagine her becoming enthusiastic or responding warmly to anything Peter said or did, but one could imagine her treating both his bizarre and his normal behaviour in exactly the same noncommittal way.

By the end of the second session her original defensiveness had turned to overt aggressiveness. She became angry and refused to accept another appointment. Contact with her after that became extremely limited both in terms of frequency and attempted depth of intervention. One result of this is that we knew virtually nothing about Peter's early history. All we knew was that he was a somewhat restless sleeper in his first year and that, from what his mother stated, he reached all his milestones at the normal times – whatever that meant to her.

The school inevitably became increasingly worried about Peter, particularly his aggressive attacks on other children. We involved the Educational Psychotherapist who presented a similarly perturbing picture to our own: of a boy who flapped and twitched, dribbled and panted, grunted and moaned. A boy clearly in deep distress, who elicited a response of sympathy and desire to help in all who came across him, except apparently, his mother.

It was with this background that I became involved again and suggested that I might see him in school on a weekly basis, without trying to involve his mother at all. She agreed to this. I felt at this stage that Peter was one of the most unusual children I had ever met and I was interested in getting to know him better and to try to make some sense of his behaviour almost for my own satisfaction. It would also serve to assuage the anxiety of the school, I hoped and to give his teachers some feeling of being supported in what was obviously a very difficult and worrying task for them. It would, I felt, have been over-optimistic to have hoped to have achieved more than this under the circumstances.

The setting as a whole was about as far from ideal as could have been imagined, without becoming totally untenable. Our times together were restricted to school terms, missing half terms, day trips, teachers' strikes, Christmas parties, sports days, etc., all of which seemed inevitably to be arranged to clash with the session. We contended, over a two year period, with three changes of room plus the unscheduled arrival and departure of different pieces of furniture and equipment in those rooms. We were interrupted physically by teachers, other children, window cleaners and plumbers, and aurally by telephones, televisions and general school noise. The only islands of constancy were myself and Peter's box of toys which arrived and departed with me.

I started seeing Peter individually in October 1980, and looking back, I can see three distinct phases in the work we did together.

I felt from the start that Peter latched onto the sessions with the tenacity of a drowning man and almost immediately invested them with a wealth of meaning and emotional warmth. I and the box, were the bridges that he could use to explore and make sense of his "mind pictures". Mrs Harris helped me to understand that the box was a concrete representation of the mother's body and that it was my role to be the external representative of the mother's mind in reverie – to hold his projections and to hand them back to him, maybe not fully sensibly ordered, but at least not stonewalled or left attended, and at best a useful spring board for future work for both of us.

The first phase was the most difficult to record and remember, perhaps because it was essentially non-verbal and also because although I knew he was acutely aware of my presence and was "playing" for me he was so distant and seemingly unreachable with words that there was little sense of a direct relationship within which to order things in my mind.

He didn't speak at all for the first three months. He then began to mutter to himself but was careful not to let me hear. Finally I was allowed to hear and he would address questions to me as long as he was facing the other way and they were addressed to the air.

He summed up his feelings in the beginning with the very first "mind picture" he brought. He stood with two tears of sheer fear on his cheeks, turned, picked out some pieces of lego and built a tower. He put a small perspex window on the top, ran his fingers up to the top of the tower and looked around the room through it. He seemed to be saying that only with this perspex barrier could he dare to be in the room with me. It also, though, carried another meaning – that of intrusive spying from a safe distance. This was more immediately indicated by a mannerism almost constant during this period, of his two hands on top of his head wriggling like antennae or horns – the dual function of both intrusive wriggling-in and self-protection of a "qui vive" kind, being fulfilled in the one gesture.

The next "picture" to emerge was closely centred on the box. He took two little men and hung them on the side of the box. They were screaming and sobbing in distress and trying to get into the box which resisted their entry. They were being attacked from below by the bull, hippo, lion, polar bear and elephant. I suggested (or to be more accurate, Mrs Harris suggested) that this was a picture of the baby at the breast, feeling unhealed and in danger of falling out of mummy's mind, while at the same time feeling attacked from below, in the bottom, being punished for his felt intrusiveness into the breast and having his projections thus pushed back into him in a hostile way.

There was always a difference in emotional quality between this presentation of his "mind pictures" and the times in the sessions when he became frightened by external events. His mind-pictures, I felt, were ways of approaching his internal terrors which had meaning and could be understood and the terror therefore ameliorated eventually by our work in the sessions. This was very different from the fear of external events that he would display: as when for example the thermostatically controlled fan heater would turn itself on, or the wind would make the door bang, or furniture would disappear and then reappear from week to week. For him such events were "heart-stopping" moments. They would be apparently be followed by such a bombardment of frightening sensations that he would literally be sent spinning round the room. Every gesture was a twitch or a contortion, words would disappear, there was just a blocking noise of explosions, screams, moans, and animal grunts. Everything around was involved in an orgy of distraction – all his lego constructions would be hurled across the room. Although many of the mannerisms and verbal mutterings would be the same during the presentation of a mind-picture, somehow he seemed more accessible, as if waiting for my interpretation. With the other kind of fear I often felt I could do nothing but wait quietly until the moment had passed and we could talk about it.

Then suddenly it happened the school was being closed down, so the room we used did look different every week as it was being used as a store room. Peter was going to a different school and the summer break was approaching. But it was amazingly under the pressure of these events that Peter began to talk directly to me. At this point I didn't know that it could be circumstances like this that might actually rupture the transference irrevocably. It was Mrs Harris who commented on this as a remarkable growing point, demonstrating both Peter's tenacity and his capacity for forgiveness.

Very poignantly in the first session after the summer, when we were talking about my reappearance, he said "I thought you was lying" (when you said you'd come back). He also questioned me about who else I saw and whether anyone else used the toys in his box. When I told him they didn't, his face became transformed with joy. He put his arms round his box and said "just mine, only mine, all mine". It was both the action of a starved child who is at last being attended to, and a possessive child wanting to keep the breast all to himself.

He began to indicate in his own words his valuing of the sessions. He asked me: "Was I moved to this school so that you could go on seeing me?", and then gave his understanding of it: "I come here to you to sort out my mysteries" and "I've got a lot of work to do."

Then there was an incident that again indicated Peter's capacity to turn a potential disaster into an opportunity for growth and learning. A designated mummy spaceship became broken up in the box between sessions without my knowledge – to be immediately discovered by Peter at the beginning of the next session. He was understandably absolutely furious. "You're hopeless, smelly and stupid – you can't look after anything, you didn't look after it – you break things up on purpose – you do it with your words – your words break things up – shut up, shut up." Perhaps here can be seen the anxiety that had to be overcome before he could even use words at all with me: that they are dangerous in and of themselves, they can be used like sledge hammers to destroy. Their power for good or evil seems tremendous and my capacity to withstand his harsh words seems immensely important at this stage – to go on using words to understand and make sense of things and not to be deflected from that in spite of his screaming at me. Eventually my non-deflection from the task in hand seemed to take away some of their omnipotence, so that two weeks later at the end of the session he can say, when putting away his spaceships, "I must put them away myself, carefully, because it's my hard luck if I don't and they get lost" – which seems to be taking responsibility for his actions and suggests the idea that saying the words can help him to be that careful, thoughtful person. He can be in control of the words rather than vice versa.

This was my very first experience of a real verbal attack by a child that was to a great degree justified. I do remember a strong desire simply to apologize but also having an equally strong sense of a Mrs Harris at my shoulder telling me to stick to my analytic stance of just continuing to observe and comment on what I was seeing and experiencing, without bringing my own feelings into it ie remaining steadfastly in the transference.

Soon after this the energy of the play with the lego spaceships began to diminish – it became more routine and far less anxiety provoking to him, and the theme with the animals that had been around for a while rose to occupy pride of place. These animals were exploring the inside of a cave-mummy – an interpretation that he accepted right from the start. This cave had monsters in it – also ammunition and then guards. He, firstly in the shape of the camel and lion, couldn't get out. Camel wanted to hide his head in the sand to avoid looking but lion wanted to continue to explore and find a way out with ropes, down a long steep hole.

This expanded session by session – the walls would fall in, there would be a light at the end of the tunnel, there was a force field to be negotiated and there were prickles in the tunnel and blue boxes that fitted inside one another and others right inside. It wasn't hard, with Mrs Harris' help, to see this as being his first permitted exploration in phantasy of mummy's body and his infantile phantasy – put clearly into words – of what he might find there, including other babies (blue boxes) and daddy's many penises (the guns, guards and prickles).

All this was explored with some fear and trepidation but with relative freedom up until the second session after the Christmas break when he had had to cope with yet another change of room. He had seemed sad before the Christmas break and had wanted to know where we were going to meet which I wasn't actually able to tell him as I didn't know myself until the last moment. He had for the first time been consciously worried about the break and the change of room. We actually moved out of the school and into the Health Centre next door. I was lulled into a false sense of security when in the first session he continued where he had left off but then …

In the second session, I saw again the child I had seen right at the beginning of our contact, in terms of the terror and desperation flowing out of him; but much more devastating in its impact as so much of it was now verbalised. He spent most of his time rushing shrieking and screaming, twitching and dribbling, round the table that I was sitting at. The main play was with the small spaceships which he got out and placed on the table – but then he clearly was one of them. He bombed, he invaded, he crashed, he banged his hands on the tables. The antennae were back, along with another contortion of grabbing his jumper at the shoulder and pulling it as if there was something on his back. The words flooded out of him but were mostly incoherent.

He became mesmerised with the wall outside that got bigger and then smaller, sometimes had a hole in it and sometimes didn't. Towards the end he began dropping things, frantic about everything being broken up and not being able to mend it. I was useless, I was a "stupid cow" and a "fat tit". Both clear "mummy" images, but ones he felt both desperately out of touch with and disappointed in.

The object he had been exploring over the last few weeks had turned on him. He clearly felt frighteningly trapped inside a persecuting and fragmented object, and to have totally lost his good object, There were only two moments when I felt he was in touch with me. He suddenly said "I'll kick anyone who tries to take my time away and who comes here". My response of "People who aren't very well" – like perhaps he wasn't feeling very well at the moment – seemed to comfort him and he came to rest from this endless spinning for a brief moment.

The theme of the wall came up over and over again in subsequent weeks. He talked about it becoming broken with holes in it, then it didn't have holes but it was floating about. He pointed to his breast and said "This is what it is." He was clinging on to it, he said – holding on to a twig-nipple but that wouldn't and couldn't hold him safely. It is hard to see how he could have stated his internal position more clearly. His exploration of his mother's body have made him feel that he had been dangerously intrusive when the body/room changed. He had damaged the breast – broken it up and holed it – and it could no longer hold him. The nipple could not bear his weight.

Mrs Harris explained this as Peter's internal world being laid out eloquently and compellingly in front of me. It made perfect sense although I couldn't have seen it on my own.

Somehow the working through of this material – the long drawn out process of putting together his fragmented good object, concretized by the wall – brought another leap forward. For a couple of weeks he seems mesmerised by the wall and the quality of his middle-distance gazing at it made me wonder from time to time whether he was actually hallucinating something. In his mind he climbed up and down the wall that he took apart and then put back together. At times it was something to cling on to, at other times it was a barrier. "If you take out one brick you can see through, but there's nothing there, just another wall but the same wall only different!"

He began to play over and over at being trapped and escaping. He fell onto the highly polished lino floor when he saw his reflection in it. He scrabbled at it frantically saying "I'm trapped inside this floor, help, help, I can't get out, I've fallen inside." He brought the two movable arms of a chair in towards himself while he sat on it screaming that he was trapped. He went in between two sets of doors, one with a glass panel, and tried to climb up them. Exactly the same actions as the little boy that I had seen at the beginning but with a totally different quality now. He could choose to play this game and he could choose to stop – he was in effect no longer trapped, but the fear had to be worked through over and over again.

When I first started seeing Peter, the pictures he painted of his internal world had the evocative quality of mime to them. They were plays without words in which one could marvel at the intensity of the emotion transmitted and the richness of the material thus revealed, but at the same time feel distressed for the little boy trapped in the concreteness of the phantasy. Now Peter has words – often extremely poetic words – and the phantasies can be thought about and symbolized rather than having to be enacted.

My initial expectations of what could be achieved working under the circumstances I have described were altered dramatically during those two years. I felt there were certain aspects of Peter's make-up that facilitated a gathering of the transference – his capacity to work and concentrate, and his relative lack of sadism, being two that readily spring to mind. A revealing example of this was when I managed to lock us out of the Health Centre so that we had to use another room for the session. Peter's response was to call me a stupid fool, but then nothing more until the end of the session when he admitted he had been distracted by the different objects in the new room and said "It'll be better when we're back in our own room next week, won't it?" This admittedly came quite late on, but even had he not been able to verbalize it earlier, his basic emotional response would have been the same: i.e. that it was a nuisance because it interfered with his work, but that I hadn't done it on purpose to hurt him. There was no vindictiveness in his response to me and his transference relationship with me could remain intact.

There is no doubt that sometimes the experience of supervision, especially when one is in training, can actually be quite persecutory, and sometimes one has to make a determined attempt to leave the supervisor at the door of the consulting room to avoid becoming paralyzed or wanting to say the "right thing". I can honestly say that I never felt that with Mrs Harris. I always experienced her as a supportive and encouraging presence. I can still after all these years hear her voice clearly in my mind, and some of her interpretations she made about both Peter and other patients that I took to her have remained with me ever since.

Her conviction about the reality of the internal world and how that was demonstrated in children's play was unshakeable and compelling and that I feel above all has been her legacy to me and countless others.

Dr Meltzer used to say that you can't give back, you can only give forward; and if any of my patients have gained from my work with them it is due in no little measure to my immense good fortune to having had the opportunity to work with both of them, but particularly Mrs Harris in this context.

Note

The case of Peter is discussed by Martha Harris in her paper "Growing points in psychoanalysis inspired by the work of Melanie Klein" (Harris, 1982).

CHAPTER SEVENTEEN

Revisiting some lessons learned from Martha Harris

Dina Vallino

I met Martha in the mid-1970s when, invited by Lina Generali Clements, she used to visit the Centro Milanese di Psicoanalisi. I had the great fortune of having both the supervision of Martha Harris (assisted by Donald Meltzer) for an infant observation, and of attending seminars led by her. Martha's supervision of Luca alternated on a monthly basis with that of Lina Generali Clements. During this same period, Mattie also supported me through her supervision of a number of severe cases that I had in psychoanalysis at that time. When she was unable to stop over in Milan, I used to go to the airport where, between flights, she would give me her supervision over a cup of tea. She always offered me, unfailingly, all the understanding and help that a young analyst might hope for when starting out. Profound and firm in her ideas, Martha was also kind and approachable, and I feel an enormous sense of gratitude towards her.

In 1989 I published, in issue 18 of *Quaderni di Psicoterapia Infantile* – which was devoted entirely to Martha Harris – several supervisions which she gave me on the case of a girl called Lucia.

Lucia was ten years old and affected by severe epileptic seizures, and had started intensive analysis with me (four sessions a week) at the age of five. The session and supervision from 1981 of which I here provide the transcript was recorded by some friends who were also present; and transcribed by Maria Pagliarani, Adele Pavia and Iolanda Galli. In my view it is highly representative of Mattie's style of working. I have also added a few comments on how I developed as an analyst and on the significance, to me, of Martha Harris's teaching.

Supervision of a session with a ten year old girl

[The child has been cutting small pieces of paper, including a picture of a lion and a flower, and sticking them onto a flat sheet of paper.]

M. H.: I think it's very important what you say to her here, that you mustn't forget the embryo she once was: that she cannot yet cut the analysis-placenta, otherwise the child inside falls to pieces. I would think what's happening here is that she doesn't really remember what you have done for her, but she is determined that she is going to cut it up and put it together – that's one thing she is doing here. She is cutting up the placenta and then sticking it on the paper in her own way. There is a part of herself that realizes that you do hold her together, that you do remember her, and that is very important to her; but she also resents this and would like to cut it apart and put it together in her own way. She does resent being kept to the definite. That you have a diary, that you remember when she comes, that she comes at certain times, that she goes away at certain times. In one way that's very important to her but in another she also resents it. She doesn't want to be kept to those particular times, to particular days. She would like to cut it up, re-arrange it and have it just the way she wants. I think that's the other element here. She says one cuts up the placenta so that one can demonstrate that it exists.

D. V. This cutting the placenta seems to me exciting the function of the mother in me.

M. H.: The mother doesn't hear her unless she really provokes her, insists and so on. She has to keep on projecting herself in an excessive way in order to get a response from the mother. She has to get under the mother's skin in order to stir her up. Is that what you mean? The desire to make something for you is obstructed. Her strong desire is to destroy everything. Yes, I'm not quite sure how to put what I'm thinking about this. I think there's something else in this: the feeling that you have done things for her and you do as it were act as a placenta, a life-line for her, and that you do remember her and she wants to do something for you. Now she says "You too should have something, something of our own to keep" – is it "our own" or "your own"?

D. V.: Our own.

M. H.: You see what is in this is something of a rivalry – wishing to be able to do the same kind of thing that you do for her. She says "We should have something of our own to keep" as if she wants you and her to be together like a kind of mummy and daddy who come together as equals to make the baby. She would like to take things apart and put them together in the way that you do. As if it feels a bit uncertain and humiliating to have to be like a baby dependent on the link with the mother.

I wonder about the placenta. I think there's something here about a progression from placenta to diary: because the baby needs the placenta when it's inside, but when it's outside, then time exists. This would mean that sometimes it is with the mother at the breast, and sometimes it's put down and separated from the mummy. She's trying to work out the difference between a fantasy of being inside you all the time – attached by a kind of placenta, in a dream – and being outside. If she's inside, she doesn't have to notice when she's here and when she's not here. She's not then an outside baby. It's puzzling, because she is the lion and the paper flower. The lion clearly indicates the rage.

D. V.: About the absence of a sense of time and sticking on the little pieces of paper: I was wondering if these could be related to the sensations that the child felt during the session – that she didn't connect together. Her feelings are like the small pieces of paper that she's stuck onto the sheet of paper. These make her sure that I am here and that she is here. But she cannot hold all these things in her mind. I was wondering whether this cutting, cutting everything she can find, is an advance for the child – showing that she is managing to express herself, all the pieces of sensation that she has.

M. H.: It's the placenta that she cuts and it's also the diary – small pieces of paper that are stuck on. It seems to me a bit more to do with a cutting-up of what you give to her – you representing the link with the breast, or the link with the truth. The link with things she does find painful. So she cuts and puts them together rather in the way that she *wants* them to be put together. I would think it's connected much more with an awareness of being outside, with the separation between sessions and I would think probably with the painfulness of this separation, and something of a protest at being kept to the definite times and being an outside baby.

I'm just so puzzled what she means by "one cuts up the placenta so that one can demonstrate that it exists". I wonder whether she is saying that when her placenta's cut she goes away at the end of the session, as if she's painfully aware that she does need you as a life-line. Maybe in the session she can sometimes let herself feel that she's inside and not really be aware that you're there – just take you for granted. But if that life-line – this placenta – gets cut, she then realizes that it does exist: that there is a very necessary life-line or link with you. But I would think that this is one of the problems of living inside an object, as it appears she's trying to do a lot of the time. You don't notice the relationship with the object you're inside: you're encapsulated, you're lost in it and you don't notice that it does exist. It's only when you're outside that you become aware of it and aware of the need of it. Because it would seem what's coming through is a painful awareness when she's not with you of needing you. That would also mean that she does remember you when she's away. That maybe she's not able to cut off and not long for you and pine for you. That she's aware of missing you, and that's painful, and she feels a bit hostile to that pain.

D. V.: After this period she was being very hostile towards me and she didn't want to stay with me during the session. She wanted to come but as soon as she was in the room she wanted to go out. I was wondering whether this behaviour had something to do with what you were saying before?

M. H.: I would think it probably does.

D. V.: When she is away she feels the need to come to me but when she's here she doesn't realize that I am here.

M. H.: I would think it's probably that she can no longer just step inside and feel that she *is* inside. When she comes, she is now aware that she's going to have to go. The diary – the time – will pass and it will be the end of the session. When she comes she's reminded of that, and wants to go away again. It's very painful for her that you should fit her in and then send her away again.

D. V.: As soon as she arrives she starts saying "What time is it?"

M. H.: She's getting ready to go away before she's sent away, because all the time she's aware that she can't just come straight inside and be lost inside, not anymore just take it for granted.

She's much more aware of the separation, of the coming and going. But the idea that you will say at the end "It's time to finish" comes to her immediately she comes in the room. She finds it very difficult to settle down and be with you. That she's going to go away before you tell her. She is much more aware of being outside, and much less able to be lost inside you.

Discussion

Sessions with this patient were turbulent. Martha helped me to grasp the atmosphere of the session, which in turn allowed me to shake off the feeling of powerlessness that this child, often over-excited and angry, aroused in me. Martha Harris reflected on the meaning of the expression "One cuts up the placenta so that one can demonstrate that it exists." In particular, what she was able to glimpse, through the sequence of the "placenta that is cut up" and of the "diary" which Lucia stuck on to the paper, was the experience of an infant who needs the placenta when on the inside, but who begins "to exist" when the placenta is cut and she is born. For Harris, the "diary" had a meaning: it referred to the sense of time that the patient had acquired through her comings and goings: her attendance of psychoanalytic sessions and her subsequent separations from her analyst. Harris's sensitivity to the emotional and elementary needs that are already present in the newborn infant as a small, evolving person allowed her to perceive in Lucia – an extremely mixed-up child swinging between gentle and angry behaviour – the essence of the bond towards the mother and feelings of affection towards her analyst. In the session transcribed here, Martha Harris followed the patient's journey from the state of "being inside" – hidden away in an evacuative pathological projective identification – to her emergence into a situation in which she begins to feel sadness at having to leave and the need to be with her analyst.

In 1978, Martha Harris wrote:

> Introjection remains a mysterious process; how do involvement and reliance upon objects in the external world which are apprehended by the senses (and, as Wilfred Bion has pointed out, described in a language which has been evolved to deal with external reality), become assimilated in the mind into what he calls the "psychoanalytic object" which can contribute to the growth of the personality; this is a process about which we have almost everything to learn. (1978a, p.176)

Reflecting on the introjection difficulties shown by Lucia, it became clear to me, over time, that the child lived in terror of her stern and violent father who used to beat her with a belt. I thus began to think that Lucia's confusion originated from her identification with a sadistic father, who did not allow her to be a child and who punished her fragility. What could Lucia possibly derive from psychoanalytic therapy that would not have been sustained by an affectionate relationship that allowed her to be, also, a little girl? And remembering how Lucia insisted on saying "one cut up the placenta so that one can demonstrate that it exists", I began to work in a new direction, endeavouring to find her "sense of existence" as a little girl, different from her confused sense of identification with an aggressor. In so doing, I was guided by two lines of thought: first, the idea that it was necessary to distinguish normal projective identification from pathological projective identification, and second, the idea of the sense of existence as a primary matrix in the ongoing formation of the sense of self and of personal identity.

What I would like to say, at this point, is that I have embraced as my own the central lesson taught me by Martha Harris: she, through her attention to the emotional needs of the newborn as a small, evolving personality, was able to grasp the emotional significance of even the most ill and disorganized child's search for the mother and for a bond. Currently, the most convincing psychoanalytic approach for me – which I present in my book *Fare Psicoanalisi con Genitori e Bambini* (2009) – is that which helps parents to recognize their children's needs, desires and intentionality.

The extension of infant observation

Another aspect of Martha Harris's teaching, which has been particularly valuable to me, is her work with infant observation. While it was Esther Bick who invented infant observation as an active method of observation, Martha Harris (who was herself influenced by Bion) must be acknowledged as the one who appreciated and defined the importance of group discussion in this ambit; indeed, group discussion went on to become an important instrument for monitoring and containing the anxieties of the observer in the setting of the infant observation seminar. As I said earlier, I had the good fortune to have the supervision of Martha Harris (assisted by Donald Meltzer) for an infant observation.

Martha Harris also introduced another important idea relating to training: namely the idea that the group, being "a sufficiently protected and organized place in which students can study and experience change and growth, in themselves and in their patients" (1978b, p. 28), could be exploited for the training of prospective analysts and psychotherapists.

A third aspect relating to group work, extraordinarily important in the evolution of applied psychoanalysis, was Martha Harris's idea of using the infant observation model outside the family, for example in hospitals and in institutional settings generally. It seems to me – and this is how I have interpreted Martha Harris's philosophy – that this use of infant observation in the field of hospital work, in the pedagogical sector, in social work, and in medical and pediatric practice, etc., can be defined as the *extension of infant observation*. When this form of infant observation becomes a routine part of the work done by social workers in the field, the result is the creation of links – affective bonds and shared ideas – between those professionals who use observation as a working method, both clinical and social. Ultimately, the presence of all these bonds, "ordered" but not rigid, has the effect of improving institutional practices. The infant observation approach to preterm infants introduced by Romana Negri – to name but one example – in the neonatology department where she worked led to changes in the way in which distressed infants, their parents and nursing staff were approached in her hospital (Negri, 1994).

We can certainly say that thanks to Martha Harris's innovative ideas, the use of infant observation in hospitals has radically transformed the way in which child neuropsychiatrists, psychologists, paediatricians and gynaecologists work, affording the newborn the right to be treated as a distressed child – in short, as a person.

Infant observation and pedagogy

I, personally, have considerable direct experience of the extension of the infant observation method in the pedagogical sphere. I refer to its use in a training project (1991-1999) that was aimed at educators: that is, staff working in crèches for children aged one to three years, and teachers in nursery schools for children aged three to five, who will then go on to primary school. Inspired by Mimma Noziglia, then Milan's head of child education services, this training project saw me involved in observation training work together with a team of neuropsychiatrists, psychotherapists and psychologists, all experts in infant observation. We felt that we were changing the direction of teacher-training, using play situations to focus on discovering more about how children's thinking develops.

These specialist colleagues visited the different schools to discuss the staff and teachers' observations on their relationships with the children. Basically, their task was to observe the children as they played with them. My role in the project was to lead study seminars with the crèche and nursery school directors and to supervise the group of infant observation specialists. There is no doubt that what I was able to contribute to this training programme stemmed from Martha Harris's ideas on the role of the group. My objective was to help the crèche educators and nursery school teachers become intimately acquainted with children's minds, and to give them an opportunity to study and appreciate how interesting, poetic and creative children's play can be, providing the adult succeeds in offering them adequate reverie and support, thereby helping them to relax, even in the absence of the mother.

I had realized that in crèches and nursery schools, children's play can sometimes fail to evolve, mainly because they do not receive enough attention or because the educators/teachers are too intrusive. It seemed to me fundamental to make these staff members aware of the important role that they, as adults, had – not only in the sense of what they were doing for each single child, but also in the manner of their play: how they helped them to develop their intentionality and express their feelings through play.

This training approach, which I named "Training using observation", has been referred to in various meetings and publications (see Noziglia et al, 1997; Vallino, 1995). It is conducted in three steps, each essential for the one that follows. In the first step, one of the teachers presents a written observation of the play of one of the children she looks after. The second step is a group discussion with teachers, led by a specialist, in which colleagues consider how to apply for their own use the observation that has been presented. The group leader is a psychotherapist or neuropsychiatrist with expertise in infant observation. The third step is the monthly meeting between the team of educators' group leaders and the leaders of the training programme (Noziglia et al, 1997). These three steps are complementary and essential to training *with* observation.

This pedagogical approach would not have been possible without Martha Harris's teaching. For this reason, it seems appropriate to conclude with her words:

Helping a child to be himself does not, of course, mean encouraging him to act upon the impulse of any given moment. Nor for the matter, does it necessitate immediate response to his demand for attention even in early infancy. In the first days his impulses are expressible almost exclusively in action, but as soon as he has begun to introject, to find within himself a comforting understanding presence, this can help him to hold, however briefly, the urgent demand or pain or need until perhaps the necessary external aid comes to relieve him or to assist him to bear the painful state of mind which is afflicting him. (Harris 1978, p.168).

CHAPTER EIGHTEEN

Reminiscences of an infant observation with Martha Harris

Angela Goyena

In November 2010, on the occasion of a homage to Martha Harris in Paris (by the GERPEN)[1], Meg Harris Williams asked me if I would like to write a paper based on my experience of infant observation when I was supervised by Martha Harris. I was lucky to find some of my notes and typewritten records, and also tape-recordings of a few of the supervisions, which I have pieced together in order to describe this immensely important learning experience I am so grateful to have had.

Just before beginning my psychoanalytic training in Paris I was working as a psychotherapist with adult and adolescent patients. I attended with a small group of colleagues seminars given by Dr Herbert Rosenfeld, who was supervising our clinical work. He strongly advised me to consider doing an infant observation as this would help me to gain understanding about the development of young children. He also emphasized that the experience of infant observation was very helpful in developing awareness of infantile experience and non-verbal communication

---

1 See Chapters 5 and 6 of this volume.

in our patients. Some time after, taking up Dr Rosenfeld on his suggestion, I asked Martha Harris for supervision of my observations which were due to begin a few weeks later. She agreed to see me for individual supervision on a monthly basis.

I was already attending the GERPEN meetings in Paris and had been particularly inspired by the very creative joint seminars of Martha Harris and Donald Meltzer in supervision of infant observation and child psychotherapy. At that time in France, the history of infant observation based on the method inspired by Esther Bick was in its early stages. I was, however, fortunate enough to be able to attend the seminar for the supervision of infant observations, directed by Dr Geneviève Haag; and also seminars of infant observations and child psychotherapy supervised by Hélène Dubinsky.

It was very important for me to have the support of my analyst for this project, enabling me to confront and understand the inevitable countertransference issues. However, this aspect of the observation is not gone into here as it is beyond the scope of this paper.

For the purpose of this paper, the following material includes an edited transcript of the observations and the supervisions of which I have tape-recordings.

Meeting the family

I was contacted by Marie who had been given my name by Dr L, their family doctor and a colleague of mine. Marie had heard about infant observations and was quite disposed to lend herself to this sort of experience. She was expecting her second child in six weeks time. We met to discuss the project and I was introduced to Pierre, her partner, and to James, aged seven years, Marie's son from her first marriage which had ended in divorce when James was only eighteen months old. They welcomed me in a friendly and relaxed manner and expressed interest and enthusiasm for the observations, agreeing with the idea of weekly visits lasting one hour. Marie was going to a private clinic for the birth of her baby, where she had been followed throughout her pregnancy. She was attending classes in painless childbirth at this clinic which she found very reassuring. She was on maternity leave from her job but would return to work when her baby was three and a half months old. I thanked them for the opportunity of observing their baby. We said goodbye and I left the two of them who were smiling.

Thomas from birth to three and a half months

Marie telephoned to announce the birth of baby Thomas the previous day at 11.30 a.m. He was placed in an incubator until the following morning "because he was too cold", she explained. She said she would be going home in a week and I could come to the clinic whenever I liked.

> When I arrived for this first observation Marie was sitting up in bed reading. I had the impression she didn't recognize me at first but her tone of voice told me that she was expecting me. Baby Thomas was asleep in a cradle between the bed and the door to the left of Marie. He was lying on his front with his head turned to his right side, facing his mother and the window. I shook hands with Marie and congratulated her. She smiled, and turning towards the baby, said: "Thomas was born last Wednesday, he is five days old today. I am breast-feeding him seven times a day, one of which is during the night. He changes every day." I looked at Thomas and saw that the whole of his body and his limbs were moving and I heard a little noise, a sort of squeaking from the throat which accompanied these movements. Then he became quiet and still. His skin had a pinky-red mottled appearance. Marie pointed to a chair where I could sit. She told me that everything had gone well and the contractions were not too hard to bear. The most difficult moment was the delivery when she was torn. Pierre was present at the birth and visited her every day with James who was very pleased with his little brother.
>
> While his mother was talking baby Thomas was sleeping, but not very deeply. He was lying on his front and every so often he would turn his head from one side to the other and in doing so he raised it up, throwing it backwards with great

force. He moved his feet and legs also from time to time, kicking them up behind him. His hands were clenched and each time his head was turned to his right he sucked his right fist and seemed to be trying to get it inside his mouth. When it was time to leave, Thomas was sleeping peacefully, lying quite still on his front, arms and legs spread-eagled, his head turned to the left, away from his mother. Marie looked at him and said, "I hope he will stay awake when you visit him at our home."

On returning home, Marie began to run a temperature and was sent back to the clinic where Thomas was born. There was no room in the maternity ward so Thomas was placed in the nursery. Breastfeeding was temporarily interrupted as a precautionary measure. Marie's milk was drawn off but not kept for baby Thomas. After two days, Pierre took Thomas to his sister who looked after him until Marie returned home five days later. She told me how hard it was for her to be separated from her baby. He had cried a lot during their separation and when reunited with his mother, was constantly searching for her breast.

Faced with this dramatic and alarming news, I wondered how this newborn baby had managed to survive on his own without his mother, separated from the breast. I remembered that I had seen Pierre, thoughtful and affectionate in a paternal role with regard to James. Therefore, I could imagine and hope that his sister, Thomas' aunt, was also a loving, caring person and sufficiently containing to enable this baby to feel held together. This constant search for the breast, which Thomas's mother spoke about, seemed to illustrate the young baby's unintegrated state and need for a containing object as described by Esther Bick (1968). Fortunately, even after such a dramatic disruption, breastfeeding was re-established quite easily.

During the initial observations it was remarkable how baby Thomas would sleep peacefully, seemingly unbothered by ongoing noise coming from the building site close by the family apartment, or loud music which was playing over the radio. He seemed to like the regular rhythm of a noise which was something predictable, perhaps like the noise experienced inside the uterus and therefore to do with primitive memory functioning and a feeling of containment linked to the security of a safe place inside the womb. In fact, we have learnt from research (Walker, Armitage and others) that the "fetal environment is rich with acoustic stimulations coming from the inside of the mother's body (through her eating, drinking, breathing, and cardiovascular and gastrointestinal activity), from her vocalizations, and from the attenuated environmental noise" (D. W. Walker, cited by Piontelli [1992], p. 35). I saw that through all this noise, Thomas would react to the sound of his mother's flip-flops as she crossed the floor. He stirred a little, moving his arms and legs in a gentle, relaxed rhythm, then continued sleeping, which suggested he was feeling held by the signs of his mother's presence he was getting to know. However the sudden, sharp sound of the coffee grinder coming from the kichen or a door slamming would startle him, plunge him into a very frightening situation. Then he would begin to cry and writhe around. He arched his back, moved his arms and legs rapidly as if he were attempting to hold himself together, to stop himself from falling apart.

The first time I saw Thomas feeding was during the third observation. He was one month old:

> Marie gave him her right breast, guiding her nipple into his mouth with her left hand. He sucked slowly and regularly looking into his mother's eyes as he did so. His arms were outstretched along the side of his body, he was very relaxed and he fed like this for ten minutes. Then he brought his arms up to his chest, closed his right hand tightly, took it in his left hand with his fingers spread all around. He sucked a little more quickly for a few minutes then shut his eyes for the last ten minutes of the feed. Marie had brought her left arm out in front, across Thomas's knees to meet her right arm so that Thomas was really surrounded, cradled in her arms. She looked at him very tenderly and seemed moved by the intimacy she had with her baby. After this feed Marie didn't help Thomas to bring up wind and this was a regular pattern seen in other feeds. I also noticed that as he sucked on the breast, Thomas opened and closed his toes in a regular rhythm as if he were feeding with more than one part of himself and using every bit of himself to make the most of it.

When Marie removed Thomas's soiled nappy, he trembled a little and made noises of complaint but didn't cry. He brought up some milk which his mother wiped away. Throughout the change Thomas's eyes were fixed on his mother's eyes. She picked him up and held him close for a moment or two then tried to interest him in a mobile but baby Thomas seemed completely oblivious of everything but his mother's face, as if he was actively attempting to keep in contact with the good containing mother during this frightening situation.

At the first observation after an interval of seven weeks (due to the summer vacation), both parents were full of smiles and asked after my holidays and my family.

Pierre was bare-chested, wearing pyjama or track suit trousers. Marie was wearing a bright blue jumper and a skirt of a red and gold colour. This was the first time I had seen her wearing make-up. In the living-room Thomas was asleep on the sofa. He was lying on his back, feet towards the window and his head was turned to his left side, towards the back of the sofa. There was a small cushion on the edge of the sofa to prevent him falling off. When we went into the room Thomas stirred, making little noises of complaint and started to cry. Marie sat on the sofa at his feet and put her hand on his tummy to soothe him. He continued to cry, moved a little then calmed down and went back to sleep. Pierre went out of the room, then came back having put on a T-shirt. They both told me about the progress that Thomas had made. Pierre said proudly: "He's grown a lot, he recognizes people well, he chatters and smiles." Marie added: "and he even smiles at his brother now."

I saw that since the last observation before the vacation, Thomas had gained weight and length, but above all his body had an aspect of being more held together than before. Marie continued to talk and after half an hour Thomas started to make sucking noises. He seemed to be sucking his tongue. Then he brought his right hand up to his mouth, his fist clenched, which he began to suck. When Thomas started to move and to cry a little Marie picked him up and sat him on her knee facing her. Thomas calmed down but tried to get hold of his mother and seemed to be searching for her breast with his mouth and his hands. She laid him down gently on his back holding him in her right arm with the left side of his body against her. Thomas took hold of her necklace and then her jumper with his right hand. Marie gave Thomas her right breast, he took the nipple into his mouth at once and began to suck. He was clutching on to his mother's jumper and began to open and close his hand repeatedly at the same time as he slid his hand to his right, coming to a stop between his mother's breasts, still clinging tightly to the jumper. He fed peacefully for ten minutes. During the feed she told me she didn't really want to start working again the following month because she will have to take Thomas to the day nursery. She also told me about her older son James, the vacation he had with his father and how he was pleased to see his friends again at the beginning of the new term. Next week he will celebrate his eighth birthday by inviting some of his friends to their home. Marie had been talking almost throughout the feed with only some brief pauses.

After about twelve minutes, when Thomas had stopped feeding, his mother sat him on her lap, his left side next to her body. He burped twice and brought up a little milk. Marie wiped his mouth and put the bib round his neck. Thomas looked at me for a moment then turned his head to look at his father. Marie lifted Thomas up and sat him down on her knee facing her. She smiled at him and he returned her smile uttering a little cry of contentment. Marie was radiant and visibly moved. It seemed that the exchange between herself and her son was very intense at that moment. Then Thomas looked around. Pierre got up, took his son into his arms and sat down in the chair opposite me. He lifted Thomas up and held him in the air above his head. Thomas cooed with pleasure. He seemed to like this game. "You like to fly the aeroplane, don't you?" said his father. Marie said: "Be careful Pierre he's just been fed", and she went out of the room. Pierre continued the game with his son, lifting him up in the air and lowering him again. Thomas laughed and gave little cries of pleasure. Afterwards his father stood Thomas up on his knees.

Thomas straightened his legs then bent his knees, lifted himself up again by pushing on his feet and he repeated these movements several times being held safely by his father.

Suddenly his father got up, came and put Thomas on my knees facing me. I held him and said that I could see how much he liked to play with his Daddy. He looked at me with a serious expression on his face. Then I said to him, "You don't know me very well yet, do you?" He smiled at me then looked around, his expression becoming serious again. I lifted him up and turned him round so that he was facing his father. Thomas smiled at his father as soon as he saw him and I handed him back to his father who began the aeroplane game again. Thomas looked pleased, continuing to smile. Then his father kissed him on the nose and held him so close that their faces were touching. Thomas brought up a lot of wind and some milk which landed on his father's mouth. "Oh, he's dribbled on me", said Pierre wiping his mouth; "I'm going to change him."

In Thomas's room Pierre laid him down on the changing table and began to undress him. When taking off the nappy he commented that it was not soiled. Thomas looked at his father, kicked his legs and smiled. Pierre, using a damp towelling cloth, wiped Thomas, insisting on the parts between his legs and his genitals. He dried him and put on a clean nappy. Then Pierre leaned over and kissed Thomas. I could no longer see their two faces because Pierre's hair was very long and thick and hung down in such a way that it hid them both. Thomas caught hold of his father's hair with his right hand. "You're pulling my hair", said Pierre, lifting himself up and smiling, then he began to dress Thomas, holding him by both his ankles with one hand and putting on his pants with the other. Thomas lifted himself up from the shoulder blades by arching his back and kicking his legs in a forward thrust movement. Then he let himself down again on to the table. He did it a second time with a very concentrated expression on his face. "Look at that, you are having fun", his father said, laughing: "Do it again." This was a moment of intense communication between father and son. Marie came into the room to see what was going on and smiled at me. "He lifts himself up by himself", said Pierre: "Go on, do that again." And Thomas did it again as if he understood what everyone was waiting for. Then his father finished dressing Thomas and took him in his arms.

Supervision

Martha Harris: This game of holding the baby above the head is something fathers are very keen on. It is interesting, the moment of intense communication with his father is when his father is changing him and when he does seem to be trying to co-operate. He lifts up his body, as if he were trying to help. That would seem to be a moment when he's almost, somehow, being given the opportunity to take the initiative to be helpful, and seemed to be doing it to please daddy; and then, when his father says "Look, he's lifting himself up", he does actually seem to understand and does it again. I take it they've both been on holiday and baby will have had both of them all of the time?

Donald Meltzer: Are they not married for ideological reasons? because they seem very united. I suppose this running about in his pyjama pants is a little bit seductive towards you and he is a little bit seductive towards the baby too, but it seems mainly warmth really. This degree of welcoming you – it's a bit unusual for both parents to be so welcoming to the observer.

M.H.: I wouldn't have said so, but would think it is an indication that they are – both of them – very interested in the baby and interested in your being interested in the baby, and welcome you as a kind of addition to their interest. You talk of the baby and his body and how he seems more held together than before. Well of course it is seven weeks and he has developed a lot, but I think perhaps that does reflect the baby's feeling of really being held together by the attention of the parents. You could have described him as holding himself together, but there is a feeling of him being very safely contained by his mother, by the parents. In this game of father playing the aeroplane, he doesn't seem to be at all apprehnsive about it. And the father doesn't really seem to mind when he brings him close and the baby burps up his milk, as one might expect. I would guess it's a bit of a problem for a father, after the mother has been feeding the baby, to find something himself to do actively for the baby. This game of lifting baby up and down is something father can do. And he does seem very happy to do the whole changing business afterwards, when he thinks the baby needs changing and the baby seems terribly happy to try to co-operate. He co-operates very actively in the feeding – the clasping of the mother's jersey and the opening and shutting of his hands. It's a very active feed on his part. The older son does seem to be very much part of it. He's not here, but he's brought into the conversation, so they do give the feeling they are very much together as a family.

D.M.: They seem pleased that the baby has shown some friendliness towards his older brother.

M.H.: One would guess that it is really awfully important to them to be feeling that the baby is outgoing and being friendly to people as in a month's time he is going into a nursery. I take it that the mother does have a job from which she has had leave and then has to go back.

D.M.: You wouldn't see many fathers having their mouth vomited on without recoiling. He's even a little disappointed that the nappies aren't soiled. It's a nice space they make between them, very welcoming, quite firm, supporting.

M.H.: And the baby is very deeply responsive to both of them. And when he's handed to you, he seems to be quite happy about that, but noticing it.

It's a little bit sad because he will be in the nursery all day. I should think it is quite difficult for a baby of this age. Although they are trying to do their best to settle him in. I would think this is always one of the problems for the mother, not to run away from her own depression and her own guilt – from her own feelings about it.

D.M.: Run away from those accusing eyes.

M.H.: I think the observer can help that by not being accusing.

D.M.: You often see there is a tremendous dumping of depression into the observer by exaggerated flippancy and carelessness. The observer leaves the observation absolutely loaded and this seems to help the family. So fasten your seat belts, here we go.

M.H.: When children go out early to a nursery after having had a very close relationship with the mother, I think they probably do suffer more than if they haven't really established a very intimate relationship. I mean their development may suffer more if they have never had this intimate relationship, but the child who has, suffers more pain at the separation.

Thomas aged three and a half months

In this next observation when Thomas is three and a half months old, we see his reactions to the beginning of weaning.

> Marie was working in the kitchen. The radio was playing very loudly, with a programme of pop music. Marie said: "He's got a cold and is completely unsettled. He can't be very well. I don't know what the matter is and on top of it, on Sunday I started to wean him."
> Thomas was in his bedroom, asleep in his cradle, lying on his tummy with his head turned towards his left, facing the window. His arms were spread out at shoulder level, his elbows bent and forearms on each side of his head. His hands were loosely closed with the thumbs under the fingers. His mouth was open and he was breathing regularly. His mother came into the bedroom and asked: "Is he still asleep? He can't be feeling very well. He woke me up at one o'clock this morning and then he slept until 10. He is really upset and if he starts to wake me up in the middle of the night..." She didn't finish the sentence and went back to the kitchen. After 15 minutes Thomas began to wake up. He moved his arms, his legs and his bottom. He bent his knees, bringing them up underneath him, pressing on his feet, almost as if he was trying to crawl. The top of his body remaind stuck to the mattress but with a great effort he lifted his head and turned it from one side to the other. He was sliding his hands to and fro across the mattress in semi-circular movements. I could hear grunts and splutters coming from his nose and throat. Then he stopped and continued to sleep. He repeated these short periods of activity several times.
> When Marie returned to his bedroom, Thomas happened to be moving at that moment. She gazed at him tenderly

before taking him into her arms. Thomas woke up, seemed a little agitated and began to cry. Then he brought his left fist up to his mouth and began to suck it. Marie put Thomas on the changing table and said to him: "I'm going to put some saline solution in your nose to clean it, otherwise you won't be able to suck." When the drops fell, he started to cry and waved his arms and legs but his mother picked him up and he calmed down. "It's coming, young man," she said to him, walking into the kitchen. Thomas was searching on the shoulder and the breast of his mother for a place to suck. He took a mouthful of her jumper, rejected it and began to cry loudly. "No, that's not it and it's not going to be the breast either", she said to him. She sat on a stool with Thomas on her knee and removed the bottle from the heat. "You'll have to wait a bit longer my little father", she said to Thomas who was crying with despair. When the bottle was ready we went into the living-room. Marie sat on the sofa and put a bib on Thomas. With her left arm around him, holding him closely against her, Marie gave him the bottle. Thomas began to suck hungrily. While he was feeding Thomas held on to his bib with his left hand, tightening then loosening his grip repeatedly as I had seen him do with his mother's jumper when he was being breastfed. With his right hand he was holding on to his mother's fingers which were around the bottle. He shut his eyes.

Marie began to speak: "What a state he got into when I gave him the first bottle. He only drank a little and I finished up breastfeeding him. His father gave him the second bottle and he absolutely refused to drink it. The third time, I gave him the bottle and he took it. He accepts it when it's me. I always give him the breast first thing in the morning and last thing at night. I shall continue to breastfeed him morning and night for some time after I have started work again. My son James was bottle-fed. He was never breastfed." Thomas finished the milk and his mother withdrew the teat from his mouth. He began to cry. She sat him up and he calmed down, burped and started to cry again almost at once. "You are really hungry aren't you. I shall have to get a little more." She got up and put Thomas down on the sofa on his back, his head and shoulders resting rather precariously on a big cushion. He was quite near the edge of the sofa and moving his body while crying. Marie looked at him, then turned to me and said "I'll be right back", and she went into the kitchen. I understood that she wanted me to keep a close watch over Thomas during her absence. I sat on the sofa next to him to prevent a fall. He was crying very much, it seemed to me from anger and frustration. He was moving his arms and legs with such force that his whole body was rocking a bit. I held out my hand to him so that he could catch hold of a finger – which he did – and I told him that Mummy was coming straight back, but that did not calm him. His mother did come back very quickly and gave him the milk. She said, "He's taken two hundred grams in all. It's funny, with the breast he takes as much as he wants but with the bottle one has to measure it." She sat him up on her lap and he started to cry a little, but not as if he were still hungry. It was more like he was hindered by something and even a little sad. She took him in her arms and held him right up against her, with his head resting on her left shoulder. She patted him gently on the back as she rocked backwards and forwards.

Supervision

D.M.: It's not as bad as one feared. When you arrived hearing pop music your heart must have sunk. I was wondering if this washing-out of his nose seemed a little unnecessary to you.

M.H.: The feeling is that the mother as well as the baby, seems to feel that something is coming between, that it takes much longer for the more intimate relationship to be established, as I think it is re-established towards the end, when she holds him really close against her. But there is a feeling that something is getting in the way. Whereas with the breast, she could trust him to take as much as he wanted or as much as he needed, but now with the bottle she has really to measure it. There is now some kind of external criterion – the world is coming in and things have to be measured or disciplined. In her attitude there is almost a feeling that the baby has to adjust to reality. No, not the jumper that's not it, but it's not going to be the breast either. You're going to have to learn something else. "You're going to have to wait a little longer my little father", as if the baby has already grown up.

D.M.: "You've got to be your own father!" His hands seem very important, both holding on and searching round.

M.H.: And then he seizes his mother's fingers on the bottle, as if that helps him, to have contact with her fingers.

D.M.: She's hardening him off.

M.H.: I would think she is also feeling, pressing in on her, this business of going back to a job and having the baby; if the baby wakens at night what's she going to do. We get the feeling that he has been a pretty adaptable baby, because he lost the breast for a week and then took it up again; he is capable of adapting to changes. This business with the bottle – when he won't take it from the mother first time, and not at all from the father, but then from the mother – it's as if he registers a protest. One would think that his cold is also an expression of the disturbance – that he does feel there is something coming between him and this intimate, very intimate relationship that he had with his Mummy. You can see that, after having the bottle, in his crying and moving his body. When he has the bottle in his mouth he sucks away and doesn't at that moment really think about what he's missing, but when it's finished, he does realize what he's been missing and really cries about it. When he cries afterwards, it's not that he wants more of the bottle, but he wants to have this indefinable something that he's been missing in the feed, which I think is the closeness to Mummy. He somehow seems to recover that closeness when she holds him close, and then he seems to waken up and looks around. That's when he looks at you and smiles at you and can take you in and recognize you at that moment. It seems that in this observation you do get a very graphic feel of what an intense business it is for the child to adapt to these changes; and how intense the anxiety is also for the mother – what a task she has to deal with.

D.M.: "I'm not going to feel too sorry for you because there are children who don't have a breast at all." The first time when she put him down on the sofa, there was a cushion placed to prevent him from falling off. This time he is placed in some jeopardy and delegated to you to catch him before he hits the floor, as it were. This is part of her own preparation to have to delegate his safety to other people. It really is the end of the honeymoon. "We can't go on meeting like this." The general feel is of resilience in both of them. They are both being resilient.

Thomas aged three months and three weeks

In this next observation, when the baby is aged three months and three weeks, we can see more clearly my role as observer in containing the anxieties of the mother and baby, just prior to Marie returning to work and baby Thomas going to the crèche.

> The baby was in his reclining chair which was on the floor next to some shelves. His mother said, "You've got a visitor, Thomas." When I said hello to him he stared at me for a few moments then smiled a faint smile behind the three first fingers of his left hand which he was sucking. Then he made a rather plaintive cry and looked at the mobile suspended above him. His mother touched the mobile to make it move and said, "He loves looking at mobiles." Then Thomas kicked his legs and spread his arms out either side of him, then brought them back again on to his chest. After this he lifted his arms up into the air, more or less in the direction of the mobile which was out of his reach. He looked at it as if he wanted to catch hold of it. There was loud music resounding through the living-room. Thomas was vocalising contentedly but soon his tone changed to one of complaint. Then he stopped and stared at the mobile for a few seconds and looked in our direction. He made sounds of discontentment, became agitated and fidgety.
>
> Marie turned off the music and said to Thomas, "You want to be picked up, don't you?" She picked him up and sat down with him on her knees, facing her. Thomas looked at his mother with an expression of contentment. Then he turned towards the window and became very interested in some

indoor plants which were within his view. His mother asked him what it was that interested him so much and he turned back to look at his mother, beginning to rock his head and shoulders backwards and forwards towards her.

The telephone rang. Marie put Thomas back in his chair and went out of the room to answer it. Thomas remained calm and looked at the mobile. He puts the first three fingers of his left hand into his mouth and turned to look at me. He stared at me with a rather serious and questioning look. Then he smiled at me, took his fingers out of his mouth, spread his arms out either side of him, kicked his legs, cooed and gurgled a bit. He stayed quiet for a few moments, dribbled and began to blow bubbles with his saliva. He folded his arms back on to his chest and held his hands together. Then he yawned and started to fidget, spreading out his arms and kicking his legs. When his mother came back, she sat him on her knees again and he fell forward on to her breasts searching for somewhere to suck. Thomas buried his head in her left breast then started to suck his left fist. He began to complain a little. "You're doing nothing but complain today. Do you want me to walk around with you?" said Marie. She began to walk backwards and forwards, round the room, with Thomas in her arms, his head looking over her left shoulder. Thomas calmed down, was very alert and looked around with a contented air. Marie said to her son, "I know you like this but soon you'll be at the crèche and I don't think they will do this for you there." Looking at me she said, "There is one person for five babies, so there is plenty for them to do during the day." Thomas looked at me intensely and Marie said to him, "That's Angela, and she will come to see you every week."

The telephone rang again. This time Marie put Thomas on his tummy next to me on the sofa. "There, next to Angela there is no risk of you falling and you can look at the holes", she said to him. (The sofa had a white lace cover draped over it.) Thomas gripped on to the lace cover with both hands, sucking each fist alternately. Marie came back and took him on to her knee. She held him between her breasts, he was on his stomach with his body outstretched. He searched on her left breast for a place to suck while clinging to his mother's silk scarf. He put the three first fingers of his left hand and a little bit of the scarf into his mouth and began to suck. His eyes were almost shut and he began to doze. Marie said "I think he is going to sleep. He always sucks a lot before he sleeps." She put Thomas in his cradle which she wheeled over to the shelves underneath a musical mobile which she set going. Thomas didn't look at the mobile but looked at his mother very intensely. Marie went out of the room and Thomas looked at the little figures of the mobile which were turning round up above him. Then he looked at me and at that moment his mother came back and said "He must wonder why you look at him like that."

Supervision

M.H.: The part that you are playing for this mother – which I think is something very important – is as if you are something that is going to enable this baby to look at the holes, to deal with the absence, and to deal with the separation. As if you somehow, for her, represent some kind of buoyant internal object that will always be there and always return to help deal with the weaning and the loss that it is taking place. She talks about the nursery where he's only going to have a fifth of a maternal object, but "Angela is going to come and see you every week."

D.M.: Yes, she certainly is directing his attention towards you as another person who is interested in him, lest he suffer from feeling neglected. She refers to you at the very beginning as his visitor: "You've got a visitor."

M.H.: She is also really trying to direct his attention, noticing when he gets interested in his environment. She provides this mobile for him to look at. She is directing, encouraging his interest in the outside world. There are all kinds of interesting things to see. You see him lying in his chair where he puts his arms out, then he brings them back in again to his chest as if he himself is really trying out expanding and then coming back to be held closely again. Then when she sits him on her lap, looking at him, he seems to laugh, they both seem to like looking at each other. Then he turns to look round at the plants. Later on, when he seems to be falling forward onto her breast, searching for something to suck, she says to him "Oh, you are always complaining", then she picks him up and walks him around to look at things. "Don't just complain because you're losing this, there are other things to look at." And the fist that the baby seems to have been sucking right from that first observation, is coming in again as particularly important; he sucks it and shuts his eyes, then he opens his eyes, as if he tries to reconstitute the feeling of being with the breast, in the sucking of his fist before he goes to sleep.

D.M.: "Next to Angela there is no risk of your falling, and here's your guardian angel and there's the place where Mummy used to be. Now you watch that space, you'll see, she'll come back. It's very interesting (she hasn't verbalized it yet, but we've heard it several other times) that at this point, the mother feels she has to direct baby's attention to how many other nice objects there are in the world, because it dawns on her that the baby could lose her, permanently. Something could happen to her. She is very identified with the baby whose mother is going out into the world and of course may get lost out there, down at the end of the town and hasn't been heard of since.

M.H.: I would think it's a situation you do get whenever a baby is weaned, even much later: that a mother can live for a longer time, if she doesn't have to go back to work, in some rather enclosed place with the baby, with the outside world kept outside. But this mother is having to go back pretty quickly, pretty abruptly, and the outside world is impinging on her as well as the baby. So she is doing her best to try to draw his attention to the interests that will help him in this.

D.M.: It's a bit like the business about her first boy not having the breast at all, as if she would say to the baby, "Oh yes, you may lose your mother in three months, but remember there are children who don't have a mother at all." As if that's real consolation.

M.H.: The music – I would think that's filling the space that the depression might occupy. Also it's very much an adolescent thing to have this ongoing sound.

D.M.: This maternal souffle, the mother's boom, boom, boom right under Mummy's heart as it were. I think it has a very intrauterine quality to it. I was just saying it's a bit as if she were preparing him to lose his mother. As if she would say to him he's lucky to have had a mother for three months. Some children don't even have mothers at all. This is her approach to reality – to remember that there are people worse off than you.

M.H.: Yes but I would think it's not only that, but that people also survive. She does seem to feel pretty happy on the whole in her relationship with the older child and he didn't have the breast and yet, there he is.

D.M.: It's very difficult when the thing that comforts him most – being put between her breasts – also torments him. Both his comfort and his torment. He is comforted, then he begins ferreting around, looking for the nipple. So the solution is to put him close but with his head over her shoulder so he's looking elsewhere.

M.H.: Which I would think is a very developmental thing to do. As if she were saying, "Well you can't have this nipple in your mouth any more, but if you look over your shoulder and look round, there are all kinds of interesting points for you to look at and take in.

D.M.: It probably also has a bit the meaning of looking backward and remembering. Some children like to sit in the front of the bus, and other children like to sit in the back and look out the back window to see where they have come from.

M.H.: I would think at the very end where the mother says "He must wonder why you look at him like that", it's as if she herself at the moment is finding it quite difficult to be looked at – to really look at what she is feeling about this whole business of the weaning; and trying to get away from it. The painfulness of the whole business, for him and for her, is something that she finds very hard to really look at.

D.M.: The observer can be sucked in to such intimacy and not allowed to have enough distance to observe, to really find the right distance.

Thomas aged eight months

After Thomas started at the nursery, his mother seemed to be running away a bit – being absent more than necessary, going to yoga classes, political meetings, etc. At the same time, it was noticeable that Thomas's health began to deteriorate. He suffered from bad colds, bronchitis, ear infections and had a very nasty nappy rash. At the suggestion of the crèche he was completely weaned by the time he was five months old. These somatic manifestations were some indication of the difficulties baby Thomas was struggling with: coping with the distressing emotional experiences he was enduring, while attempting to come to terms with losing the breast, adapting to his new environment and facing up to the harshness of reality. His mother was very distressed herself and therefore unable to contain her son's anxieties.

In the next observation, Thomas was almost eight months old; he was teething and verbalizing more and more. I saw him becoming increasingly mobile and curious. When on his stomach, although not yet crawling on all fours, he could pull himself along the floor by his arms, with his legs outstretched behind him. The observation begins:

> Marie was not yet home from work and Pierre was looking after Thomas. He showed me into the living-room and Thomas looked up in our direction, wide-eyed, open-mouthed with a beam all over his face. Thomas's father offered me a chair. He told me that they will leave Thomas with Marie's parents for two weeks. He will be looked after by his maternal grandmother. After that, all four of them will go skiing for the period of the school holidays. Pierre went out of the room. Thomas pulled himself across the floor to the shelves where the gramophone records were stacked. He looked at them for a few moments and touched them with his left hand then noticed a magazine in a plastic wrapping amongst the records. He pulled at it with both hands as if he was trying to get it off the shelf. Then he moved over to a pile of newspapers and magazines. He pulled some of the newspapers and they fell to the floor revealing a knitting basket

with needles and wool in it. He took hold of a knitting needle so I lifted him away saying that knitting needles are for Mummy and that if he plays with them he might hurt himself because they are dangerous for babies. Pierre came back, picked up Thomas and sat down on the sofa with Thomas on his knee facing him. He kissed him and lifted him up into the air and down again several times. Thomas was smiling and obviously enjoyed his father playing with him.

Then the doorbell rang so he put Thomas back down on the floor and went to open the door. Thomas started to cry a little. Then he pulled himself towards a low table on which a number of bottles of alcoholic beverages were standing. When he reached his objective he touched the bottles with his right hand, steadying himself with his left hand. At that moment, Pierre, a lady visitor and a little boy came into the room. Thomas was attracted by their entrance and overbalanced, knocking his head on the corner of the table and he started to cry. His father picked him up and said "Oh it's nothing he often knocks himself ", and he put him down on the floor. At that moment Marie arrived home from work. I heard her talking to Pierre in the hall. Thomas made another attempt to reach the bottles so I give him a toy key-ring with plastic keys of different colours, saying to him "You can have fun with these." He looked at me, took the keys and started to play, shaking the keys, putting them in his mouth and chewing on them. Pierre came back into the room, picked up Thomas and sat down on the sofa with Thomas on his knees. "Do you know who has just come home?", he asked Thomas, who didn't appear to have realized that his mother had returned.

Marie entered the room, greeted me, and took Thomas into her arms saying "How's my baby ?" She held him close for a few moments, kissing the top of his head. Still holding Thomas, Marie talks to her friend, giving her news of James and their forthcoming holiday. Then the lady and the little boy left. Marie told me she was very tired and needed a break from looking after Thomas. "It's my mother who suggested looking after him, I hope he will stand the separation all right. I think it will do me good", she said.

There was a short pause in the conversation when Marie seemed to be preoccupied and then she said to Thomas, "I think you're feeling tired, it's time for your bath." Thomas started to cry as soon as his mother began to undress him. "His bottom hurts and he doesn't like being undressed", she said. In fact his bottom was really raw. It had been like this for sometime now and I had only once seen her use a soothing ointment. Thomas stopped crying when the undressing was finished but started to cry again when he was put into his plastic bath. The water was too hot. Marie looked at the thermometer floating on the water. I noticed that the gauge was well above 37° centigrade. She put in some cold water. Thomas stopped crying but looked rather anxious and sad as he held on to the side of the bath with each hand. Marie washed him quickly and I noticed that Thomas was not playful like he usually was when in the bath. While his mother was washing him, using both hands Thomas grabbed hold of the shower hose which was dangling into the water. He put it into his mouth and chewed on it throughout the bathing and did not smile at all. "He chews everything at the moment and his two bottom teeth are through as well", said Marie. She stepped back a little from the bath and watched her son in the water. "He will be away rather a long time, I don't know how I am going to feel without him", she said to me rather thoughtfully.

Thomas whimpered again when she lifted him out of the bath. Lying on the changing table, Thomas took hold of the side of his towelling bath robe, pulled it out from underneath himself and held it with both hands in the middle of his chest. Marie dried him skimpily and reached out for a bottle of gentian violet. It was empty. "I'll have to use this disinfectant. He will cry because it stings, but I must put something on it", said Marie holding Thomas by both ankles in her left hand, as she proceeded to dab his sore bottom with cotton wool soaked in disinfectant. Thomas began to cry very loudly and pulled the bath robe up to his face as if to bury his face in it. He was really screaming loudly, but his screams were muffled by the bathrobe. I found it difficult not to intervene and suggest she use some soothing cream as I had seen her do on one previous occasion. "There you are my little one, you'll feel better now", Marie said to Thomas and he calmed down quite quickly. She reached down for a clean nappy but there weren't any so she asked me to keep an eye on Thomas while she fetched one from the other room. Thomas looked at me as I moved close up to the changing table. His mother returned almost at once with the nappy, put it on and dressed Thomas very quickly. "Ah, you're tired tonight aren't you Thomas", she said, picking him up and holding him very close to her. "You can have your supper and then a good sleep." Her chin was resting lightly on the top of his head and I had the impression that this was perhaps the first moment of a more intimate contact between them during this observation. Thomas was sucking the first two fingers of his left hand and staring into space. The three of them accompanied me to the door. Thomas's gaze fixed upon me for a few moments. I caressed him lightly on his cheek as I said goodbye. He looked tired and had a faraway expression on his face. I left this observation feeling very anxious and depressed.

Supervision

Martha Harris made the following comments on this observation:

M.H.: The mother seems to harden off. There seems to be a terrible turning away from that earlier intimate period. It would look as if she is finding it very difficult to deal with the depression and guilt about this and in a certain way she probably feels it much more than the father, but she hardens off more than him. So it may be easier for him to be affectionate to the child and she has had to cut herself off. So many mothers do have problems with weaning, for themselves as well as for the baby and if they can't manage it for themselves, they can't help the baby with it. She hardens herself off from her separation anxieties and depression and is the same way to the child. What is a little impressive on the whole, is the degree to which he does make the best of what is available. He doesn't seem to realize his mother has come home. Sometimes another child would be hanging on to Mummy coming home. He doesn't do that, but makes the most of what does come to hand. It's also clear that once she is home, he can't actually count upon her being with him for any long or connecting time, and it takes her some time before there is a moment of intimacy between them. And one wonders if it is a moment of intimacy, because he's got these fingers in his mouth and his eyes are looking far away. It's not Mummy, it's something else, and he's making his own kind of breast. Being held by Mummy but making his own kind of breast and nipple and looking into space is not a real intimate interaction.

Concerning the fact that the house didn't seem to be set up for the development of children – records, beverages etc. within the baby's reach, as if the child has to fit in – Martha Harris commented :

M.H.: At a time when he was more or less immobile, they didn't have to think about how he was developing. They seemed to be able to be much closer, to be able to create that space before he really begins to stir and move around, and she is then having to move away. In the earlier observations, they seemed to be able to be very close to him, be interested in him, and to identify with him as a baby; but not since the separation has taken place. I suppose the crèche can't have helped very much, insisting that she give up the feeding which seemed to be something she really, in a sense, fought to keep on; because afer that month away, many mothers would have given up. To have a close physical contact with the breast seemed to be something that she felt somehow at home with, and it probably was a loss to her when she had to give it up as well. But again it seems to be so usual; maybe especially in France and Italy, as far as I can see, the emphasis is not to go on too long breastfeeding; mothers get no encouragement at all. He would have been nearly five months when she stopped breastfeeding. The crèche pefers to have them younger because they are easier to break in.

What is impressive about this baby so far – it seems to me he is not broken in. I don't know whether this faraway look he gets into is going to increase or not, because he is friendly – he beams when he sees you, he is interested when this other woman with the child comes in. He is lively and outgoing and in a sense, turns to what is at hand to amuse himself. He turns to the toys, he's got a resourcefulness. I would think he's got an experience of such unpredictability that he doesn't look forward to and hang on to his mother, because when she does come home, it's quite a while before she really is able to fully attend to him. She says she is so tired, as if she is really projecting her feeling of tiredness into him and not quite seeing him, and not quite able to really enjoy or draw something from him. And I would think she is worried about this going away and leaving him with her mother. She wonders how she will be and she is very mixed up in her mind.

It seems to me so common – this problem of both mother and baby managing, and mother being able to face the baby, help the baby to feel and work through depression at the separation and weaning and so on. I suppose it's a society where people don't actually help on the whole, and a problem of the whole crèche atmosphere. I think the trouble is, you've got to deal with the problems of the crèche workers who are no more able than the mothers sometimes to really face the pain and depression of the baby, and really try to bundle it under. It is very hard and is something that needs some kind of ongoing support as it comes up, because you can't prepare people to deal with that experience. You have to be with them to help them how to think and work their way through it. I would have thought the answer would be some much better ongoing education for crèche workers, and help to put them and the parents together a little bit more; because when there is some sort of understanding and mutual support between workers and parents, it is amazing the degree to which even little children can be looked after by someone else – even a lot of the time – if there is some kind of understanding and getting together between parents and the crèche personnel. I would think with this child, with a friendly child, that more awareness on their part could help, because it seems to me that he is responsive and adjustable and in a sense, tries to make the best of what's going on. I would think he is probably more responsive than his mother. In a sense, she's got greater difficulty, and she seems to be the one who can't quite face the guilt of leaving him. She is steeling herself because she is saying "He's gotta have this even if it hurts." The stiff upper lip as it were. He is very investigatory, busying himself exploring and differentiating. It's interesting how he goes for the magazine with the plastic cover, picking out something specific – even the knitting needle. It seems to me that they rely on the fact that this is an adaptable child, who doesn't go on whining.

Thomas aged eight and a half months

This next observation is just after Thomas's two-week stay with his maternal grandmother.

> Pierre opened the door, he was smiling. He took me into the living-room where I saw Thomas who was with his brother James and a friend. Thomas looked at me very intensely. He was holding in both hands, a thick shiny coloured band of paper from a skein of wool which he was sucking with the first two fingers of his left hand. Then he took his fingers and the paper out of his mouth and looked at the paper he was holding with both hands. He was sitting very firmly with both legs stretched out in front of him. He appeared to have put on some weight since the previous observation just over two weeks earlier. He had a better colour, his complexion was less blotchy and he seemed to be in very good spirits. "He can crawl properly now", his father said proudly and then he went out of the room. Thomas continued playing calmly with the piece of paper, chewing on it then looking at it alternately. Then he turned his attention to the two boys and to the buckle on James's friend's belt. Thomas caught hold of the buckle with his left hand. He pulled at it and tried to move it up and down. Then James's friend played with a wooden rattle, the sort used at football matches. The loud noise as the boy swung it round and round seemed to fascinate Thomas. The boy noticed Thomas's interest in the rattle and gave it to him.

Thomas watched the two boys as they went out of the room. He put the handle of the rattle into his mouth and took it out again and holding it with his left hand he managed to swing it round a little. Obviously pleased with the noise it made, he swung it round once again. Then he put the handle of the rattle back into his mouth with the first two fingers of his left hand. He sat still for a moment then he caught sight of a basket which was on the floor. There were two plastic bags inside. Thomas took hold of one of the bags and began to wave it up and down. It made a rustling noise and Thomas moved it more quickly, looking at me then at the bag. Then he put some of the bag into his mouth and I proposed he take one of his toys instead – a small rubber giraffe – saying that he could chew on this instead, as plastic bags were not suitable for baby boys to play with. He took the giraffe quite willingly and crawled over to his rug. There were several toys on it including some plastic coloured rings which attracted his attention. He chewed on the giraffe for a few moments, discarded it then picked up the blue ring and started to chew on it.

At that moment Pierre came in carrying a tray. He had made some tea and offered me a cup which I accepted. He told me that the two weeks with his maternal grandmother had gone very well for Thomas. He had even been skiing on her back. "He didn't want to know me when I arrived to fetch him. He went over to his granny. But when we arrived back here, as soon as he saw his mother, he went straight into her arms", said Thomas's father. He reminded me that they were all going away for the school vacation and I told him that I would be taking vacation in April. "Oh well you won't be seeing much of Thomas then. First we go, then you go, but you will be here all through March won't you." The door bell rang and Pierre went to see who it was. Thomas followed his father out of the room crawling on all fours. It was Marie.

She came into the room carrying Thomas in her arms, followed by Pierre. She told us how that morning, when she left Thomas at the crèche, he had cried. "When we arrived, Thomas saw another child crying and he immediately started to cry too", Marie said laughing. "I'm sure he wouldn't have cried if the other child hadn't been crying." Then Pierre said, "and apparently he often gets fidgety and excited and climbs all over the other children and makes them cry. He also takes the dummies away from the other children and puts them in his mouth." Both Thomas's parents laughed and Thomas started to laugh too, opening his mouth wide, and he said "Daa da da" with a big smile on his face. His mother then said "He really likes to join in the conversation. The other evening we were at a restaurant and he did the same thing." Marie went to get Thomas's bath ready. Thomas crawled over to the shelves where the records and hi-fi equipment are kept. His father leapt up and said "No Thomas, don't touch, I'm making a recording." Thomas then caught sight of some electric plugs and wires which he went straight towards and sat down just in front of them. His mother came back to fetch him and said to Thomas's father: "You mustn't let him touch that, it's dangerous", and picking up Thomas she beckoned me to follow.

As she undressed Thomas on the changing table he was kicking so hard that his mother stepped back in order not to be kicked in the breasts. As she took off his nappy his kicking increased. I saw that his sore bottom was healed and the nappy rash had gone. When Marie picked up Thomas to take him to the bathroom his body stiffened and he held his legs stretched out as far as they would go. Once in the water, he sat firmly, his body lost its stiffness and he seemed very calm. He picked up the thermometer and started to chew on it. His mother washed him with soap and rinsed his hair with water which ran all down his face but he didn't seem to mind very much, though I noticed that at that moment he put his left arm out and grabbed hold of the side of the bath. While he was being washed he was chewing on the thermometer, seemed rather withdrawn and passive, unlike previous times when I have seen him bathed and he was very active. When Marie had finished washing Thomas she said to him "Are you coming my baby?", as she held out her arms to him. "He holds his arms out now", she told me; but this time he did not, and she lifted him out of the water and put on his towelling bath robe. His body seemed quite relaxed and he was still holding on to the thermometer. As soon as he was lying on his back on the changing table he began kicking as before. He was looking at his mother, then at me, and seemed very alert. When Thomas was dressed Marie put him down on the floor. I crouched down to say goodbye to Thomas and he held out his arms to be picked up. Marie, seeing he wanted to be picked up, did so herself and we walked towards the front door. I said goodbye to Pierre as we went past the kitchen where he was preparing supper. I wished them all a happy holiday and left.

Supervision

M.H.: Well it's just general improvement and relaxation all round. The parents seem to be looking forward to their holiday. He seems to have learned to crawl properly and he's learned to put his arms out. This time he seems to get really lost in this experience of being inside the bath. When his nappy is taken off there is this terrific kicking as if there is a kind of excitement, as if he is looking forward to getting in the bath. It seems to be different from the last time when he cried. His sore bottom must have been uncomfortable when he was in the bath and must have been a pretty constant persecution.

The father seems to assume that you really are coming for Thomas. It is the father who is working out how often you are going to be coming. He does regard you as very important. It is clear, this picking of the buckle out of the belt, so very precise. It's that he wants to get at, and take, as if it is linked with wanting to take the nipple. And I think that these two fingers that he puts in his mouth may represent something like that. So he seems a little bit obsessed by where these nipples have gone, in the same way which he chews and then has a look at what he is chewing, as if there is a kind of puzzling about what happens when you chew something. As if there may be some kind of worry that he has chewed these nipples up and they have disappeared and he is looking for where he can find them and get hold of them. He certainly tries everything in his mouth, as a lot of children do, and he is interested in what happens to it. I was wondering why he was sucking on the thermometer in the bath, as if there too, he seemed a little obsessed with it.

I was also thinking about all the hi-fi equipment. He seems interested in the music, wants to join in, as at the restaurant. They seem to be fairly casual. He does seem very friendly towards other children. He is able to observe James's friend with a rattle. He does have an urge to enter into life and what's happening round about him. It is as if he does somehow feel that in the bath he has a little holding space that allows him to be introspective. This chewing of his doesn't just seem to be that kind of mindless sucking that takes a child into another world. He does seem to be investigating as well, because earlier on he had a bit of paper in his fingers. When he takes them out and looks at both, as if there is some kind of recognizing of differences or different qualities and trying to work something out – what happens to this paper when he chews it. He accepts you taking the plastic bag, then when you propose he has the giraffe, explaining to him, he takes it quite willingly, as if he is quite reasonable and willing to accept a substitute. It's interesting what the father said, that after being with his grandmother he didn't want to know his father, but when he is taken home he immediately welcomes his mother as if he does have a very definite relationship with her and has forgiven her. He may actually have intuitively recognized that granny is his mother's mother, a good object. Children often do this and do accept the grandmother as mother's mother. There often is a kind of resemblance between mothers and children and perhaps he would have experienced her as a Mummy who has a bit more time for him. She seems to be a very spry grandmother, taking him skiing on her back.

Thomas aged nine months

In the next observation baby Thomas was nine months old and he and his family had just returned from a skiing holiday of two weeks:

> The music was playing loudly. Pierre, who was holding Thomas in his arms, told me that the vacation went well

except that he injured his leg. He explained that Thomas was very grumpy but he didn't know what the matter was. When he went to fetch him at the crèche Thomas was crying and other children were crying also. I noticed that Thomas was dribbling a lot, his nose was running and he was wheezing quite loudly. He coughed a bit, spluttered and whimpered, seemed uncomfortable and wanted to change his position. "He cries as soon as he is put down", said Pierre. In fact Thomas looked very tired, he yawned and remained fretful and restless until his mother came home.

As soon as Thomas spotted his mother he gave a cry of pleasure and smiled for the first time since my arrival. Marie took Thomas in her arms and kissed him and I noticed for the first time that observation that he put the two first fingers of his left hand into his mouth and started sucking. He stayed calm for a short while but it didn't last. Marie spoke briefly about their vacation saying she had enjoyed the break but that it wasn't much of a rest. Thomas began to wriggle and started to cry again. "What's the matter with him today? Has he been like this for some time?" she asked Pierre. "Yes, since I fetched him from the crèche", replied Pierre. Marie gets up and walks to and fro across the room, jogging Thomas gently in her arms, but this doesn't seem to make him feel any better. He became more agitated and his crying became louder. "What's the matter?" she asked rather impatiently, "you're giving me the shits this evening." Marie decides to get the bath ready for Thomas and she gave him to me to hold.

I stood in the bathroom doorway holding Thomas with his back to me so that he could watch his mother. He was sitting on my right arm which I was holding in front of me at waist level. My left arm was folded round in front of him. I could feel the vibration of his wheezing as he breathed. He became very calm and sat quietly watching his mother, his two arms resting on my left arm. "He looks comfortable in your arms", said his mother as she tested the water with her hand. She was filling the big bath and called out for James to come too. When she had undressed him, Marie sat Thomas down in the bath. He got up immediately and went to the end of the bath where an assortment of bottles were placed on the shelf.

He started to examine them, then picked up a pumice-stone and put it into his mouth. His mother took it from him saying that it would hurt his gums and gave him a plastic bottle instead. Then James came running into the bathroom already undressed and got into the bath. We all watched Thomas who continued to play with the bottles. James took hold of Thomas and sat him down on his knees. Thomas became playful, splashing in the water with his hands. James sat him down in the water and Thomas nearly went under. He kicked his legs, splashing water into the air. Then Marie washed Thomas and James helped with the rinsing. Thomas stood up holding on to the end of the bath. He picked up the soap and put it into his mouth but his mother took it from him and he started to protest for a moment but then turned round, went down into the water again climbing on to his brother. The two boys enjoyed playing together. James handed Thomas a blue, round rubber object which looked like a perfume spray. Thomas examined this very carefully, feeling it, pressing it and patting it with both hands. "That's what he wanted", said James. Marie lifted Thomas out of the bath, wrapped him in his bathrobe and took him into his bedroom. When he was dry and had on a clean nappy, Marie held Thomas's feet in her hands, bent forward and blew on his toes, put them up to her mouth and kissed them. Thomas laughed and she did it again saying to him "You're only laughing half-heartedly tonight aren't you", and she put on his pyjamas. Thomas yawned and started to grizzle a bit. "You're really very tired tonight. You can have your supper now and then go to sleep."

Marie, holding Thomas in her arms, accompanied me to the door. Thomas was sucking two fingers and looked very sleepy but watched me as I left.

Supervision

M.H.: James is certainly very nice to him. He understands him very well. He knew what Thomas wanted – this rubber perfume spray that he presses and pats, a breast-like object.

(I remind her that James was not breastfed. He had a bottle and was fed from a spoon from the age of two months.)

M.H.: That's interesting because she did seem to enjoy breastfeeding Thomas. Perhaps she'd learnt something, or fashion has changed a bit. Her circumstances were very different with James, because her marriage was already on the rocks.

I'm not sure whether Thomas is also responding a bit to his father's injured leg. But he would have had both parents, and more particularly his mother, all day, all the time they were away, so it is hard going back to the crèche – it's more upsetting. He got used to having Mummy all the time. The question of the beam he gives his mother when she returns home: this visit he hadn't smiled until then – he didn't smile at you. He was really looking out for his mother coming home. He seemed to have enjoyed the vacation with his grandmother and he may very well have enjoyed this vacation with his parents, and got used to Mummy being on hand all the time, which may have been hard for her as she seems to relax better by not having the baby at home. But it would seem in this observation it's his mother he's missing. He is very decidedly fixed on her. It may be that when she is home, he feels more able to go to sleep – that when he wakens up she'll be there. But it doesn't last for long, as if he still isn't quite happy because she says "You're giving me the shits", almost as if she is feeling he's projecting into her a kind of upset and depression which she actually can't stand.

The period leading up to the summer vacation was marked by several events including Thomas's first birthday and his parents' marriage. Thomas had his adenoids removed in order to improve his breathing and he had a drain in both ears. However, in spite of his recurring health problems, during the observations I saw that Thomas had a good appetite and appeared to be a playful and good-humoured child. He was "the terror of the crèche", which his mother was both proud and worried about. So at this stage he was keeping his rage, aggression and hostility away from the family, but it was breaking out at the crèche. He was starting to walk and becoming familiar with the family routine and the spatial order of things in the home. He had got to know me and I felt that I was present in his mind.

Coping with loss

Resuming the observations after the summer vacation wasn't easy for me. The tragic accident which happened to Mattie Harris came as a terrible shock to me and I was deeply saddened to know that Mattie, so generous and life-giving, was now battling for her own life. My pain and anxiety due to this terrible loss was coupled with the grief following the death of my father a few weeks earlier. I was lucky to have the love and support of my family and the sustaining containment of my analyst to accompany me through such a difficult period. So in the autumn following that fateful summer of 1984, when Thomas was sixteen months old, I asked Susanna Isaacs-Elmhirst for supervision of my observations and she agreed to take me on through to the end of the two-year period.

In the spring of 1985, my husband and I visited Don and Mattie. I recall how intense my emotion was when we entered the room where Mattie was resting in her chair. As I held her hand, I saw a look of recognition in her eyes and she said "Thomas", showing me she was remembering. Indeed, Mattie was a person who had that wonderful capacity to hold in her mind, with understanding and respect, people and moments of life's experiences.

CHAPTER NINETEEN

Family consultations in the footsteps of Martha Harris with toddlers at risk of autism[1]

Maria Rhode

Mattie interviewed me for the Tavistock child psychotherapy training in May 1969. Everyone who is asked about her mentions their first interview, and I am no exception. It didn't feel like an interview – I remember the easy informality with which she bent over the piles of papers on her desk in search of some document or other. She was often to be seen arriving at the Tavistock clutching enormous armfuls of papers, smiling wryly at the overflowing files, in winter perhaps wearing a crocheted hat – a headwarmer, as she called it. But however voluminous the files, we students all knew we lived in her mind – our aspirations, our strong points and our weaknesses, someone's wish to work in a hospital and someone else's problems paying the rent. In those days, the student intake was much smaller than it is now, and we didn't get beautifully printed diplomas when we qualified: we'd be told about that if we happened to bump into Mattie in the ladies' toilets.

Mattie supervised my first intensive case: nine-year-old Laura, a matchstick-thin little girl with translucent skin who ate

---

1 This chapter is based on a presentation at a conference in memory of Martha Harris at the GERPEN, Paris, November 2010 (see Chapter 5).

nothing but tea and toast. In one of Laura's paintings, a girl's eyes were black circles filled in half in pink and half in blue. Mattie thought she was using her eyes as an anal sphincter: as a means of exerting control over the pink-and-blue parents. As you will gather, the language of part-objects came very naturally to her, but it was always linked to emotion and never formulaic. Laura once composed a story that started out, "In the beginning it was very cold." She accompanied this first sentence by cutting little snippets out of a folded piece of paper, as children do in order to make a "snowflake", except that this particular snowflake had only four small holes in it and looked decidedly like an attempt gone wrong. Mattie knew otherwise: "Now this", she said beaming, "is really very interesting. Look, here are the eyes, here is the mouth, here is the genital …". She was showing me how Laura seemed to experience birth – the cold beginning – as being literally cut out of the matrix. Later, I remembered this in the context of Laura's profound conviction that we must be negatives of each other, so that she could not identify with me as a maternal figure; much as she yearned to be on good terms with me, this would threaten her own survival.

The atmosphere Mattie created in supervision meant that we students could talk about our own associations without feeling that this was irrelevant or silly. A propos of nothing in the material, I said to her one day that I had had the thought that Laura would find it impossible to transfer, unlike my other patients. I added that this didn't make much sense, as I wasn't considering transferring her. Mattie encouraged me to take the thought seriously. In the early days of a baby's life, she said, the continuity of its existence depends on the continuity of the mother's knowledge of it. It was that primordial level of Laura's sense of self that she thought was triggering my countertransference fantasy. As she wrote in her paper on "The early basis of adult female sexuality", the child must be "able to feel that he is well enough known for what he really is, to develop the kind of internal containing object which can help him to feel at home with himself" (1975c, p. 193). Conversely,

> In so far as the infant is unable to bring parts of himself to the mother to be expressed, held and thought about, he is

likely to feel that there is something unacceptable about himself. These parts are then likely to become alienated, split off and projected to some distance from his good objects: with the ever-present threat that they will return to endanger these good objects. (p. 193)

Mattie stresses that the father or some other "ongoing parental figure" may be able to provide this acceptance if the mother cannot.

In this chapter I want to illustrate the central importance of the parents' unbroken knowledge of their child by describing family work with two toddlers at risk of autism. Mattie did not herself see children on the spectrum: the theory that informs this work derives from Tustin, Meltzer, Haag, Houzel and Lechevalier. Mattie did however pioneer family consultations for toddlers. In her paper on "Therapeutic Consultations" (1966), she describes her work with Willie, a little two-year-old who was driving his parents to distraction with his hyperactivity, claustrophobic anxiety and major sleeping problems. His mother felt tyrannized over and imprisoned by him; his father was overburdened by working additional hours so that the family could buy a house, and both parents were at their wits' end. Mattie describes listening to them very carefully, eliciting details, reflecting their feelings back to them. Willie, who was not yet speaking, took no notice of her presence.

It turned out to be one of those "miracle" consultations that can sometimes happen with toddlers in united families. When the mother brought Willie back for the second appointment, she reported the first proper night's sleep she had had since he was born. The parents had continued talking after their appointment, and had followed through on Mattie's question about anything that Willie liked that might settle him before bedtime. They remembered that, when relatives had come to visit, he had been fascinated by the baby's cradle; so his father rigged up an indoor swing for him that his mother put him into after meals and before bed. It gave Willie a containing place to be – one that responded to his movement without provoking claustrophobia – and allowed his mother some respite. She reported to Mattie that she felt for the first time that she had been able to get through to Willie. With this encouragement, she had spent two days teaching him to go down the stairs backwards, so that she could be confident he was safe when he wanted to leave the flat to play in the little private garden. She and Willie were both relieved of their claustrophobic over-involvement. Interestingly, Willie now engaged with Mattie over the toys, and used some words appropriately. As Mattie commented, "It would become more worth his while to talk when he felt greater confidence in being understood" (p. 303).

Brief work is of course not appropriate for children with autistic features, but I think that Mattie's conceptualizations in this paper are highly relevant to them (as is her comment to me about the way in which the mother's ongoing knowledge of her baby provides the foundation for his sense of continuous existence).

First of all, she stresses that she did not provide an "expert" opinion, but concentrated on eliciting the details of the parents' experience. The implication was that it was their own resources that would help them to resolve the problem. She underlines that it was the father's intuition that led him to provide a swing, and that it was the close marital relationship that made this way of working possible and fruitful. Next, she suggests that mother's feeling of being able to get through to Willie for the first time followed on her experience of getting through to Mattie in the consultation. This simple statement implies a great deal: it makes the link between an unresponsive child and the parent's unresponsive internal parent, though "ghosts in the nursery" were not Mattie's immediate concern. She was not addressing the parents' internal constellations: instead, she was working in what Daniel Stern (1995) so aptly called the "good grandmother transference". In this family with many resources, we can trace a sequence from the parents' experience of getting through to Mattie to the mother's justified optimism about getting through to Willie, and onwards to Willie's new feeling that there were people he could himself get through to by speaking. What could be mistaken for a relatively ordinary new experience led to a cascade of developments, a benign circle of interactions that brought about important shifts in the whole family.

This can of course work the other way too: ordinary mismatches can have major, cumulative consequences. In a pilot research project (Rhode, 2007) on therapeutic infant observation with toddlers at risk of autism, following the model pioneered by Didier Houzel (1999), we could see how easily mother and child could get caught up in a vicious circle of discouragement so that the contact both desired always went wrong. The mother would attempt to comfort her son, but the little boy would wriggle free. By the time he climbed onto the sofa, his mother was so disheartened that her arms remained at her sides and she commented to the observer: "This is where he usually starts head-banging." We could also see – which links to Mattie's point about the importance of the whole child being known – how easy it was for the toddler's capacities not to be noticed, let alone amplified. This was true of the observer, not just of the mother, which is one of the reasons supervision was so important.

Two toddlers at risk of autism

I will now discuss family work with two toddlers at risk of autism. The first resembled Willie's family in that the parents had a loving relationship, the "good grandmother transference" was easy to establish and maintain, and the child seemed to blossom naturally while the parents talked. After a year's work, Oedipal issues were manifest on a whole-object level. The second family was far more fragmented, and the "good grandmother transference" alone could not outweigh the many factors impeding the child's development. Linking up with the mother's therapist provided what I think was an essential enactment of a co-operative couple. Oedipal issues are discernible on a far more primitive level than in the first case: we can see the little boy beginning to integrate maternal and paternal aspects of the family envelope, as described by Didier Houzel (2001). This happened more particularly with regard to the senses of vision and hearing. I am emphasizing Oedipal phenomena partly because of the importance of the parental relationship, as emphasized by Mattie; but also because the closure of the Oedipal triangle makes possible what Britton (1989) has called the "third position" of the observer, who can also imagine being observed. This makes it possible, in his words, "to reflect on ourselves while being ourselves", a capacity strikingly lacking in children on the autistic spectrum with their characteristic Theory of Mind deficits.

A child at medium risk of autism

Isabel was born in England of Argentinian parents; her older brother was developing well. Both parents came from supportive families, though Mr G was the only child of a single mother and Mrs G's next-youngest sibling had died in childhood. She had herself suffered a potentially fatal illness soon after arriving in England, and the possibility of a recurrence remained a shadow in her mind. The atmosphere between the parents was loving and co-operative, and their vitality and sense of humour became more evident as work progressed.

Mr and Mrs G referred Isabel when she was 17 months old. All had gone well until she was seven months, when they felt they had suddenly lost her. It turned out that Mother had had a brief but painful illness at the time (not related to her previous serious one), and had worried that her medication might have harmed Isabel. They did not feel that she knew who they were, and described her as a vegetable, though they said that she responded better to professionals than to them. When I took up how painful this must be, Father said that, on the contrary, it was a relief that she was capable of it: she would have to be a great deal better for them to have the luxury of feeling jealous.

At 17 months, Isabel could sit but not crawl. She made no eye contact and was not babbling. She clutched a spoon that she used as an autistic object (Tustin, 1980), and reached for her parents' hand to perform difficult tasks. With insistence, I could just elicit fugitive eye-contact if I imitated her actions. She stared blankly into a corner or out of the window, though she liked pushing down and releasing little wooden men in a Galt pop-up toy so that they came back into view. She tapped repetitively on hard surfaces, like the table or the humming top. She had no interest in the dolls' house, and seemed frightened of the teddy in her box. When tested, she fell in the medium-risk category of the Checklist for Autism in Toddlers (Baron-Cohen et al, 1996), which carries roughly a 50% chance of an autism spectrum diagnosis at three and a half.

Gradually it became possible to draw her into the group of adults through imitating the way she used the little wooden people or tapped on the table: this could be amplified into simple rhythmical exchanges. Isabel needed our total involvement. She once cast a delicate, tentative glance over her shoulder in her parents' direction, became disheartened to see them talking to me, and then remained impossible to engage. Mr and Mrs G responded eagerly when I described the delicacy of her glance: "She's always been like that." I could see just how easily a vicious circle of mutual discouragement could have arisen.

Isabel appeared to take no notice of us: in fact, she was exquisitely tuned to the atmosphere. She was beginning to practise pulling herself up to a standing position at the table, but suddenly collapsed when our tone of voice changed as we discussed her parents' refusal of permission for me to liaise with other professionals. They remained politely sceptical when I pointed out this sequence, but they quickly identified with my observing function and began to tell me new things they had themselves observed her doing at home. At this stage it seemed that one of them would take the risk of detecting meaning while the other expressed doubt.

With my support, they encouraged Isabel to be more forceful with the toys, and amplified her growing enjoyment in banging the table and growling fiercely. Isabel's increasing pleasure in this shared activity was regularly and unpredictably interrupted by frightened looks out the window and into the corner that she had previously stared at blankly. While she appeared to have located something dangerous in these places, her play around the table moved ahead steadily as her parents talked. She began to babble, to imitate sounds and songs, and to point. Her use of the toys became more clearly symbolic. At the end of a session during the second term, she had been sitting on the floor "feeding" the teddy with one of the little wooden people. I described this to the parents as they were clearing up, and, no doubt sensing their pleasure, she turned with a beautiful arching movement and raised her hands from each side of the pop-up toy to clasp her mother's face instead.

She had by now relinquished her autistic object, and no longer reached for a parent's hand to perform a difficult action. She was producing words in both English and Spanish, including "mummy" and "daddy"; her first word, "light", accompanied her pointing at the bulb inside the fridge, which struck me as an apt representation of her parents' increasing hopefulness. She beamed at me on arrival each week, played peek-a-boo when it was time to go, and once burst into tears at the end of the time. I was encouraged when occasionally, after a separation, she could be wary of me, even cross, though usually the "bad" thing remained outside the window rather than located in a human being. Mattie's split-off part of the personality comes to mind. Interestingly, although her play was clearly symbolic by the end of the year's work, she remained worried by an adult's "mock angry" face.

Increasingly, her play focused on rivalry and exclusion. The little wooden men jostled each other in competition for a hole in the pop-up toy. Isabel piled little dolls and animals into the dolls' house, then threw it crossly onto the floor. Sometimes she then collapsed onto the floor herself, as though identified with the maltreated toys. Two of the four little wooden people became mummy and daddy (she chose the colours to match her parents' clothes that day) and they kissed at great length while the other two were casually discarded.

After a year's work, Mr and Mrs G decided to return home: a measure of their confidence in Isabel's continuing progress. The following week, for the first time, Isabel proudly took several steps towards me along the corridor. In the room, she made the little wooden 'parent' dolls kiss, then repeatedly threw them on the floor, crouched down to retrieve them, and stood up again showing us that she had a firm grip on them. Her parents' newfound confidence in facing another migration seemed to sustain Isabel's own greater confidence in retrieving internal parents whom she had thrown away in Oedipally-inspired anger, and who could now support her in walking on her own two feet.

Work with this family proceeded very much on the model of Mattie's paper on Willie. Isabel seemed to blossom out naturally as her parents talked. Towards the end of the year, they said that our sessions were the only place where they could discuss their own feelings about her progress and the various interventions that she was having: I think they had the experience of "getting through" to me, and must have sensed that I found them and their little girl tremendously endearing. The "good grandmother transference" was easy to maintain. Like Willie's parents, Isabel's had a strong, loving relationship, and what Didier Houzel (2001) calls the bisexual elements of the family envelope were well integrated. One consequence was the speed with which the parents identified with my observing function, and the ease with which the three of us could take turns in pointing out to each other the developments that Isabel was making. During the whole year's work, I felt discouraged only once, when Isabel was still not walking at the age of two; I had to remind myself of what I frequently told the parents, that she undoubtedly remained delayed but was moving in the right direction. Mr and Mrs G, like their daughter, needed ongoing encouragement: even when a paediatrician told them categorically that Isabel was still delayed but definitely not autistic, they found this hard to believe. On one occasion, when Isabel had participated with gusto in a game, they raised again the spectre of her diagnosis, and I said to them that if they still thought she might be autistic after what they had just witnessed, I wondered who was telling them so. They laughed, understanding my reference to Isabel's enjoyment that could so easily be interrupted by frightened looks at the window. I did not see it as my role in this kind of intervention to probe any further.

A child at high risk of autism

In contrast, work with Andrew and his family has been far less easy. At the age of one, Andrew was showing worrying signs of being at risk of autism. He was the youngest of a large family, of whom the eldest daughter had an autism diagnosis while the others appeared to be developing satisfactorily. Mother and father were high-flying professionals who had seemed to take in their stride a potentially fatal illness mother had suffered as well as the first daughter's disability. Mother told me that everyone thought of her as the strongest person they knew, but the possibility that Andrew might also be autistic had been the final catastrophe that had overwhelmed her.

With this family, the "good grandmother" transference has been much harder to establish, though I see them twice a week. Largely, this has been because the parents have never come together, and I have only met the father once; Andrew is brought by his mother or the nanny. Initially, there was no room for me to say anything: Mrs P kept up a constant stream of songs and talk designed to stimulate Andrew, and, I think, to save him from becoming autistic. Whenever I pointed out something new he was doing, she countered that his sister had done this too, and then had a massive regression at the age of two. The nanny initially felt more hopeful, and was able to follow Andrew's lead, to which he responded well. Interestingly, once his development began to pick up, the picture was reversed: Mrs P was increasingly encouraged by his progress whereas the nanny felt disheartened by how far he still lagged behind normal children. I often felt as though I were fighting a losing battle; as though there were a hostile force acting to discourage Andrew's development. At times this seemed to be embodied in references to a great-grandparent who had lost the power of speech, and to whom Andrew was compared. Here again is the link between an unresponsive child and an unresponsive parental figure.

Faced with my own feelings of despair and impotence, I frequently turned to the parent worker to discuss the case, and in that way at least to enact a mutually supportive couple constellation. She tended to smile at me and say that our obvious task was to provide an infusion of good objects to counter the despair in the system: she reminded me of Harris and Meltzer's (1976) formulation that the functions of a parental family included engendering love, promoting hope, containing despair and supporting thinking.

At the beginning of my work with the family, Andrew spent most of his time trying to climb over gaps between pieces of furniture or suddenly throwing himself off an adult's lap, so that we had to be constantly vigilant. He bit his mother and pulled her hair in a way that seemed partly aggressive, but also a desperate way of holding on. I encouraged Mrs P to set limits, but also to think about possible emotional meanings. She confessed that this was not easy: she had become accustomed to the behavioural approach in her daughter's school. Andrew's piercing screams could be unbearable, but it was hard for her to think of this as a communication: that would imply greater capacities in Andrew than she dared hope for. Her expectations were very low – as she said, she would rather not be disappointed, though she understood that this could become self-fulfilling. I was encouraged that she welcomed signs of improvement – for instance, when Andrew lay on the floor hiding his face, but allowed me to turn this into a peek-a-boo game. He also learnt to use some Makaton signs, which his sister never had. Still, when he was given the CHAT (Checklist for Autism in Toddlers) at 16 months, he came in the High Risk category, and we had to work hard not to lose sight of recent steps forward.

As with Isabel, symbolic play was the first area in which Andrew showed substantial improvement. He developed a pattern of climbing onto the table, sweeping all the toys onto the floor, and beaming proudly as his mother commented, "Who's the King of the Castle?" He then regularly flopped face down himself, as though, again like Isabel, he felt identified with his displaced rivals. He obviously felt that there was only room for one – and indeed, I learnt that this reflected the pattern at home, in which the children fought for attention and often ended up in different rooms.

The Oedipus complex and sensory integration

After roughly a year of work, Andrew began repeatedly to indicate that he wanted his mother to sing a particular action song that involves naming and touching various parts of the body ('Head, shoulders, knees and toes'). We both noticed that, while he listened to her, he watched me as I performed the actions (without singing). He repeated his request so often that it was obvious that this constellation meant something very important to him, even without his beaming smile at me as I performed the actions. I understood Andrew to be constructing the Oedipal constellation at the very fundamental level of the senses, through orchestrating the cooperation between his mother and me in which he could watch me perform the actions while he listened to her singing. This brings to mind Meltzer's discussion of sensory dismantling as a means of avoiding Oedipal conflict ("the mummy with the uniform and the daddy with the bell who pass each other in the night of the child's mind"; Meltzer, 1975, p. 25). It also illustrates an emotional component in the capacity for cross-modal perception as described by Daniel Stern (1985), which can normally be taken as a given.

The autistic level of the Oedipus complex: oral competition

Against this background of constructing Oedipal cooperation between his mother and me on the level of vision and hearing, Andrew began to be able to stage his Oedipal conflicts on a part-object oral level. On the occasion his father brought him, and – perhaps encouraged by this – he rattled the Russian doll, pulled it apart so the smaller dolls fell out, and bit half of the biggest doll hard so that it seemed to remain attached to his mouth. He then used it as a cup that he filled up with water from the sink and drank from. Although I stopped him, he persisted in trying to get inside the full sink himself. He seemed to be showing us his own wish to be inside (in itself a hopeful sign in a child at risk of autism), whether inside the sink or inside the largest doll, and his rivalry with the smaller dolls contained in it. Biting seemed to be both a way of separating the two halves of the largest Russian doll so that the babies fell out, and of taking over one half of it so that it constituted a unit with his own mouth, not with the other half of the doll.

After the long summer break, during which the whole family had spent five weeks together, Andrew elaborated on both of these themes. He had for some time been turning to catch my eye or his mother's to be sure that we noticed what he was doing (social referencing); during the summer, he also began to use pointing in a proto-declarative context and to imitate adults. In one of the early autumn sessions, his mother balanced one of his shoes on her head. Andrew placed the second shoe on his own head, then held out his hand for the shoe his mother had, and gave it to me. I placed it on my head, he gestured to the shoe on his and smiled at me. He then held out his hand towards me for the second shoe, so that he had one in each hand, and "clapped" them together. Andrew appeared to be illustrating the phase Geneviève Haag (2005) has described in which the two halves of the child's body represent the integration of the two parents – a phase more advanced than that of "mother and baby in two halves of the body": we are reminded of Isabel's play with the little pop-up people in relation to walking.

I can envisage that the next stage will involve a move towards individual work – he has begun to go to music therapy and to a specialist nursery by himself, and to enjoy playing with other children. For the moment, however, I feel that the setting with two adults has a positive value for his development as it supports his attempts to work over Oedipal themes on the primitive levels I have described.

Concluding remarks

I have offered clinical vignettes from family work with two toddlers at risk of autism in order to illustrate how easy it is for a vicious circle of discouragement to become entrenched. The professional's task is then to attempt to contain the despair, while fostering links between parents and child that can lead to a benign circle. I have suggested that it is easier to work in the "good grandmother transference", as in Mattie's work with Willie's family and in mine with Isabel, when a co-operating parental couple can provide the child with a supportive Oedipal context. With Andrew, where one of my main functions has probably been to witness his interactions with many different adults and in that way to help him to integrate them, I believe that the enactment of a couple in my consultations with the parent worker has been crucial in supporting Andrew's construction of an Oedipal context on fundamental, primitive levels.

In closing, I cannot do better than to quote Mattie's comments at the Tavistock memorial event for Mrs Bick. She described Mrs Bick's vitality and enthusiasm – whether for a piece of psychoanalytic work, a beautiful landscape or a plate of spaghetti with garlic sauce. Being in the presence of this had been an inspiration and a privilege for all her students – "and to the best of our ability", Mattie said, "we try to pass it on."

CHAPTER TWENTY

Shorter personal recollections

Gabrielle Crockatt, Hélène Dubinsky, Ellen Jaffe, Judy Shuttleworth, Brian Truckle, Eleanor Wigglesworth, Ricky Emanuel, Katherine Arnold, Herbert Chaim Hahn, Carlo Papuzza, Maria Pozzi, Renata Li Causi, Torhild Leira, Eve Steel

Gabrielle Crockatt

If I had to describe Mattie in one word, it would be "human" – in the best and warmest sense of that word. I first met her while I was still at university, and wondering how to launch myself into the world of adulthood and earning a living. I had decided that I wanted to be a child psychotherapist, contacted the Tavistock, and was offered an "interview" with Mattie.

I arrived full of trepidation at the old Tavistock in Marylebone, with a welcoming open fire in the entrance hall. The experience reminded me of the children's story "Just Awful", where a little boy goes to see the school nurse because he has cut his finger, and comes out having had his finger washed and dressed, and been given a big hug, saying "I think I'm going to be alright."

Mattie asked reasonably challenging but sensible questions, such as how I had come to think of doing child psychotherapy. I felt anxiously self-revealing as I answered "because I read Laing's *The Divided Self*, and connected with the idea that we all have our problems." She was quite unfazed both by the knowledge that I was applying for a course by admitting that I had problems, and that I had been inspired by someone who I came later to realize was not part of required reading on the course, and simply suggested that when I had got my degree I should find a job working with children and contact her again, and she would arrange for me to attend some seminars and see how I got on. I did exactly that: found a job as a remedial teacher, started weekly evening seminars at Mattie's house, and five years later was a qualified child psychotherapist – a job which has seen me happily through my entire working life.

Once enrolled as a trainee child psychotherapist, I of course asked Mattie if she would supervise my first training case, a sassy and determined little two-year-old. I thoroughly enjoyed my weekly meetings with her, and learned a huge amount. Again, she was the most human of supervisors, chatty and supportive, not critical, but able at the same time to be helpfully forthright.

I vividly remember one piece of advice she gave me, which I have passed on to generations of trainee child psychotherapists: "It is no use trying to combat omnipotence with omnipotence." This idea has been helpful to me in so many ways, at work and in life, and I believe that Mattie lived by this precept. The depth of her knowledge and experience was enormous, but she wore it lightly, and was always open to new experiences, ready to listen to the most inarticulate and faltering of students with an ear for something alive and real in what they might be trying to convey.

Hélène Dubinsky

We had just moved from Brussels to a remote hamlet in Hampshire because of my husband Alex's work. I had studied law and practised for two years, but I was only too happy to leave it behind as my interest was in psychoanalysis. I wanted to understand myself and others.

By chance, I came upon a book mentioning the Child Psychotherapy Training. On a Saturday, a few weeks after our arrival in England, naïve, omnipotent and hopeful, Alex and I drove to London to explore the Tavistock Clinic, without having made any appointment. I hardly spoke any English, had read a few books by Freud, never heard of Melanie Klein and I had no experience with children.

I asked the porter – the long, thin, sarcastic, legendary Lofty – at the downstairs reception, whether I could speak to someone about the child psychotherapy course. Unperturbed, Lofty made a phone call and told me to go to the first floor and this is how I met Mattie.

Mattie listened to me attentively, perhaps with a sparkle of amusement in her eyes but also with real interest and this made me feel so hopeful. She said that I needed to get experience with children. This is how I became assistant house mother in a children's home in Hampshire, collecting children from school and helping the house mother to give tea to the children. I attended Mattie's work discussion seminar every other week. A while later, I embarked on a five times a week analysis in London, travelling four hours every day to and fro. After a year, we moved to London and I worked in a school with small groups of difficult children. In a later interview with Mattie, before starting the Observation Course, I talked of some of my shortcomings. I ended up saying "I am not sure that I like children", unconsciously paraphrasing Jack Lemmon desperately saying "I am not a woman" in the film *Some Like It Hot*. Mattie looked a bit taken aback but reassured me that to be in touch with one's darker side helps one to understand people and she quoted Shakespeare.

During the years that followed, through supervision, seminars and her readiness to listen when I had a difficulty, Mattie was at the centre of my experience as a trainee child psychotherapist.

I always so admired Mattie's depth of insight, her absolute trust in the importance of the psychoanalytic understanding of unconscious phantasy, her courage, her love of beauty, her generosity and her invigorating rebellious spirit.

She gave me unfailing support and encouragement and thanks to Mattie, I am able to do the work I value.

Ellen Jaffe

When I think of Mattie, the idea of learning from direct experience – including the learning that goes on in seminars between teacher and student and among peers, as well as from books and from one's own clinical work – is one thing that stands out clearly. Although I never had Mattie as a supervisor, I was in some small seminars and larger group teaching situations with her, and she interviewed me when I applied for the Child Psychotherapy Training, in September 1974. During that interview, I felt that Mattie could see into me, not exactly reading my mind (being intrusive) but making contact with my soul in a way that was both clear-seeing and extremely kind (though certainly not sentimental). Although at first she said the course was closed for that year, she then called a few weeks later and accepted me, and I believe she knew how important starting the course was for me at that time. I had come to London from New York in 1972 on a one-year fellowship to study open-plan education; then decided to stay and teach for a while. When I discovered and attended a Work Discussion seminar offered by the Tavistock, I felt I had emotionally and intellectually come home, and wanted to apply for and immerse myself in the full child psychotherapy training. I had recently been through an unsettling personal experience (did I mention that in the interview?) and somehow knew the course could help me deal with ghosts from my own childhood, as well as provide rich ideas and help me do meaningful work. I am grateful she trusted me to begin.

I think Mattie's combination of clarity, compassion, and honesty was the source of her integrity (I think she was a person of great integrity), and these qualities made her a good teacher. When she was in a room, her presence radiated with a pure light. She helped shape my thinking, helped me think and feel for myself and also learn to listen to good teachers and explore ideas in a rigorous way – not fighting authority nor blindly accepting it. The experience of learning and teaching at the Tavi felt more authentic than my experience at university – and came at a time when I was open to that growth, hard as it sometimes was.

I remember another, younger seminar leader talking about internal objects and the process of internalizing as opposed to projective identification. He said that if we admired Mattie and wanted to be "like" her, this would mean becoming the best person we ourselves could be, not a carbon-copy of Mattie. This made a big impression on me. I also came to see that, despite occasional appearances of distraction, Mattie's mind was actually sharp, clear, and deep, and her respect for people around her as human beings was an essential part of her nature. And Mattie showed us that creative chaos and not-knowing is necessary, too; as Marion Milner wrote, sometimes we have to walk in the fog for a bit. As a poet and writer, I was glad that she, too, loved poetry and literature, integrated literature and other arts into her teaching, and helped students see the value of this. I felt I did not have to "hide" this part of my life; rather, my training as a psychotherapist also helped me develop as a writer.

In both Infant Observation seminars and Work Discussion seminars, she was very sensitive to everyone's needs – the infant/child, the parent, the student, and yet could be "ruthless" in the way a knife needs to cut sharply to be effective – just as a writer or artist needs to be ruthless in dealing with characters and plot; sentimentality and evading the truth are not helpful, and (in the end) only offer a false kindness, something Mattie did not do.

Judy Shuttleworth

I was in my early twenties when I first met Mattie and I think that if I hadn't met her at that point I might well have done something very different with my life. She gave me an idea of a certain kind of child psychotherapist that became both a starting point from which to strike out on my own career and later, an object to orientate to during the vagaries of what has turned out to be quite a long working life as an NHS clinician.

I remember that it was snowing when I arrived for an interview following my application to train as a child psychotherapist. I had only just left university and in my growing up I had not come into any contact with psychoanalysis. I had stumbled on the training by a series of accidents but it seemed to give form to my vague idea that I wanted to work with people in emotional difficulties, with only the thinnest of veils between that and my own post adolescent struggles. I had read *Envy and Gratitude* and "Our adult world and its roots in infancy" and I had found myself a job in a children's residential assessment unit in Birmingham but that was the sum of my preparation for that first meeting.

I remember enjoying the interview and the chance to talk about what I had read with someone who appreciated why I would have found these psychoanalytic ideas such an exciting, and enlightening revelation. It was like no other interview before or since. I left feeling I had had a highly significant conversation with someone who had understood and taken seriously my barely formed hopes. It left me thinking that if I wasn't accepted it obviously wasn't the right thing for me and that I would find other ways to pursue my new found interests. Surely I was wrapping myself up in a protective blanket against possible disappointment, like the blanket of snow all over the car park outside as I emerged out of the building, but I think it was also a response to Mattie's style of talking about deeply important matters in ordinary unspectacular language. I hadn't gone expecting a therapeutic consultation but I had been offered one and it has remained with me always. Even the briefest of clinical encounters can be significant. What I didn't know then but came to know later was that Mattie had only recently been widowed.

I was accepted and I had many opportunities to hear Mattie talk in delicate particularity about the human condition, in a lecture series on Human Growth and Development, in Infant Observation and later in clinical seminars. Though she would mark passages in a presentation as it was being read for us to return to for more detailed attention in the discussion, sometimes towards the end of the seminar she would link the issues in the material to broader themes that must have been preoccupying her. I thought of these as homilies, moral but not moralising. She had at this time a memorable way of talking in a simple lively manner about deeply serious matters, a way of linking psychoanalysis to wider human concerns.

In one seminar, I was presenting with another student some work we had done jointly with a family who had been bereaved; it was thought a rather novel venture at the time. We had somehow strayed into taking a moralistic attitude, as if there were good and bad ways of experiencing bereavement. Mattie said sharply, "Look, people get through something like this just however they can." I'm sure I was mortified at the time but it also helpfully cut through some misconceived way of being psychoanalytic. I felt stripped of some pretensions to knowledge and set down to try again. Over the years I have often had cause to remember and to be grateful for that moment and for having come into contact with Mattie as a teacher who gave me something enduring to aspire to.

Brian Truckle

My first experience of Mattie was when, as a student on the one-year Advanced Course for Social Workers at the Tavistock Clinic, I attended open case conferences of the Individual Psychotherapy Programme in the then Department for Children and Parents. These were huge meetings co-chaired by Shirley Hoxter and Jean Leared where staff and trainees presented cases in treatment. At the end of wide-ranging discussion, Mattie would often intervene with a few well-chosen words, summing up the situation and succinctly pinpointing the essential issues. This was impressive. Who was this Scottish woman who spoke with American inflections?

As part of the course we all attended a series of lectures on human growth and development, and I well remember the impact of Mattie's lectures on infant emotional development. This included material from her treatment of a toddler girl who talked to her about "ach-ach-bosoms". Much to my surprise, this material made some sort of intriguing sense and encouraged me to try to tolerate fascinating but terrifying new ideas.

At the end of the year, I approached her with trepidation to ask if I might attend some theory sequences on the observation course so that, as I thought, I could understand more. Twenty minutes later, I emerged from her room, slightly bewildered, fully signed up for the whole course and scheduled to attend her Infant Observation and Work Discussion seminars as a starter (but no theory).

Subsequently, what then became invaluable were her insights into the internal worlds and conflicts of the children brought for work discussion seminars. Her capacity to elicit from the material and from discussion, ideas and hypotheses which so often could be collaborated by further information from the presenters, was astonishing and enriching.

When I commenced the clinical training, Mattie agreed to supervise what was to have been my first (adolescent) training case. Unfortunately, the young person concerned only agreed to come twice per week in order to discuss a "close encounter of the third kind" never to be achieved. Nevertheless, joint supervisions, together with Elizabeth Tuters (then a senior social worker at the Tavistock and now a psychoanalyst in Canada) were great fun and we both learnt a lot.

This was also my first direct experience of her philosophy of offering a little less than was needed so as to encourage (or force) independent thought. This I imagined to be evidence of a Calvinist upbringing; it could be very frustrating.

By now I was teaching on the one year Advanced Social Work course and running a sequence called Direct Social Work with Children and Adolescents. For both courses, Mattie's book *Thinking about Infants and Young Children* was seminal reading. The capacity to communicate in ordinary language the everyday dilemmas of being a mother and/or a baby, is very rare. This book has had an enormous impact on hundreds of readers over the years. Students would tell me (and still do) how situations sensitively described in these brief pages had resonated not only in their work settings but also in their personal lives as parents in a most life-enhancing way. She writes of human dilemmas in early relationships and how to approach them but, characteristically, indicating that the person or couple concerned need to work at possible solutions themselves (including the baby). At one stage, demand for the book was such that I bought 20 copies to lend to students: at least a few came back! I am sure the other copies have had good use too.

Eleanor Wigglesworth

I first met Mattie in the early 60s when I was accepted on to the Child Psychotherapy Training at the Tavistock Clinic then based in Beaumont Street in Marylebone. She had taken over the running of the course from Esther Bick fairly recently and she was determined to base the training on firm psychoanalytic principles as espoused by Mrs Bick and clearly based on Melanie Klein's work. At the same time she needed her considerable diplomatic skills to negotiate the complex political currents at the Institute of Psychoanalysis and the Tavistock Clinic, where clinicians of other persuasions were concerned to broaden and, perhaps in her view, dilute the impact of Kleinian thought.

At that time there was no requirement to complete any preclinical child psychotherapy courses, other than to have gained a degree. The course numbers were very small, the group of tutors close-knit and the atmosphere extremely friendly, relaxed, and enjoyable. Mattie took enormous trouble to help us in every way possible. In my case as I was particularly raw, in my very early 20s, straight from a first degree course in the provinces and new to London and to psychoanalysis, I was thrown in at the deep end from the start. Mattie supported me by offering very generous practical help, such as putting me up at her house whilst helping me look for accommodation and finding various forms of paid work for me to do in order to support my training.

Mattie's commitment to a training that enabled the students to make sense of what was, for some, an initially alien psychoanalytic way of thinking about disturbed babies and children, led her to work for us with amazing empathy and her usual energy and flair. She shared her enjoyment of detailed clinical work and observation in a most exciting and adventurous way, gradually awakening our capacity to tolerate and eventually work in close contact with primitive, turbulent, often violent and erotic, unconscious processes in disturbed children and young people. She introduced us to the new developments in psychoanalysis of

Bick, Meltzer and Bion in such a way that we were able to take in and digest what were then very complex revolutionary ideas.

I think it was the very substantial experience of Mattie's own capacity be attentive and receptive, to hold one in her mind and then to respond with considerable sensitivity and acuity as she did with her patients that provided her students with the essential template for making contact with and enabling development in our patients. She was as clear-sighted in seeing our deficiencies as she was in touch with her young patients' destructive impulses, and yet she could work with the best in us as she did with her patients. I was hardly the most dedicated of students, determined as I was to enjoy the swinging 60s to the full, but my respect for Mattie's input resulted in some quite hard work on my part and I did develop a deep interest in child development and psychoanalysis and have since been privileged to belong to a profession that has kept me interested for many years and where I have worked with some challenging and fascinating children, adolescents and adults.

The Child Psychotherapy Training at the Tavistock went from strength to strength in the 60s and 70s and the numbers of students swelled. I am always struck how those child therapists who trained with Mattie each had had the experience of benefiting from her full, thoughtful attention in a unique way, and how this experience is reflected in the way they work with their patients.

Ricky Emanuel

A recollection of Mattie that has always stayed with me is of my interview with her in 1976. I had been doing a PhD in Edinburgh in artificial intelligence, using computers and robots to catalyze communication in autistic children, in an environment they could control. It actually worked well, but unfortunately my supervisors contacted *The Guardian*, and they published an article (without my consent or knowledge) saying "a cure had been found for autism"!

After the betrayal of the *Guardian* article, I decided to leave Edinburgh and apply to train as a child psychotherapist. I already was more interested in the children than the computers and was reading a lot of psychoanalysis. I knew nothing about child psychotherapy training, nor anyone involved. I rang all the training schools (there were four at the time in London), and at the Tavistock I spoke to the admin person. When she asked me what I was studying, she told me to forget it as my degrees were in computer science, economics and artificial intelligence. Being young, I did not take no for an answer, and asked if at least I could speak with someone teaching on the course to find out more about it. I was put through to Mattie, who asked me to come to London to meet her. I arrived with some trepidation, but found she was interested in my work with an autistic child who had begun speaking for the first time ever. She offered me a place there and then, which amazed me. I felt I had come home! I had already made contact with Frances Tustin, and was offered a job in the unit for autistic children where she was working.

My next anecdote comes from when I asked Mattie if she would supervise my intensive adolescent training case. She offered me a time at her home at 5.45 am! and I think I may not have even been her first supervisee or patient. At my first supervision, in her inimitable way, she said she wanted to make one thing clear: people come to supervision to learn, and I should not present work to her with the intention of being praised. I have always remembered this, and at no time did I feel she was critical in a negative way, neither did she give much praise. I encountered the same openness as when I first met her, which allowed me to find my own path and also was true for the patient. The task was to understand the material and follow the transference and countertransference. She was rigorous, but allowed freedom of thought and expression. I will always remember her chairing the Bion conferences at the Tavi, and the palpable way in which she put Bion's ideas of eschewing memory and desire into practice.

Katherine Arnold

I was fortunate to be in Mattie's Infant Observation seminar in the preclinical course, in her Clinical seminar later on, in the Work with Parents seminar which she took with Dr Britton, and to have her as my supervisor for my latency age training case. I was training from 1975-1979.

I learned about the training form Lynn Barnett who was in the same postgraduate anthropology seminar as me at University College London. I asked to see someone to learn more and found myself having an interview, and being accepted to my joy.

I went to meet Mattie and I remember her asking me what sort of person I was. I answered "a happy person", which I was not aware of being, but I think she had that effect on me immediately. I was already troubled by my father's severe mental illness which was to cast a shadow over my own life. Looking back, I think Mattie's hopefulness and pleasure in new life has remained deeply with me.

I remember Mattie as always encouraging and interested, even when she had to point out to me that my contribution to a clinical seminar was "very complicated", which was said with a laugh. I had talked at huge length about the meaning of a house number in a child's drawing. I also remember vividly her telling me she only had one regret in her life, which was that she had not spent as much time with her children as she wished she had. I always felt supported in the inevitably difficult choices between work and children and other aspects of life which later confronted me. I am forever grateful for that remark, though of course I was still left with impossible choices which I was bound to get wrong!

I also remember Mattie talking animatedly and fervently in the common room, I think about her struggles to establish an adult top-up training for child psychotherapists. Once she said – laughing though clearly describing a real struggle – that there is nothing so helpful as a good bad object. Nearly 40 years on that may be my creation of course. But I took with me a sense that it is possible to struggle on, perhaps failing outwardly but being strengthened and cheerful even so, and being able to find comfort from others' companionship.

In my personal supervision with her, which lasted a year, I remember how much she helped me to think of ways to put things to my patient – a girl of eight – which would open up our situation together. She was so generous with helpful suggestions which I felt I could use if I wanted to, or forget if not. I felt she wouldn't mind telling me again, which was such a fresh and immediate experience for me. She used to constantly slip into her conversation the phrase "You see I think", meaning, let us make time and space to think about it. I also remember her saying the mother of my patient was a silly woman for saying that she was special so couldn't be expected to keep to the time arrangements of her child's sessions. I saw Mattie able to clearly disagree with someone, but with only tolerance and sympathy for such a "silly woman".

As I write this on my 64th birthday things come together in a joyous and light hearted way, just as they did then with Mattie nearly four decades ago.

Herbert Chaim Hahn

It was the experience of meeting Mattie that enabled me initially to dip a toe into what became the best and longest professional training and development of my life. This also provided multi-faceted opportunities for my personal development to which she generously, actively and creatively contributed; and for establishing longlasting friendships.

When I first met her "for a chat" in the early 1960s in relation to developing my interest in psychoanalysis, I was uncertain about my future professional direction and hesitant even about going through the application process to train as a child and adolescent psychotherapist. At this meeting she communicated an attuned friendly interest in my personal and professional development and, sensitive to my caution about committing to a long and expensive training, generously invited me to "sit in" on a couple of her seminars to "get a taste and a feel" of what might be on offer. This taster inspired me to proceed with persistence and determination to what became a seven-year part-time training under her aegis.

Over the years of my training, I experienced Mattie's deep commitment to Kleinian psychoanalysis as being accompanied by a breadth of friendliness, warmth and respect towards me and my peers as people, and individuals, in our own right. It also became clear that over the years that her wide ranging and effective social skills were resolutely inspired by her deep commitment to her professional beliefs and values, in ways which were widely and deeply crucial and effective for the survival and development of the Tavistock child and adolescent psychoanalytic psychotherapy training.

Mattie's courage, zest and commitment to her professionalism *and* to truth were crystal clear when she unilaterally made firm surgical decisions when she decided that her training was under threat; and at other times, trustingly shared her hard-won, ongoing, "forbidden" questioning of various "holy cows" in the areas of both mothering and child analysis.

Mattie effectively raised my horizons, after I completed my training, by encouraging me to apply for a senior staff role at the Tavistock, then a principal at the London Child Guidance Training Centre, and also to train as an adult psychoanalyst at the London Institute. It was through Mattie and my time at the Tavistock that I was able to engage with and learn from Winnicott, Bion, Bridger and Meltzer, who also all changed my life. And although the Institute adult training was interesting and useful, it lacked the rigour, warmth and inspiration of my training with, and under, Mattie.

Shortly before I was invited to write about my recollections for this book, I was conversing with a colleague here (in Melbourne) about a workshop on helping people to differentiate between violence and assertiveness. It brought back a vivid memory of a seminar led by Arthur [Hyatt Williams] in which he told us how quickly he had to think and "interpret" when he was working in a cell with a person convicted of murder, and who suddenly projected the person he had murdered onto Arthur himself. When my colleague contrasted assertiveness and violence with "passivity", I pointed out the contrast between passivity and receptiveness; and my conscious memory was of Mattie revealing this different to me all those years ago, and profoundly shifting my understanding and insight, to include matters such as phallic versus breast-centred conflicts; the controversies bubbling in Hampstead between Finchley Road (the Tavistock) and Maresfield Gardens (the Anna Freud Centre); and the Tavi psychoanalytic psychotherapy training versus that at the Institute. All deriving from a few clear and inspired words from Mattie, spoken lightly to our small training group, in which she bridged theoretical concepts with the symbolic potentialities of sexual intercourse, pregnancy, and birth, and from there all internal and external relationships.

I also have a lively memory of Mattie's "apprehension of beauty" (to borrow Donald Meltzer's phrase), which – reinforced by Meltzer himself – has become deeply internally established.

Thank you Mattie, I miss you. And writing this piece has also lovingly re-minded me that you are alive and well in my inner being.

Carlo Papuzza

My memory of Martha is very clear. Above all I was struck by her ability to sense the state of mind of our specialist workers, and to translate profound concepts into simple terms. I was also struck by the grace with which she expressed her interpretative hypotheses and gave technical advice.

Still vivid in my memory is something she once said about the powers and limitations of psychoanalytic therapy. A successful analysis, she said, makes the patient aware of and able to use his natural potential, getting rid of all that prevented him from being himself. It is like a centrifuge, dispersing the dust that covers over the gold and bringing out the gold within in all its splendour. But be aware of the fact that if there is no gold but only some less precious metal, the analysis will not have the power to change the baser metal into gold. An analysis can only bring out what already exists in terms of natural endowment.

Maria Pozzi

I remember being in a clinical seminar of hers in which she talked about her patients' material (some recent patients and others from the past) with great clarity as if they were alive in her mind and in the room. In fact her way of looking did not seem to be focussing on the people present in the seminar room, but as if she were focussing in a communicative encounter – verbal or non-verbal – with the patient at the precise moment that she was telling us about it.

I also remember her and Donald Meltzer running a seminar in Perugia in 1978 or '79 (the year before I came to London to train at the Tavistock); it was like a duet and I was deeply touched by the way they worked together.

Renata Li Causi

When I first arrived in this country to do my training in child analysis a friend of mine had let me use her room, as she was away. The room was in a house in Hampstead where Martha Harris and her family lived. She showed interest, wanted to know who I was, and invited me to a big family do. Not being sure if I was really wanted, or if she had just invited me out of kindness and politeness, I arrived late and behaved in rather an off-hand way. So that when, at some point, they were discussing the ethics of raising battery chickens in a farm they were involved with, I very aggressively and self-righteously intervened, saying that they should be worried about the workers being exploited in factories, and not the chickens.

Nevertheless when my friend claimed back her room and I had not yet found a place to rent, she suggested I stay in the house for a few more days until I had found one. As there were no more rooms available, a bed was prepared on the living room sofa.

Her generosity, warmth and availability made my transition from Italy to London much easier. And my transference to London was only positive – at least until I started my own analysis! Mattie was to become my baby observation and work discussion seminar leader and then the supervisor of my first child patient. She had a remarkable capacity for opening up one's mind to different ways of seeing and understanding the clinical material without making me feel stupid or inadequate and I felt free to express my thoughts and valued for what I was able to contribute. She was one of the very few people I encountered who could link theory and clinical material without forcing the one to "prove" the other. She had a hesitant way of talking as if her thinking was being arranged as she spoke and was allowing connections to emerge. I would leave these sessions full of ideas and renewed passion for the work I was doing, however difficult.

Once, a few weeks after my baby was born, she came to visit. The baby started to cry, I thought she could not be hungry as she had been fed recently, and anyway I did not want to be offering food as soon as the baby cried! I tried all sorts of ways to pacify her but finally only feeding stopped the crying. Mattie was quietly watching, hardly breathing I thought, and then when the baby was peacefully feeding she let out a large sigh of relief. She had been experiencing the emotional impact of the interaction she was watching but had not intervened nor given advice, until I found my way to the baby. Later while thinking about it I reflected that it was a poignant example of the analytic stance.

I have a final image. Arriving at her consulting room I encountered her watering a large, beautiful flower bed filled with a great variety of plants. I remember the leaves always green and flowers full with blooms. It can't always have been like that, and I am sure that Mattie, too, cannot always have been warm, sensitive, facilitating, and clinically astute. Yet I cannot think of any instance when I felt disappointed, let down, not kept in mind. It was terrible when we lost her as the result of the accident.

Torhild Leira

I got to know both Martha and Donald when they first came to Norway, to a congress in the early 70s, invited by my former husband, Svein Haugsgjerd. Then there were visits over many years, lectures and supervisions. As we started a child analytic group, Donald also supervised all four of us child analysts to be. Both of them were present at meetings in the analytic society. Martha was the one who went to basics in the discussions, keeping the way clear to infancy, shedding light on issues confused or hidden – she was much treasured for her comments.

Also in the 70s Svein and I met Martha and Donald in London, and we drove with them to the house at Mersea. They insisted we borrow Martha's car to make a trip to Constable country. In the morning – I was late for breakfast – Martha gave me a pitta-bread containing a fried egg and bacon together with my coffee. This was ages before such an exotic dish came to Norway – I can still taste it! Most of all that morning she was eager for Meg, who was pregnant, to arrive, with her husband, the doctor. We also stayed at Buttermilk farm, another lovely house made by Martha. For dinner she made a fabulous dessert, and Donald said (exactly): "Martha, you have done it again!"

In the summer of 82, after my divorce, my son and I went to visit Martha and Donald in Gromignana. Meg and her family were there, and Morag, married to an Italian; also Françoise Begoin and her family were there, camping. Martha and I bought some trout from a farm nearby, that tasted delicious; another day we went swimming in the river.

Back in Norway a while later, I read Martha's article in the *Journal of Child Psychotherapy* about her grandchild, Morag's daughter. I guessed from small bits of information. When Martha and I talked about it next time we met, she was astonished that I had understood this connection – it was not meant to be recognized by readers.

In those years, when coming to Norway, Martha always brought small gifts for my son. I remember some very nice blocks – red, yellow, blue. What struck me was the delicacy of these bricks and the strong colours. A beautiful gift, not just useful or functional. Writing this, so many good memories have come back to me, making me feel thankful.

Eve Steel

Mattie helped many people to gain experience in various settings before starting the Child Psychotherapy Training; then the Work Discussion seminars were set up where those working in a variety of places shared their work experience with a member of the Child Psychotherapy staff. Mattie sent me off to consult with schools and speak in various settings, where she saw the need – matching this with who could do it and get on with it. She was intuitive and active in the social sphere, and also savvy politically with such a light touch. She set things up that grew, and did not create rigid structures that she was possessive of.

I have memories of Mattie's sensitive receptivity and saying what needed to be said straightforwardly. I remember seeing a big young West Indian girl, bursting out of her school uniform, depressed and silent and Mattie saying something simple about her being black and me being a white woman. Obvious and unspoken and we came from such different worlds. Mattie's extraordinary gifts were not only clinical, but also political. Her disarming hesitant manner belied a strong will and clarity about what she thought was best. She usually got her way without any conflict and with good will.

I remember when her husband Roland died, the shock reverberated through us. I dreamt of Mattie running frantic through a dark and green wood, then she came to a clearing and stopped, as if pulled by a silent presence that led her to sit quietly and be at peace. I knew she would be alright.

CHAPTER TWENTY-ONE

Memories of Mattie

Valerie Sinason

> A luminous vagueness ... a democratic elitist ...
> a compassionate perfectionist ...

For many of us child psychotherapy trainees who had the fortune to train in child psychotherapy at the Tavistock Clinic when Mattie was there Mattie *was* the Tavi. When you did not know her or before you knew her personally she was the renowned writer, psychoanalyst and child psychotherapist, Mrs Martha Harris; just as, when you first approached it, the concrete building rising up in Belsize Lane was that rare NHS teaching and training place, The Tavistock Centre. Then, slowly and almost imperceptibly, there was the transition to affectionate abbreviation – "Mattie" and "the Tavi".

My memories on the feelings about those two different states of closeness are still vivid – embarrassingly so! Although 30 years old or so on approaching the training, there was an adolescent quality to my amazement that this soft-voiced woman, with her unique kind of elegant clumsiness, deep insights and accessible writing could be called "Mattie" by her trainees. Not only had she (together with John Bowlby) created the only NHS child psychotherapy training, she had also followed Winnicott in caring to write articles and books for the general public about all the complex issues involved in bringing up children. She was deeply committed to the NHS and to child psychotherapy as a profession.

In a way that seemed similar to Anna Freud, to me, she had cherished us child psychoanalytic psychotherapists and poured into our training and baby observations a quality that we did not think then existed in the child training at the Institute of Psychoanalysis. Indeed, whilst most entrants to the adult psychoanalytic training already had an adult psychotherapy qualification, most child psychotherapists (including myself) had no wish to add on any further child training. We considered we had experienced a most full training. Where we sought further training it was to add on an adult qualification.

After being home-based until my youngest child started full-time school I was excited at the thought of developing a new career. Despite an English literature degree and a teaching diploma for secondary English and drama I knew I no longer had the wish to undertake a PhD in literature. (I had been only six months into a PhD on George Gissing and his treatment of the working class in his novels when my loved tutor died and I first became pregnant.) Also, despite coming from a teaching family and having loved both infant school and secondary school teaching I knew I was more concerned with the children in the class who had emotional problems.

Moving next door to Tavistock Clinic Consultant Child Psychotherapist Susan Reid at this significant moment became the catalyst to change my life. In hearing my readiness for a new career she said she could see I loved being with children and wondered if maybe I would be interested in the Tavistock Child Psychotherapy Training. As a neighbour and a mother she was inspiring and I read the brochure and decided to apply. My parents were delighted I was interested in applying to the Tavistock because of the presence of John Bowlby. As a teaching family, they would have otherwise preferred me to have applied to the Anna Freud Centre as we had all read and enjoyed Anna Freud's Lecture Notes for Teachers.

I left a message at the Tavistock Clinic saying I was interested in applying for the training and expected to get an application form through the post. None came. A week later the phone range and "Hello" said a friendly voice. It was Martha Harris ringing me to ask me about my application. I felt a frisson of terror as my five and seven year old unerringly chose that moment to have a heated argument. How would Mrs Harris have a positive view of me when she could hear arguing children in the background? Making theatrical signs to my children to be quiet did not work at all. Indeed, obviously, it caused an escalation. Surely this would be a black mark against me. "Half-term isn't it!" she said sympathetically with a tinge of humour and I could hear the kindly grin.

I relaxed and we made a time to meet. At the Tavistock, she asked me about my English degree and what I enjoyed reading and told me that she herself had an English degree and she had fought the Department of Health each year to make sure they included a literature degree as part of what was seen as a useful pre-requisite to training, along with medicine, psychology and social work. Indeed, she said she felt an English degree was more useful in helping you understand human nature and her late husband had been deeply involved in literature and teaching. A postgraduate diploma in teaching in addition to the English degree meant I could fulfil the requirements.

She asked me about my teaching practice and background in a kindly interested way that allowed me to respond. When it came to talking about analysis, something I had never had, Mattie said "It might be hard for you to start analysis when you have not had to come to it through personal need and have managed without it. It can be easier for people who have longed for understanding because they were in such difficulties and chaos."

When I said I wished I had come for it honestly as something useful for me rather than have it acceptably hidden as part of a training package, Mattie gently replied that I was saying the same thing as her, that personal need had not been pressing enough. I realized, just as in her writing, how she could effortlessly be kindly to completely different groups of people at the same moment. People who came to training desperate for analysis were bathed in approval for doing what they needed and people who had not needed to do that were also bathed in approval. This is not to minimise her rigour and sharpness over clinical meaning but to highlight the non-shaming way she spoke.

At the end of the interview, as I left the room, she smiled at me and said she could not see any reason why I should not be accepted for the training. As the door closed all my worries returned. I was paralyzed with doubt. What did she mean? In great anxiety I asked my nextdoor neighbour, Susan Reid. "That means she has accepted you", said Sue with a big smile on her face.

After waiting nervously for what felt like endless days I rang the Clinic and left a message for Mattie asking when I would formally hear the results of the interview. And then, of course, I thought I would now definitely be rejected for being so needy and such a troublemaker! A message came back saying I was accepted and a formal letter would follow.

At the summer meeting for newly accepted trainees who would start in the autumn, Mattie said three particular things which I have never forgotten and have continued to have an effect on me. Firstly, in warmly welcoming us and telling us about the library, she added, "And please don't steal library books like last year's trainees did." In my state of idealization I could not believe that professionals like child psychotherapy trainees could ever commit such acts.

At a far deeper level her comfortable awareness of the universality of disturbance made it easier for me to later deal with situations where trained NHS professionals behaved abusively. She did not split the world into those who had been analysed and others.

Indeed, her second unforgettable comment, for me, from that introductory talk was: "Do not idealize analysis. You will meet some people in the world who are the wisest people you could ever go to for help and have a depth of understanding which is peerless and who have never ever read an analytic book or had a single session of psychoanalysis or psychotherapy and, of course, you will meet people who have had years of psychoanalysis and you just hope they must have been infinitely more disturbed when they began!"

In almost any lecture or teaching to lay groups I quote that from Mattie, as well as my favourite definition of adulthood from her, "Being an adult means acting your chronological age for at least half the day." Mattie's ability to say profound things in humorous and everyday language meant her books were invaluable for parents. In *Thinking about Infants and Young Children* almost any page provides an example of the way she avoids splitting and makes the reader feel accepted. For example, note her inclusive language in thinking about weaning: "The difficulty of helping to wean the baby, in general ways, from too great a dependence upon us is one which, as mothers, we nearly all feel at some time or another." She was always part of the "we" and the "us".

My own willingness and interest in writing a monthly column for the *Guardian Weekend* newspaper for four years on family problems had its precedent in Mattie's welcoming such educational chances. Her deep delight in what psychoanalysis could give to people was one that she clearly felt should be shared. Not everyone could afford such a chance, even if they wished for it, and she saw it as part of her commitment to psychoanalysis to educate the general public.

At that time I edited an illustrated poetry magazine called *Gallery* and, knowing that both Mattie and Isca Wittenberg (my tutor) were welcoming of creativity, I started a House Journal for the Tavistock, called *The Tavistock Gazette*. It is hard to convey now what terror there was at the idea of a House Journal at the Tavistock. The building was beset with two terrors – the impact on patients of reading what their therapists wrote should they see it, and the impact on therapists and trainee-therapists of knowing that their analyst might read it! Including poetry, art, interviews, reviews, it soon found a safe home and lasted for years after I gave up editing. It helped to pave the way both for the increase in book and papers published at the Tavistock as well as the development of pantomimes (whose scripts were published in the *Gazette*). Being humorous was almost as dangerous as being in print. Mattie's creative support was to show itelf in many different places in the fabric of the Tavistock, way outside the remit of training and teaching! Additionally, in seeking to bring literary events to the Clinic, I invited D. M. Thomas to come and give us a reading from *The White Hotel* which led to a packed 200 plus audience in the lecture rooms. Pantomimes were also to follow as well as the *Understanding Your Child* series.

Having been asked by a publisher to produce a series focussing on the developmental needs of each age, I followed Mattie in thinking this would be an excellent chance for the Tavistock Clinic. In linking the publisher with the child psychotherapy training to ensure something more permanent, a highly successful series followed. Without Mattie's books for the general public as a precedent this would never have happened.

Indeed, in looking at the profusion of books from workshops and individuals that come from the Tavistock now it is hard to believe how little was published at the time I was a trainee and what a major example Mattie had set. Her lightness of touch combined with passionate educational ideals was accompanied by a great sense of humour.

In fact her sense of humour enlivened seminars as much as her insights and pleasure in listening to our accounts. I will not forget her vivid description of doing Scottish dancing reels with John Bowlby or the size of Melanie Klein's hats!

When baby observations began in the autumn I was startled to see women who had only just had a baby going out to observe someone else's. I could not understand how they could switch off from their own baby's needs. My parents reminded me of the fact that Anna Freud did not allow mothers to join her training until their children were in full-time school.

In a both naïve and arrogant way I raised this problem with Mattie. I said it upset me to see mothers doing training at this stage when it meant leaving their little babies with nannies. In addition, how could they leave their babies to do a baby observation when the observation of babies was so powerful? Mattie looked at me very gently and said, "Has it ever occurred to you that you are lucky because you enjoyed being at home with your babies until they were five? Has it ever occurred to you that these mothers will be better mothers when they go home because they have done something that enriches them?"

It had not occurred to me and it transformed my attitude. It also affected my clinical work. When patients spoke angrily of how other people in their life did X or failed to do Y, I almost repeated Mattie verbatim. "Has it ever occurred to you that you are lucky because…"

Mattie was luminous, warm and wise. She could transmit a sense of meaning in the behaviours of children of all ages and their parents and a sense of pleasure in the work. She was also passionate about the training. She was disturbed that, at that time, there were few paid trainee posts so that class and economic issues affected who could train as a child psychotherapist. She did her best to help. She also had an inclusive view that if someone really desperately wanted to work with children, they would do so anyway and so it was better to make them as well-trained as possible. Unlike the Institute of Psychoanalysis, where there was a complex process if somebody wanted to change their analyst or supervisor mid-training, Mattie helped it through as smoothly as possible.

Her philosophy of self-selection was that she trusted in the innate awareness of trainees to know if, after the observation course, they felt they had the patience and capacity to go through the whole rigours of the training. The Work Discussion groups were her invention and they allowed us all to explore our own work settings whilst learning from other people's. Every year a small number would decide that from what they had understood and learned they did not wish for the task of a complete training but would be happy with the difference the observation course had made to them.

This was to have a huge impact on my development of courses for people working with learning disability, or later, for people working with ritual abuse and dissociation. I kept a policy of self-selection, feeling that even where there might be the occasional individual who was not appropriate for the particular training, the damage caused was far less than the hurt and rivalry and fear and waste caused by interviewing.

At the time of my training Mattie was married to Donald Meltzer, then possibly at the height of his theoretical powers, and when she quoted from him, we felt privileged we were having access to the wisdom of a couple. Indeed, Mattie and Meltzer's joint theoretical model, *A Psychoanalytic Model of the Child in the Family in the Community* was brought to us in our weekly theoretical seminar so that we had the experience of watching a remarkable body of knowledge form itself through a serial (rather like listening to Dickens, chapter by chapter!). Mattie and Meltzer were keen in their teaching to respect other paths to learning and wisdom rather than to privilege psychoanalysis, but in a way they each underestimated their own brilliance although they accepted their partner's. I liked the modest and social ideological model in which they both stated "One task of the analyst is to find his way into the world inhabited by his patient, but this is just as true of parent or teacher." I also resonated to the idea that "A person or part of the personality trapped inside an object can usually be helped and enticed out… given at least one person interested enough to seek him out in his claustrum."

A highlight of the training was the summer picnic Mattie provided at her home in Mersea. All trainees and staff were invited, together with partners and children. It was rather precious that children were acknowledged to be important on such a course. However, I was not alone in having worries about how mine would behave there as well as joining in the enjoyably rivalrous feelings about the food we all brought to take there. People signed up to bring main courses, salads or deserts and everyone did their best dinner party cooking! In department parties Mattie always said that child psychotherapists made the best desserts.

Her summer parties, open equally to staff, students and their families, allowed us access to people we had previously only met through their writing. Wilfred Bion was a regular guest and I remember with particular pleasure his comment that at least no-one could accuse him of being Bionic! Donald Meltzer hospitably carried on conversations with adults and children alike and I could discuss with him the reality of ritual abuse survivors who lived in a concrete claustrum that exactly matched his description of the inner one. Unlike many others at that time, he could take in the reality of such traumatic experiences but was keen to point out that if the claustrum was not internalized someone still had the freedom to move out.

I did not have the personal experience of being supervised by Mattie but I could see her impact on my supervisors and teachers. In the children's department at that time Margaret Rustin and Susan Reid, who many of us saw as her successors, were beautiful brilliant young women with lustrous waist-length hair and as well as admiring them clinically we could see that Mattie was able to provide succession planning in a nurturing non-envious way.

When it came to qualifying Mattie was as confusing for me as she was when I had applied. "I see no reason why you can't qualify", she said. After several years of analysis I now had the capacity to ask directly what that meant instead of waiting in terror. She picked up her pen and pointed to my exercise book. "You have qualified" she wrote. There was the obvious wait for the Association of Child Psychotherapists' formal letter and certificate but that was it!

A particular highlight for me was the picnic where I sat chatting to a sparkly creative woman about her artwork and writing. As a poet and the editor of *Gallery*, I was always looking for illustrations. She turned out to be the writer and artist, Meg Harris Williams, the daughter of Mattie and Roland Harris and step-daughter of Donald Meltzer.

In thinking with gratitude of what Mattie gave to child psychotherapy and to British childhood with her own teaching capacity, books and personality, I am also grateful to see the familiar luminous quality shining in Meg's eyes and for the Harris Meltzer trust to continue educating us.

CHAPTER TWENTY-TWO

Mattie's legacy

Asha Phillips

One of the remarkable influences Mattie had on so many is that learning from her occurred in a very organic way. The French word for training is "formation", that which forms you. It is hard to say specifically what she taught; you just know that she helped to shape you. I believe this is what Bion (1962) referred to as learning from experience rather than learning about. Mattie taught so that you learned from the process, from how she addressed you and how she thought and spoke about the material, as much as from what she said.

I always associate Mattie with development, with things that grow. You could present her with the most depressing cases. Where others saw a derelict emotional landscape, pathology and despair, Mattie somehow spotted the one tiny green shoot in the desert that showed that internal life had a chance, often in dire external circumstances. She once gave me some gladioli bulbs from her garden and I remember lifting them carefully to transplant whenever I moved house. For me they symbolized her legacy, as one of her students, to see potential development and help children grow.

The other noticeable aspect of being one of Mattie's students, in great contrast to the world of child psychotherapy training today, was how informal and personal the whole process was.

I actually came to the UK from Paris to study psychology at university because I had heard about Mattie and the Tavistock Clinic and wanted to do the child psychotherapy training. I met with her as soon as I graduated, aged 21, expressing my wish to join the course. I thought I was going for an interview and my boyfriend came with me for support. To my astonishment Mattie invited me to what was then the bar, on the fifth floor, and asked if my boyfriend would like to join us rather than sitting in the waiting room. I declined! We had a friendly chat and she suggested, in her wonderfully straightforward and factual way, that I was rather a bit too young and might want to get some experience with children first. I therefore did a Postgraduate Certificate in Education in nursery/infant teaching so that I could obtain work with young children, as this has always been the age group that most interests me.

Once I completed the course, I was back knocking on Mattie's door, and in 1978 I began the extraordinary journey of training. She suggested I apply for a job in what was then called a Young Family Care Centre. This was a Social Services run day care centre for under fives and their parents. The families were very difficult, the innumerable problems (alcoholism, drug addiction, domestic violence to name but a few) stemming from a terrible cycle of deprivation going back many generations. The aims were to promote healthier family relations, offer an alternative model of parenting to both children and parents and to look after the children in a day care setting. Staff were involved in all the general tasks undertaken in an ordinary nursery as well as counselling parents and liaising with other agencies. It was a real foundation for the rest of my working life. The centre had a large number of Tavistock pre-clinical trainees as staff and was run very much with the families' emotional health and development in mind. We also welcomed students to carry out their Young Child Observation there. Looking back I realize that this input was very much Mattie's idea, to bring psychoanalytically informed minds to settings where the children and parents would be very unlikely to access psychotherapeutic services directly.

One of the most formative experiences for me at the centre was having individual sessions with some of the children. These were known as "special times". The original special times, already in place when I started work, were short periods of time where children would get special attention, going for a walk to the shops or spending time with a staff member playing with them on their own, some such ordinary activity they might do with an attentive parent. I was able to offer special times to many children, usually on the basis of when they became particularly difficult. We would go to a room for an uninterrupted 20 minutes and I could attend to the child's play and try to understand it. There was opportunity to bring these sessions to the work discussion seminars. Additionally, I was fortunate to be able to turn these into regular three times weekly sessions with one child, which I have written about (Bhownagary, 1983). This was what I like to call psychoanalytically flavoured work. I was very privileged to have weekly supervision with Lisa Miller. I look upon it as a real preparation for the training cases that would follow and know that I would have made no sense of the material nor survived the child's attacks without the combination of Lisa's passion and patient help. I did not know it at the time but this was an idea initiated by Mattie. Neither Lisa nor I remember exactly how it came about; it could well have originated from a brief chat with Lisa in a corridor, with Mattie wanting to offer a recently qualified Lisa more opportunity to supervise and me the extraordinary chance of one to one supervision at such an early stage of my pre-clinical training. It is typical of Mattie that she would plant the seed as it were and then let us get on with it, taking no credit for the concept nor interfering with its progress. If it worked it would be a useful experiment and if not we could draw lessons from the experience. She was very keen that psychotherapeutic work not be restricted to the consulting room. The "special time" model has now been used in many different contexts and countries.

Once on the clinical course, for me, as I imagine for many, the training was inextricably linked to Mattie. I was also fortunate in that I asked her if she would supervise my first training cases, a latency boy, and she accepted. I was slightly chastised for not going through my personal tutor with this request but Mattie's whole approach made it seem as if there were no rigid rules and regulations, so one was never quite sure whether there was a protocol. I remember that when any of us, on what was then called the pre-clinical course, asked how we would know if we would be accepted on the clinical training, the answer seemed to be that we would know this for ourselves. Over and above the training case supervision, the Work with Parents seminar and the lectures she gave at the Tavistock, I attended a group she ran for those who had already done an infant observation but wished to revisit the process once qualified.

I would like to reflect a little on my training case and draw out what was so special about Mattie's teaching style.

Joseph was a very withdrawn, bright but chronically under-achieving seven year old. I saw him for two years. His teacher found him quite provocative in a passive/aggressive way and described "wanting to put a bomb under him" to get a reaction. He spent the first term of three times a week therapy not saying a word and then speaking very little for a long time after. He tended to keep his coat on and mostly fiddled with his pockets, his coat zip and his clothes, occasionally bringing in tiny toys from home. For over a year he did not look into the toy box I provided. One might imagine that as a student right at the beginning of training, I would have panicked and not known what to do; but Mattie saw a wealth of meaning in the detailed description I gave of his behaviour and its impact on me. It was very akin to infant observation. Joseph's play, if one can even call it that, had a terribly stuck, dense and impenetrable quality. It is through this case that I gained some understanding of Klein. Like most of my peers, with eyes new to psychoanalysis, Klein could seem "way out", very hard to believe or relate to. However in the treatment room with young children she makes so much sense. Mattie helped me to see, in the here and now, how children locate themselves in parts of the body; with Joseph this was very much the bottom. He gave the sense that he had far more interesting things inside himself, thank you very much, and didn't need me at all. His attitude could be very superior and condescending towards me. Mattie taught me to help him move, up the body in a sense, from "poohs" to thoughts, and from inside to outside, to open himself to the world of others.

In contrast to the therapy sessions the supervisions were lively and dynamic. With her guidance I found much to talk to him about. Even though he didn't speak back, he seemed pleased that I was trying to reach and understand him. In time he responded by nodding or shaking his head or smiling and giving me other non verbal signals to help me on my way! I learned to work with what he brought as Mattie did with me, however little I felt was happening or I could say to him and however unpromising my interpretations and the hope of change.

Mattie's style of supervision was quite unique. She simply focused right in on the material and spoke about it. She was most unsentimental and never tip-toed around technical mistakes, interpretations which were clearly off the mark. She just talked about what she felt the child was communicating. In her paper "The Tavistock Training and Philosophy" she writes:

> Even if one is quite convinced that a student recurrently fails to comment upon or even see material that is asking for attention, one can be useful only by trying to approach the material again and again – by describing it ever anew from different angles as it recurs in different contexts. (Harris, 1977, p. 14)

She certainly had to do that a lot with me! Somehow she managed it without ever making me feel criticized, diminished or judged. The point I believe is that it didn't matter to her too much at all whether I got it right or wrong and it would be wasting time to linger on it. What mattered was the child and understanding him. It has been a great lesson to me and I hope I have internalized this capacity to focus on the child and his feelings.

Her approach has had a major impact on my work ever since, particularly the use of infant observation in the service of understanding patients, adult and child alike, closely allied to rigorous monitoring of the countertransference.

Mattie also had a strong "common sense", so helpful when working with parents. She writes simply about when to say no: "There is a time for yielding – but it is not all the time!" (Harris, 1975a; 2011, p. 78).

With children who fought to run out of a session, I remember her telling me she was a large woman and just placed her chair in front of the door. It was neither frightening nor threatening but a reminder of who was in charge of boundaries and also a communication that one could tolerate their fear without being so infected by it that one lost one's own capacity to think clearly.

For most children, the therapist giving in to the fear can turn both the room and the therapist into persecutory objects and encourage a phobic reaction to the sessions rather than the opportunity of working through the phantasy. The importance of boundaries resonated deeply with me and led me later to write a book for parents about it (Phillips, 1999).

In addition I feel Mattie fostered in me the freedom to take a chance and voice my thoughts, in a "thinking out loud", sharing hypotheses kind of way, rather than handing down interpretations from on high. Mattie often started sentences by saying "You see, I think" and although it might have sounded like a rather compulsive tic at times, it captured the essence of her. It addressed you (you see) and genuinely offered her pondering (I think).

She was strikingly non-dogmatic. She writes:

> The furtherance of the work of Freud, of Melanie Klein and of other inspired contributors to the science or art of psychoanalysis, depends on each student living through in his own way that path of discovery – of the interaction between the internal and the external world, the influence of the unconscious upon conscious activities. The journey is made a little easier by using the maps of those who have crossed the wilderness before. But maps read in the cosy safety of home are no substitute for the journey itself. Such cosiness prevents not only further inroads into unknown territory, but the maintenance of ways that have already been cleared. (Harris, 1977, p. 16)

This approach brings to mind Bion's (1970) call to refrain from memory and desire. What is stressed is the importance of being in the here and now with the patient, in what we might now call a mindful way. My analyst always spoke of analysis being forged in white heat – far from cosy. Mattie was adventurous, in her thinking, in her application of psychoanalytic thought to settings far wider than the consulting room. I believe she hoped to see and contribute to psychoanalysis growing and transforming and developing. She loved it, in and of itself and transmitted this passion for the process rather than fostering an admiration of her as practitioner or obtaining narcissistic gratification in teaching people to "do it her way". She had a true interest in trying new ways.

Later in the same paper she writes:

> Theoretical teaching and seminar discussion would aim to present theories not as sacred or final, but convenient. They should illuminate methods of organizing observations, of naming and generalizing, and bring order out of chaotic experience – yet leave the space and freedom to admit new data. (Harris, 1977, pp. 21-22)

It might be due to this lack of dogmatism and demagogy that Mattie's work and writing has now taken such a discreet, almost backstage place in today's training. However she has taught so many of us that I hope her legacy lives on. I, for one, am eternally grateful to be one of those she helped form.

CHAPTER TWENTY-THREE

Mattie on maternal containment

Anne Alvarez

Mattie was big-hearted, intelligent, curious, and passionate about psychoanalysis, literature and the people she loved. She was also a wonderful and exciting teacher. There was an incredible sense of abundance about her – her cooking, her garden, her wealth of ideas, and her generosity in her clinical write-ups of observational or clinical material. She clearly hated oversimplification and pathologization, and thus there is always a fully rounded picture of a session or of an observation. Not that she was ever obscure – she was clear, but she stuck to the detail of the rich complexity always. I wonder if this is one reason her writings are less well known than those of Donald Meltzer or Esther Bick, because they are not easy to pigeonhole conceptually. She did not think in headlines, she always thought of the rounded picture of the patient. This can be frustrating when you want to get at the theme or the main idea, but her style was so deeply open to subtlety, and somehow so understanding and forgiving of pathology without ever flinching in the face of destructiveness, that we have to be willing to search for the very important and often quite original ideas embedded in the writing.

She had a beautiful soft Scottish burr and seemed very lady-like. Yet I do remember our very first clinical seminar in 1962 when she showed the things that her little girl patient had done with the pig and other animals, and told us how she spoke to her of her "little pig part", as being an absolute revelation: that, of course, was nothing compared to what was to come. She could talk about the most savage of feelings and doings in our patients without batting an eye or losing the gentleness in her voice – except when she rowed with Sarah Rosenfeld of the Anna Freud (then Hampstead) Clinic about the issue of whether babies were born object-related or not; then I remember her showing her teeth and us seeing a certain ferocity in her passion).

There was something about her wisdom and understanding and forgivingness which always balanced her judgments. When my under-five training case, a little girl named Lara, was due to terminate, she got the chicken pox, and missed her last two weeks of treatment. I was very upset, and wanted to offer more sessions to make them up after she recovered. Mattie pointed out that was perhaps the only way she could end: Lara had been, and up to a point still was, a very controlling little girl. And Mattie felt we needed to respect that. (I think I persuaded her to let me see the child for one last goodbye session.)

She was of course a demon for work; you could be having the most intense of conversations about psychoanalysis or Shakespeare or politics, and all the while she would be weeding between the paving stones at the farm.

Her papers offer the same sense of abundance. They can sometimes be frustrating because of the lack of clear conclusions but yet they are full of ideas. To take one shining and typical example, "Some notes on maternal containment in 'good enough' mothering" (Harris, 1975b). It does a brilliant job of linking up the Bick concept of maternal "containment" with Winnicott's "good enough mother" (Bick, 1968; Winnicott, 1960). It identifies some important constituents of containment which can lie within the range of good enough mothering. She does this through the medium of two wonderfully detailed and moving infant observations, and then some clinical work with a disturbed mother. Both concepts – that of maternal containment, and that of good enough mothering – are getting filled in, but although the theoretical introduction is very clear, the paper's conclusion gets so interested in the details of the cases that the theoretical point gets forgotten. Actually, to be more precise, she is so bent on encouraging the reader to study the details, that she is by now less interested in the theory. Yet we do get to see how much of the two theories are being filled in, and how we dare not be simplistic in our thinking about the two. The material allows us to infer that one of the mothers is more "good enough" than the other who is somewhat burdened by depression, but Mattie's incapacity to be judgmental doesn't even let her say that. But we do definitely get shown the difference in two ways of being good enough.

As I said, she simply cannot think in headlines; and so unlike Bick and Meltzer, her theoretical statements can go unnoticed. One example, just tucked away and almost invisible (p. 141) is the distinction between Bick's (1968) and Bion's (1962) concepts of containment. I wrote a paper about this a few years ago (Alvarez, 1998), and I wish I'd re-read this paper of Mattie's, because she'd already said it!

To come to the material on the two babies, Charles and Anthea. Although Charles's mother was very experienced and loving, the reader gradually becomes aware that she did tend to put him back down into his cot after almost every feed, and unlike with Anthea's mother, there was little holding of him in order to play with him or simply to chat to or comfort him. Yet, although Mattie does contrast Charles's mother's sense of being burdened (three other young children, no grandparents alive, and a concern about stirring too much jealousy in the other children), at no point does she comment on these lacks in Charles's mother's behaviour. She does discuss, however, the level of observational detail of the baby himself that shows Charles' tendency to startle and fall apart, and his gradual development of ways of holding himself together physically. Even before he was weaned, he always seemed to be having to concentrate hard on sucking, always somehow working hard at things.

Mattie also compares the way Anthea burrows into her mother's chest with Charles's burying himself in his cot. In fact, it is interesting how important the details of his interaction with his cot become to the reader, but still Mattie doesn't underline the comparison. She simply isn't in to mother-bashing, although she does discuss the way Anthea's mother is so interested in, indeed fascinated by, her baby's personality and capacity to teach her parents how to be parents. But even here, there is no simplistic comparison of the mothers; she points out that in spite of Anthea's mother's responsiveness, she has warned the observer that she has her limits: that, after a particularly and unusually difficult day with Anthea, she doesn't know what she would have done last night if the baby hadn't finally slept and let her sleep too. In other words, Mattie suggests that this mother was also simply lucky in the good fit between herself and her baby.

I now want to turn to the theoretical contributions which as I say are not included in the conclusion, but are actually there in the paper. She begins by telling us about

> the prerequisite for mental growth of a primary maternal object who can be an adequate container for the infant's personality, the "good enough" mother about whom Winnicott has written (1965). Detailed study of interaction between individual mothers and infants may help us to formulate better the quality that underlies this quantitative differentiation; the constitutuents that make for that "good enough" (Harris, 1975b, p. 140).

She then emphasizes the importance of recognition of the uniqueness of each relationship and perhaps the importance of fit. She then moves seamlessly and brilliantly from Klein on the epistomephilic instinct to Bion on the containment and reverie that enable the infant to feel understood as well as comforted (Klein, 1921; Bion, 1962). Then she tells us that Bick looked at containment from another point of view – the baby's need for an object which can hold the parts of the personality together, which as I say (Alvarez, 1998) is very different from Bion's concept. She then adds: "Faulty development of this primal containing or 'skin' function may arise from defects in the object, or from phantasy attacks which impair the integrated (and therefore integrating) form in which it is introjected into the infant" (p. 141). The latter is the more familiar Kleinian formulation, but note the former: she is speaking of *defects in the object*. I have been writing for some while now about deficit in the object, and ways in which therapists may learn to repair such deficits in internal objects of their patients, but I had not realized Mattie had used this term so boldly so long ago!

Later, in a discussion of Anthea's baby, there are fascinating comments on the baby's partial internalization of the containing mother, and of the moment when Anthea runs out of steam and needs the real thing. Then, we get a fascinating list of some constituents in an internalized good container:

> The baby continues to show considerable capacity to find or re-create a good internal object. This has different qualities. First there is the holding, the hand on the head re-creating the function of the mother who keeps the baby's person together, while the bad stuff – the flatus – is expelled. Then there is the quality of filling the emptiness, the reminder of the nipple in the thumb which is perceived as "coming" to her aid at a moment of acute distress, as if it were the agent of an internalized object in advance of the baby's own conscious control. (p. 156)

(See examples of such benignly active superegos in dreams in Al Alvarez' book on *Night*, 1994.) Here, Mattie seems to be seeing the thumb not as a part of the self, but as beginning to be identified with an object full of otherness which can act independently of the self. When eventually the baby turns to the mother as an external object and is given the breast, she sucks heartily. Then, fortified by this experience of taking in the mother with mouth, eyes and ears, she turns to take in details of the wider world around her, one at a time, in the same wholehearted and intense fashion. It is interesting that in the final discussion, Mattie ends with the following two sentences:

> Charles in these early weeks is a baby who is – and seems to have to be – more preoccupied with survival, with holding himself together. Anthea shows evidence, at the same stage of her life, of internalizing a maternal object upon which she can rely for some containment of her distress; and although

alert and interested in her surroundings, she is already less totally dependent upon them. (p. 162)

Mattie had told us earlier in the discussion that Charles "tended to look more integrated when attracted and held by the impingement of external sensory stimuli – the light, the sound of the clock ticking, the points of touch – and to disintegrate when these are removed" (p. 161). What an interesting distinction between ways of being interested in external reality – i.e. whether one is very dependent on it, or simply finding it interesting. A fascinating distinction, and, as I hope I have illustrated, only one among many in this extraordinarily rich paper.

CHAPTER TWENTY-FOUR

Baptism under fire: finding my feet as a child psychotherapist

Caroline Gluckman

I was interested to read that Don had described how for Mattie the child psychotherapy course was a "baby" equivalent to her own family. I know that from my earliest contact with her there was a sense of being in something like a relationship to a good parent, a good but firm mother, who expected things of you but who was hugely generous and accepting. Becoming one of Mattie's tutees did feel like being accepted into the family where to some extent it was up to you whether you sank or swam – but where one did not feel criticized in any negative sense and there was room for all sorts. I have heard Mattie use the analogy of a garden – and I believe she was a keen gardener – where her approach was not to pull out the weeds but to put in so many flowers that the weeds did not have much of a chance, letting the plants, so to speak, sort themselves out. I must admit, as a gardener myself and thinking about how tough some weeds can be, I was not so sure whether this liberal approach would succeed. The evidence from our training, however, was that reliance on self-selection seemed to work. I recall that a couple of people did drop out over the years having made their own decisions that the course was not for them.

I am sure Mattie tried to treat all her "children" equally and discouraged competitiveness and sibling rivalry. The fact is, I did feel lucky to have Mattie as my tutor and pleased also that one of my good friends was also one of her tutees. We were given to understand that one of the reasons for her taking us on was that we were both pregnant and this undoubtedly added to that sense of Mattie taking a parental, maternal role as well as a teaching one. I remember this as a happy time during the training and have visions of myself and Evanthe (Blandy, then Piper) sitting in one of her seminars with big tummies and being invited to put our feet up while we considered a presentation. It was a good marriage of the relaxed and the serious, of nurturing and responsibility, which encouraged an attitude of learning in the group.

The friendliness was apparent too at the summer picnics which took place at Mersea. I can still see Mattie and Don, hand in hand, walking up from the beach. I was there with my two small children, the "tummy" having turned into a baby boy. I probably felt a bit shy being there with my family, but again it turned out to be a lovely occasion with large quantities of marvellous food.

Mattie was not all soft and certainly not sentimental. I remember once being in a supervision with her when her phone rang and I heard her discussing a possible candidate for the CP training. I understood that the caller was an analyst who was trying to convince Mattie that she should accept the candidate. She was not to be persuaded and firmly stood her ground. I was impressed.

I tend to associate Mattie and her influence more with younger children partly because she did supervise my under-five training case, a little boy who had suffered some strange fits and had a phobia of masks. Her supervisions were always helpful and never persecuting, and the young boy quickly lost his phobia and made good progress in exploring his ambivalent relationship to his mother.

I eventually qualified in 1982 and managed to get my first job which was to work part-time as a psychotherapist in a special school. In those days it was called a school for "maladjusted" children, a title which really does date it. It was in fact a boarding school in Berkshire, an all-girls school, for girls from London boroughs. It was my first experience of working in a school, other than a nursery, and it was a novel experience also to be involved in a boarding school, very far from my own experience. It was not an entirely happy time. The task of trying to do therapy in the school setting was not easy. Gathering together a large group of disturbed children and adolescents under one roof posed particular difficulties. I was given a room to work in but had no means of protecting the space from intruders until I was given a key and henceforth had to lock the door when I was in session. Even then, it was not always possible to protect my own space and that of the child when there were present in the community of the school a few youngsters hell-bent on causing problems. Bion's work on the basic assumptions of the group made absolute sense in this context. One of my most frightening experiences was when one of the more destructive girls/parts managed to get into my room with some acolytes and succeeded in getting a blanket over my head so that I thought briefly that I was not going to be able to breathe. I had absolutely no control over the destructive invasion until one of the gang herself obviously got cold feet and called the attack to a stop. For a moment it really had felt like life or death. It was a grim moment.

Around this time, and no doubt wanting to keep some contact with my training school and with colleagues who might continue to help me understand and deal with work issues such as my encounter with the acting out adolescents at school, I got the opportunity to join a baby observation group that was going to be run by Mattie. The idea of the group was to give some of us now qualified child psychotherapists with a particular interest in baby observation a chance to have a second experience. At Mattie's suggestion we were to follow just two babies over a period of two years, meeting weekly as is the custom on the M7 observation course. I did not myself observe a second baby but had the luxury of being able to follow the story of the two babies as presented by two colleagues who took turns to bring material. I have found an account I wrote towards the end of the observation in response to a request from Mattie to try and think about the experience. When I look now at what I wrote then, in March 1984, it strikes me as a piece written rather like an observation in itself – an observation of an observation, not particularly sophisticated or theoretical but a down-to-earth account of what it was like, reminding me too of some of the difficulties of that first job when I was newly qualified. I include this piece un-edited:

Some thoughts on attending a second baby observation: March 1984

There are perhaps some parallels with any repeated experience – less of a sense of novelty but a gain in terms of understanding and insight. Most people found the second seminar a much more enjoyable experience than the first one and there are similarities to a second child – a more relaxed process free of earlier anxieties.

The first observation is undertaken as an initial step, as an introduction to psychoanalytically oriented observation, in many ways a beginning. This was the one seminar I attended in the pre-clinical phase for which I developed a strong feeling I should like to have another go at later on with the benefit of increased experience and knowledge, with more personal analysis under my belt.

Following two babies as we did in the second seminar proved enjoyable because it gave us the chance to get to know each baby really well. I can remember some feeling in the earlier larger group where everyone was presenting and all wanting help, anxiety about not being able to present frequently enough, and perhaps some possessiveness about the babies. One of the joys in being part of the group but not doing the actual observation is the freedom simply to think about the material.

The gap of some six or seven years between observation groups is important in terms of personal development. Hopefully it is a more mature, adult group of people less liable to project into the baby or parent being observed with a greater capacity for thought and space to receive the experience.

I have found the second observation particularly helpful in dealing with deprived children. The seminar coincided with my first year of work in a school for maladjusted girls where for the first time I came close to deprived children en masse. Having the seminar run currently with my experience at the school of seeing a series of quite deprived and needy children one after another was helpful.

In the seminar we had witnessed the initial difficult and cut off relationship between baby Lucy and her mother, which gave rise to some theoretical discussion about the meaning of the absent object and primitive bodily/emotional states – all highly relevant to deprived children. We could see baby Lucy searching for an object to latch on to at this stage before any sense of an internal space had been established. In her case, this shifted fairly rapidly at about six weeks, assisted by the arrival in the family of a young nanny.

In the school, I feel I am surrounded by children who have never satisfactorily achieved this all-important internal space and have compensated in various ways. For example, there is Susie, an eleven-year-old, to whom Mrs Bick's invaluable article on "The experience of the skin in early object relations" (1968) is painfully relevant. This girl is operating at a very primitive level with little sense of an internal space for good objects with the result that she alternately latches on like glue – such as, obstinately refusing to go when I say it is time, or spilling out in a totally uncontained way, causing havoc around her; turning things upside down in my room, or running out of class rooms or the school grounds. Her uncontained state of mind was vividly illustrated recently when twice in one day she managed to get to the bathroom where she turned the taps on full force, seriously flooding the top floor. In the seminar we were thinking about Bion's formulation of the containing aspects of maternal reverie, and of course the consequences of its absence. This helped me to view Susie as a such a baby thrashing around helplessly, although faced with this degree of lack of integration and containment I find myself wondering if this child, despite the understanding and structure she now receives from myself and others in the school, has sufficient internal resources to pull herself together as baby Lucy managed to do in her second month of life when help arrived in the form of the young nanny.

Review

Re-reading this account of the second baby observation seminar opens up quite a flood of memories about that time in my life when I was starting out in my new career as a child psychotherapist, sometimes wondering as I set out on my journey west to the school if I might not just drive on past the turning. Did I really want to engage with all these troubled young people? Somewhere in my head, I have no doubt, was a bit of Mattie who was quite uncompromising in her conviction that of course I should and indeed would get on with the job.

I do wonder looking back over well over 20 years how to evaluate the work of the school and how I would handle the situation now. Undoubtedly attitudes in society have changed: the idea of skimming off a layer of disturbed youngsters and gathering them all together far from home and familiar things is not current accepted practice. In certain respects the school did, however, achieve. The girls tended to get on better with the adults around them and there was some academic progress. There was less success laterally: relationships between the girls were harder to shift. I could not see all the girls in the school, relying on teachers to indicate which youngsters they wished me to concentrate on. No doubt this factor fed into the hotbed of sibling rivalry that simmered away never far below the surface. I understood that extracting a child from a classroom in order to visit the "therapy lady" could stir up rivalry and distrustful curiosity. It was a constant struggle to protect a thinking space.

The image of flowers and weeds often came to mind. The school itself was set in pleasant rural surroundings. There was an attractive well-kept garden with woods beyond. I was aware that several of the girls found the view and idea of these woods quite frightening rather than beautiful. They were used to an urban environment and did not automatically take to the countryside.

Perhaps the thick trees which surrounded the school looked dark and foreboding, a place of hidden danger. I certainly had to struggle many times to remind myself of the potential for "flowering" in all the girls I saw, even the most acting-out. I knew that almost without exception these girls had suffered environmental failure, that from early on they had been strewn, so to speak, into barren ground where weeds did have the field.

I was helped in my thinking in my new job not only by the baby observation seminar but by two papers written by Mattie: one concerning work in schools and the other the role of the individual in a group. The 1968 paper, "Consultation project in a comprehensive school", contained some useful ideas about working as a non-teacher in a school. Part of my role in the boarding school was to attend staff meetings once a week and I immediately recognized Mattie's own experience where she recounts the different responses of the staff to her presence. She describes the initial reaction as ranging from one of "perfunctory politeness covering hostility towards yet another chore, another person to keep happy, or the resentful 'Who is this trying to teach me my job?' – to a very warm welcome and interest" (1968b, p. 323).

The sense of "them" and "us" was perhaps even stronger in a boarding school where the staff spent so much of their time, even academic staff doing overnight duty at regular intervals. I became aware of some tension too between academic and care staff, a tendency to hierarchical splits with consequent loss of focus on the children in question. The psychoanalytic training generally primes us to watch for splitting factors in relationships but it was helpful for me in those early days to hear it spelt out in a setting similar to the one in which I found myself, where the aim to allow for equal consideration in staff discussions to all views was accepted by all in theory but in practice could prove difficult. As the most obvious "outsider" to the staff group I found myself on several occasions used as a sort of confidant outside the meeting. Some of the feelings between staff which could not be addressed openly within the group were revealed to me outside in the corridor or the car park. If I felt the issue needed more considered attention I decided that I would offer consultation time to individual staff members as well as the girls. Inevitably sometimes personal matters blew in to discussions and I think it was helpful to provide space for that if need be. It was quite a relief to read that Mattie and her colleagues had also struggled with complex dynamics and not taken a rigid stance in their methods of responding.

The 1978 paper on "The individual in the group" was helpful at this time in drawing attention, as I understood it, to the tension between a need to have the security of one's training, colleagues, supervisors, psychoanalytic literature, to hold on to all that and try and digest it, together with a desire to identify and develop one's own mind and thinking. Mattie here describes "the pressures of the group and the thrust of the individual for development" (1978b, p. 26) as a constant theme in Bion's work and one close to her heart. It is of course an on-going tension but of particular import in the immediate post-qualification period. Undoubtedly I experienced some sense of relief when I recognized a description from a senior colleague of a difficult clinical situation. I know I did need reassurance and I think that may be a necessary basis from which more adventurous thinking can take place.

Bion's thinking about groups, specifically of group mentality and the emergence of basic assumptions, had a bearing for me in relation to another school experience. Having worked in the school for a year or more it was suggested by the headmaster that I run a group with some of the older girls as a way of trying to increase the number who might benefit from my particular form of work. It was decided that I should have a co-therapist, a young male teacher who was interested, and we had six adolescent girls picked out for our group. Even having, as I thought, absorbed some of Bion's ideas about different kinds of basic assumption such as fight/flight that can characterize a group, I was not entirely prepared for the intensity of the hostility which was rapidly directed towards me. I clearly became seen as a bad object – in my mind a bad maternal object – who had to be attacked and there was very little resistance or hesitation from any of the six girls, much to the distress of my male co-therapist. Indeed I remember spending time after the meetings reassuring him that the girls' reactions were not unexpected and could be used to help us understand deep-rooted problems. I think we managed half a dozen meetings before the teacher declared he did not wish to participate any longer because he found it too disturbing.

Mattie comments in this article that "baptism under fire at some point is an essential part of the development of a child psychotherapist" (p. 37) and I have no doubt that for me these experiences in my first job at the special school were such a point. I must admit it was with some relief that after two and a half years in the school I started another job at a "proper" clinic where boundaries were much more secure and the attitude of staff less ambivalent. But my school experience stood me in good stead and my ongoing contact with Mattie through the seminar was hugely supportive.

There is a small post-script to the school time and my thinking about flowers and weeds. When I left the school I was able to arrange to continue seeing one particularly difficult girl in the clinic for a period of time. The room I worked in there had a table outside the door which had a few plants on it which received erratic attention and could look wilted. Shelly, the adolescent I was seeing, one day tutted as she passed the table and picked up one of the drooping plants, bringing it into our room. To my amazement she ticked me off for neglect and spent the whole session busily re-potting and watering the plant. I felt guilty about the neglect but also hugely touched that this tough, difficult girl had allowed herself to display a softer and more hopeful self. I felt Mattie would be nodding her head with approval as though to say "You see, it can happen!"

CHAPTER TWENTY-FIVE

On becoming a psychotherapist

Margot Waddell

My own training as a child psychotherapist, indeed, the route whereby I eventually "became one", is inextricably related to the role that Martha Harris played in my life at the time. The tale that follows is therefore inevitably an idiosyncratic one. I first met Martha Harris in 1971. I had not yet completed my PhD on the work of the 19th century novelist George Eliot and had become deeply demoralized not only by the ardours of the scholarship itself, but also by the suicidal desperation of so many of my peers. They were among the brightest, the most interesting, most radical, and most unusual of their Cambridge generation. Yet for some the local mental hospital, Fulbourne, tended to beckon and, despite the enlightened psychiatric regime that presided there, a few did actually, shockingly, tragically, die. Others died in car crashes, or war zones as did Jimmy in Biafra, a beloved medical student and friend. But these were extreme times: privileged, political, angry, liberated, it was an age of marching, pamphleteering, acting, guitar-playing alongside the highest standards of work.

These were values, qualities and activities which remain so alive in my mind today.

One day, I was bewailing to a fellow student the psychological plight of such an apparently blessed generation of youngsters, myself included. Tamsin's disposition was more practical than mine: "You probably shouldn't be here at all. Why not think in terms of training at the Institute of Psychoanalysis in London", she said. "But it's very difficult to get in there if you have an arts degree. Ideally you should be a doctor. Why don't you go and talk to my godfather in the clinic in London where he works? It's called the Tavistock, and it specializes in children and adolescents. You might find it interesting."

I rang up the person she mentioned, John Bowlby, and made an appointment to meet him. Little did I know at the time that John Bowlby was the foremost proponent of attachment theory and was writing about *Childcare and the Growth of Love*: the adverse impact of separating mothers and children during the first two years of life. Committed as I was to contemporary feminist issues, I would not have taken to this position. But I did take to him. Within twenty minutes or so, as I remember it, of talking to this warm, kindly, intelligent, thoughtful man, he suggested that I pop up the corridor and speak to his colleague, Mrs Martha Harris. Publicly, and theoretically, they were at daggers drawn. Privately, and impressively, they were good friends. As I left his room, he said that if I did ever come to the Clinic and wanted a godfather-like person to talk to, I should feel that I could rely on him. And so, in due course, I did. And he always was utterly available and, indeed, reliable.

So, I went ahead and knocked on that door. I was invited in by a woman who seemed to me at once so strong yet, I felt, verbally hesitant and also vulnerable. She spoke with the distinct accent of the Scottish borders and I immediately took to her.

The only part of the subsequent conversation that I remember in any detail was of Mattie, as I later came to know her, asking, rather sceptically, what I knew about psychology. What was my degree? When I told her that I had spent the previous three years researching George Eliot's intellectual milieu in relation to her novels, she said, with typical forthrightness: "Oh well, there's nothing much that academic psychology can teach you then. We'll just have to fix up an informal-type link with a Cambridge psychologist to clear your credentials and then you can begin the training". PhD and much else as yet unfinished, that is what I did. I moved to London; took a job working with disturbed adolescents; began analysis and, in a sense, the rest is history.

Except, of course, nothing is ever history. For what I didn't then know was that that interview with Martha Harris, in a small room on the second floor of the Tavistock Clinic, London NW3, was to change my way of thinking forever. Until then, conventional academic qualifications had ruled the day, especially in a world that undervalued women's education and put up markers that few could achieve. Slowly, I began to realize that psychodynamic training required quite other things: not so much the kind of intellectual abilities that I had, up to that point, been struggling after in the course of my formal education, but rather, certain capacities, hard won by dint of a very different kind of work.

It took me a long time – years and years – to discover the nature of that work. I remember asking Mrs Harris, in the very early days, what was meant by the term "introjective identification". "You'll discover in due course", she said, as I thought, at the time, annoyingly gnomically. I wanted answers. "It's not an easy notion to define, unless you've felt it on the pulses", she said, also, to me, gnomically annoying. Never properly having studied English, or indeed anything, at school except Latin and Greek, I did not recognise the allusion to Keats's letters, a rich vein of wisdom that I was yet to discover in Mrs Harris's fortnightly seminars on Personality Development. Unbeknownst to me then, those seminars were to provide the infrastructure for much that was to shape the rest of my personal and professional life. The style of teaching was passionate, and, more especially, evocative – far from the didactic mode to which I was accustomed, even in thrall to. Her style was less about conventional "knowledge" than about wisdom – a distinction that so struck me in the course of one of Bion's lectures that I attended in 1979. One cannot see the wisdom for the knowledge, he said – about the noise of conflicting and competing psychoanalytic theories.

I can only think that what happened to me was that I came upon something of the process of introjective identification as having been taking place when, newly appointed to a post at the Tavistock, I was, perforce, having to carry on as a staff member in the wake of Mattie's terrible and, as it turned out, irrecoverable car crash. I was required to take over her teaching – beginning with Personality Development. This course I taught for many years, having prematurely had to grow up and take my place in the adult world of teaching and training, when, in reality, I knew that I myself still had everything to learn. In those early, anxious days, I found myself able to draw on so much that I didn't even know that I knew. For there were things that, as it turned out, I did "know" from her. Projective identification can be spotted at the time. The introjective version was, as Mattie so rightly said, only discoverable as having been taking place over longer stretches of time. It depends on a path of inner change of a kind so wisely and truly noted by George Eliot in *Middlemarch* in terms of "the secret motion of a watch hand" (1985, p. 226).

One of the things that Mattie said during the early days of Personality Development stuck in my mind with the force of recognition: the kind of "unthought known" described by Kit Bollas. It is a recognition that somehow throws everything into place. She commented that, given the extraordinary complexities of early development, as understood by psychoanalysts, psychologists and child psychotherapists, the strangest thing is that anyone gets through it at all. Later I discovered, and wholly agreed with, a similar thought articulated by Freud in the context of adolescence. Yet this was a matter of great interest to Mattie, as to me. How is it that, given the pressures, the casualties, the deprivations of all ordinary human life, most people, willy nilly, do, in their way, get through?

In fact, being in many ways a late developer, as she once described me, even at this stage, now in post, I was riven with doubt as to whether I had, in fact, "got through". Her description of me was in response to, at one point, my being held back a year in the training. Fearful of the answer, I nonetheless eventually asked "Why?" Mattie replied with the resonant sentence, never forgotten, "Development runs unevenly." Perhaps this related to my impetuosity in going to her after a year of Klein theory seminars. I announced that I simply couldn't understand Klein and that I should probably leave the training. It all sounded so mad, I said. She persuaded me not to, urging me simply to wait, to work with the children and then see. I did work and, with time, I did see.

My uncertainty about ever having actually qualified remained however and was based, among other things, on the fact that, being so panicked about committing my soul, as opposed to my mind, to paper – as I saw it – I had never managed to write a qualifying paper at all. The only straw that I had hung onto for ten years since that cop-out was Mattie calling over the wall of the adjoining loo in the Adolescent Department, "Oh by the way, you will be qualifying this summer." No ceremony then, no certificate – or had I lost it?

Never convinced, anonymously I finally rang Burgh House – then the ACP HQ – to ask if they had on their list of qualified Child Psychotherapists someone called Margot Waddell. "Oh yes" was the reply, "she qualified a decade ago." Incredibly relieved, I then set out to try, belatedly, to "earn" that qualification, to write in a different register from the past and to impart something of the immense wisdom gleaned from my early years of training. There began a never-ending road, a never-ending inside story and I have Mattie to thank for opening my eyes to the nature of that endeavour.

Treading in her footsteps, I began thinking about development not primarily cognitively, nor behaviourally, nor in terms of theories of child development or social adaptation, but emotionally, psychically, in terms of the inside story, a story that I first encountered in those early seminars. There I began to understand something of a "psychoanalytic attitude". That picture is one that puts the emphasis on the complex relationship between internal states and external tasks; on capacities rather than abilities; with the stress always on what an experience means to a person.

By the time that, at Mattie's behest, I attended a two-day summer seminar with Wilfred Bion (Bion having been invited by her to visit London from Los Angeles in the late 70s) I was just about ready properly to "cross-over". The "crossing" was to be of enormous significance to my own development. It was from what I later came to realize was an attitude of mind that needed to know "about" things to one that was willing and available to "learn from experience"; willing to be able to engage with experience "first hand" rather than simply sticking to the more cautious approach to life through second-hand ideas; willing, in Wordsworth's words, "to work and to be wrought upon" (*The Prelude*, XIV.103).

CHAPTER TWENTY-SIX

Remembering Mattie

Alessandra Piontelli

It is difficult to speak of Mattie as just a teacher. Mattie was indeed a fantastic teacher, one of my best ever, but she was also a dearest friend, a motherly figure, a deeply humane person and much more.

We met in the early 70s, when I had just graduated in Medicine, and was specializing in Neurology and Psychiatry. We were both going through very difficult times. Mattie's beloved first husband had recently died, and the pain for the loss was almost unbearable. She and Don Meltzer were not yet together. I was in my early twenties and already going through a rocky divorce while having to bring up a young child almost totally alone.

I don't know what the age-gap between us was, but age difference didn't seem to matter and we both immediately felt at ease talking about our lives. Our deep friendship started then and continued until she died.

Mattie supervised my first two infant observations and three years later, when I was living in London, the psychotherapy of a latency child.

During the early and mid 70s Mattie travelled frequently to Italy, lecturing and giving private and public supervisions. After presenting some of my observations in public, we decided to have private supervisions as well.

Soon after I started travelling periodically to England in order to have more frequent supervisions, especially as I also intended to move to London with my young son.

Mattie was still living in her house in Lancaster Grove, and I was often her guest. Despite being exceedingly busy and overworked, she found the time for cooking, sewing, embroidering, knitting, and for looking after her garden and house-plants. Mattie sewed many of her own clothes. Italians are almost by definition fashion-conscious, and Mattie was not stylish in a proper sense. Yet I found her flowery comfortable outfits particularly elegant and fitting for her tall, imposing figure.

All these extra activities helped to take her mind off the many tasks and demands of the day. The conservatory in her home was amazingly beautiful. I don't have green fingers, but still have some plants of a particular kind of geranium that have a very pleasant fragrance. She gave them to me for my mother, and now that my mother is no more the plants are well and alive on my desk.

After the supervisions, we used to spend time talking about everything, from matters of life to the changes in the Tavi that particularly concerned her.

Needless to say Mattie was extremely helpful, affectionate, and encouraging. By the time I was living in London in the mid-70s I had a job at the Tavi, and it wasn't long before I became part of its teaching staff.

I will always be grateful to Mattie for all she did for me and for trusting me from the start.

Mattie always wanted me to have "the best". She introduced me to Mrs Bick who was no longer taking on private supervisions on a regular basis. Mrs Bick accepted to supervise my young child case and another strong and affectionate relationship was formed. Both Mattie and Nusia (Mrs Bick) were particularly eager to find a suitable second husband for me, and they discussed all the possible candidates. In the end none was ever "good-enough" for me! Nusia loved Mattie, but was worried about her being overworked, and did not like the expansion of the Tavi.

Curiously, both Mattie and Mrs Bick somehow encouraged me not to drop my "scientific", medical side, but to foster it along with my psychoanalytic-psychotherapeutic-observational training.

At first, I was rather taken aback and took their remarks to mean I was not a "good-enough" therapist. Years later when I did go back to Medicine, their words made me feel less isolated and appreciate even more their deep and unique open-mindedness. Mattie and Mrs Bick were clearly devoted to psychoanalysis to which they dedicated all their lives, yet they could also foresee that psychoanalysis needed constant development. As Mattie often said, "Words and concepts can become so over-used as to lose any meaning. Vogue kills thought." She was very open to contributions coming from other disciplines, especially the arts in general, but also from various branches of science. Nevertheless, she did not like wild speculations. Given my particular background we often discussed this. She thought that psychoanalysts had to remain such, albeit open to other thinkers equally deeply involved in their particular fields. Cross-fertilization had to be done carefully, and respectfully, not speculatively or superficially. As she said, "This can only be damaging to psychoanalysis. A neurologist" (by then I was one) "will never listen to the babblings of a psychoanalyst pretending to be one. He or she will only think that psychoanalysis is not a serious discipline or anyway not grounded on any evidence."

In my medical work, I continue to be deeply influenced by the rigorous observational approach both she and Nusia taught me. Still later, when I started working as a doctor in developing countries, I was greatly helped in approaching all sorts of different cultures by the psychoanalytic methodology they had both fostered me to develop.

Coming back to less personal matters. What kind of supervisor was Mattie?

At first, I was rather shocked. While I was reading my first observation that I had typed in detail for her, I had the impression that Mattie had fallen asleep! Yet, a few minutes later Mattie seemed to wake up and came back with a totally fresh, stimulating and exciting point of view. In due time I became accustomed to Mattie's apparent "naps" and began to view them as a sort of state of "reverie" in which she occasionally plunged to better comprehend the patient's as well as the analyst's state of mind.

Besides her apparent (and only occasionally real) "naps" Mattie was often silent and apparently self-absorbed for a long time while listening to the material and taking it in. Then she suddenly came back almost towards the end of the supervision with some brilliant interpretation which gave a profound new meaning to the whole session/observation.

In this sense Mattie was a deeply "Bionian" supervisor. Bion (1962), as is well-known, called maternal "reverie" the process through which the mother internalizes the experiences of the infant, gives them a meaning and finally returns them to the infant thus making it possible for this latter to develop a reflective capacity enabling it to comprehend its states of mind. Mattie thought of Bion as an indisputable genius. However, her reverie stemmed exclusively from her temperament, not from a theoretical background.

Though Mattie was deeply "maternal" during her supervisions, she was far from being wholly acquiescent. If something was "wrong" she could be quite firm. Her "no" never left me feeling humiliated or angry. I always thought she was just right!

Despite being a Kleinian, Mattie seldom used what is considered the typically concrete "Kleinian" terminology. For instance, bad and good breasts were seldom mentioned. On the other hand, "Kleinian" feelings were taken into serious account. The accent on envy and gratitude was especially pronounced.

In this sense, Mattie differed profoundly from Don (also my supervisor) who used concrete language abundantly.

Mattie made use of the countertransference. She always asked as first question what I felt. However, as compared to other Kleinians, her work was not based on a minute and careful examination of the countertransference, but on a broader picture of the mood of the session. Her interpretations – be it observations or sessions – were targeted towards the patient or the observed subject more than the relationship between the analyst/observer and the subject.

Mattie also looked for the strengths rather than the weaknesses in patients, thus fostering ego-functions other than regression. This attitude, amongst others, probably stemmed from her attitude towards life largely based on resilience, generosity, and vitality.

Since the analytic cases she supervised were mostly children, she thought that contact with the parents was necessary. With the latency case, I met the parents once per term, but was available for extra contacts if necessity arose. Once adolescence set in, contact was avoided save in extreme circumstances when some kind of real danger for the patient was involved. In that case, the patient was usually told.

In the infant observations, she tended to identify with the infant and focus on its feelings, somewhat more than on those of the mother. Being a young, divorced mother, I was in tune with maternal anxieties perhaps more than the average student. Mattie noticed that and commented on my comprehensible anxieties. She added that the majority of students tended to identify with the baby and its helplessness, a condition that according to her we continued to try to avoid throughout life. However from then on my personal anxieties were shared too!

Another feature of Mattie's thought always struck me. Due to her particular sensitivity, Mattie had a kind of foresight. This was evident during the supervisions of the sessions. If I had not picked up some relevant aspect, the patient regularly came back the following session bringing exactly the kind of material Mattie had commented upon.

Her "foresight" was even more evident in the supervision of the infant observations, and especially so in retrospect.

The first "babies" supervised by her are now well over thirty, and, albeit not on a regular basis, I have kept in touch with them. Each time I see them, I am struck by Mattie's accuracy in foreseeing the kind of young men they could have become.

One, I will call him A, was a flabby baby, with a passive, gentle temperament. His mother, a woman in her early twenties, was apparently affectionate and gentle, so much so that one could have considered her an "ideal mother". She could also be considered the ideal spouse, as she followed many of the principles in vogue in the 50s acting as the "perfect" housewife.

Mattie helped me to see behind the idealized façade. Mattie was alien to idealization and although she could pick the best in all, she was also very down to earth, and showed a great experience in life including its less pleasant aspects.

This young mother displayed a general tendency to be silently domineering. For instance, she overfed A and teased him with clearly "castrating" remarks. Soon A came to look like a Chinese Buddha, with a huge belly, never protesting or crying and perennially smiling. His genitals were invisible under the layers of his bulging tummy and his mother often commented on that laughingly. Besides that Mrs A had the propensity to never leave him alone even for a second, to look intrusively at the tiniest folds of his skin, and to inspect closely all his orifices and holes. One had the impression that A could not have any "private parts". He gave in passively to all sorts of intrusions. His mother was clearly not a "bad mother", far from it, but she was a silently domineering one.

Her husband was never present, and despite their not florid economic condition, he often disappeared for expensive holidays abroad. Mrs A never complained, and expressed very traditional ideas about male-female roles. Women had to cook, stay at home, and look after the children. Men by being the breadwinners were allowed all the freedom and the fun, including possibly philandering. Her "traditional" view of men contained unspoken elements of anger, envy, and of spitefulness. In the end, her husband was regarded as a little child with no responsibilities and no desire to act like an adult, responsible person.

Mattie envisaged for A a future of conformity and dependence on his family and particularly on his mother as well as a general passivity and difficulty in forming ties with girls.

He followed exactly this pattern making me appreciate the predictive value of infant observation as well as Mattie's analytical capacities.

Only in adolescence did A make a weak and tentative attempt to rebel by declaring that he wanted to enrol in the navy as this was "a manly profession". His wish was soon "castrated" by his mother.

He enrolled in what was considered a typically "feminine" university and continued to live at home. His mother bought him a huge dog that he used to take for walks in front of my house. I never saw any girl around.

However Mattie could not have foreseen how even the most traditional women could change. When in her forties Mrs A's husband divorced her and married a much younger girl. By then the finances of the family had become rather florid.

The change in Mrs A was incredible. One day I met her in the street, and could hardly recognize her. She had clearly undergone extensive plastic surgery, changed her hairstyle and was behaving "sexy". Soon I was to see her going around with other men.

Clearly all her pent up envy and rage were surfacing. She was now determined to be a "modern" woman, at least superficially.

Soon after A was allowed to go and live alone in a flat in the same house where his mother lived. When I met him again he was with his first girlfriend who looked exactly like his mother when he was a young child. Only this girl was openly domineering and he followed her round like a passive, domesticated animal. Soon he married her. As for work, he chose to be employed by his father.

Many other details of this observation could be discussed, but certainly, my first infants made me believe that a lot could be gathered about their future by the careful observation of their present.

Mattie and I had a project of writing all this up, but this was before the accident that made the last years of her life an agony. Up to now I have been unable to go back to it.

CHAPTER TWENTY-SEVEN

Personal recollections of learning from Mattie Harris

Pamela Sorensen

Certain memories carry more than personal narrative because they illustrate shifts in awareness that open new kinds of emotional learning. I would like to share certain moments and observations that remain vivid in my mind because they illustrate the impact that contact with Mattie Harris had on my development as a child psychotherapist and as a teacher. I think Mattie's ideas about growth and development permeated the culture of the child psychotherapy training at the Tavistock in ways that I took for granted, so that I did not understand what I was learning from her while I was learning it. Looking back I realize how profound an influence her ideas and her character had on my thinking.

When I applied to the Tavistock training at 25, I had already investigated the three other child psychotherapy trainings in London at that time (the early 1970s). I will describe these encounters in some detail because my experience of them provides the context for my first meeting with Mattie. Other people will, of course, have had quite different impressions of these institutions and the personalities that inhabited them.

First I visited the Institute of Child Psychology led by a very elderly and dignified Margaret Lowenfeld. This training was housed in a once lovely but now dilapidated building in Notting Hill Gate. The waiting room at the front of the building was large and light with two long leather sofas. I remember a cavernous hole in the seat of one, with the foam stuffing coming out. I thought that I had come to discuss the program with someone. But, after waiting a while, I was shown to the basement where children were seen. A receptionist asked me to sit at a small table and complete a Lowenfeld mosaic, which was a projective test consisting of a set of colored plastic shapes to be placed in a pattern on a board. Once this was completed, I waited again in the waiting room until I was shown into the office of a fresh faced male psychiatrist who asked me questions about my family. Upon hearing that I was the eldest of three sisters, he informed me with swift certainty that this was why I wanted to be a child psychotherapist, so that I could boss my patients around as I had bossed my little sisters around.

Dazed by the punch, I cannot remember the transition to the final part of the visit. Margaret Lowenfeld sat behind a large wooden desk with my mosaic before her. She asked me how I had constructed it. I told her that I had first placed the perimeter tiles, then the green and yellow triangles working towards the center, and finally the red circle in the middle. She rustled with diagnostic acumen and pronounced, "Nobody who is ready to be a child psychotherapist works from the outside in."

My second attempt to find out about training institutions took me to the Hampstead Clinic headed by Anna Freud. I attended a Wednesday morning clinical presentation held in a room with large, dark portraits hanging from the picture rail. The room was full of students and teachers waiting for something. Soon Miss Freud and Dorothy Burlingham walked together down the aisle between the rows of seated students and sat at the front. They were both wearing ankle length, navy blue broderie anglaise frocks with delicate collars. I can remember feeling simultaneously drawn to and unnerved by the formality of the setting. A young American girl presented clinical material, clearly eager and very nervous. Miss Freud presided.

There might have been some discussion, but by then the solemn weight of the portraits and the feeling of pressure to say the correct thing drove my mind right out of the room into the sunshine of Maresfield Gardens.

I came back the following week to discuss the program with the training director. But she met me at the door with a cigarette in her mouth, which stayed there for a good part of the conversation. I felt quite distracted by this and it added somehow to my feeling that this place was not for me.

Discouraged, but still curious, I visited the Jungian training where I spoke with an elegant and ancient Ruth Strauss who met with me in her home, which was filled with beautiful paintings and sculptures. I couldn't understand her Viennese accent very well and thought that, perhaps, she had trouble understanding mine. She spoke at length about Jungian psychoanalysis, but I had no idea what she was talking about.

So, I approached the last training destination close to resignation that I might not be suited to the world of psychoanalytic child psychotherapy. Innocent of any real knowledge about theoretical differences, I had looked at each place with raw, ignorant, awkward hope that I might find something I could recognize. It hadn't worked out.

I knocked on Mattie's door with little expectation of finding a path of possibility. When I walked into the room I was struck by the grey, plastic covered furniture and the bare, utilitarian arrangement, which, with the exception of a few plants and one picture over her desk, was clearly made for work. As were her hands. They were hands that did work. She wore a belted flowered dress and sat near the window, looking out from time to time and occasionally twiddling her thumbs. I think I talked for a while about my educational background, but this didn't go very far and I finally ground to a halt. It seemed that whatever expectations I might have had about the interview were irrelevant to its course. After a silence, Mattie asked me why I thought I wanted to do this work. I confessed that I did not know what this work really was and, carrying on in my disarray, blurted out that I had been a responsible big sister and a quick study at school and university, but that none of it felt quite real. Embarrassed, I waited to be politely dismissed. To my utter amazement, Mattie calmly said that she thought this was probably a very good reason for wanting to be a child psychotherapist. We talked about finding a setting in which I could observe young children and she said she would find an analyst for me.

I was surprised and relieved to realize that I did not have to know what I did not know. This experience of having my ignorance and immaturity accepted as a realistic, perhaps even valuable, starting point for learning seemed revolutionary to me. All that I came to understand later about Kleinian and Bionian ideas about projective identification, K and –K, began here. As a teacher, Mattie conveyed that there was no alternative to beginning where you are. I think that my own joy in teaching really comes from this lesson, remembered with gratitude for the tolerance and generosity of spirit Mattie demonstrated then and on many other occasions.

A second example of Mattie's robust and realistic view of authentic learning came during a supervision that followed Wilfred Bion's lectures at the Tavistock. I angrily complained that I had found him deliberately obscure and had understood nothing at all. I was surprised when she laughed. The tension surrounding my own limitations and the defensive anger this engendered softened and I could imagine trying again. Such experiences have played a long term role in shaping my own approach to teaching. When I returned to the United States I found myself in university and professional settings where no one had read Melanie Klein or any of the work that flowed from her discoveries. Reading these texts upset many people and stirred up hostility. I came to realize that these negative reactions were the valuable starting point and so developed a method of asking everyone in the seminar to underline the parts of the text that they hated the most. Then we read these out loud and lively discussion ensued. Really, this is analogous to welcoming the negative transference into the consulting room and is another version of beginning where you are.

It may be hard to know quite how values, methods and ideas are really passed on in a learning community. Certainly, in our learning community of child psychotherapy, great value was placed on observing and retaining detail. In clinical seminars and case supervisions, I remember Mattie's attention to the smallest particulars of a session and her boredom with jargon. It was through dwelling in the particular that Mattie entered the world of unconscious phantasy, sometimes even doing a miniature version of the non-verbal behavior being described, like moving her fingers or mouth to get the feel of it. This physical means of imagining the feel of the inner world seemed so connected to the baby inside us all. Getting the feel of things in the inner world meant that theoretical ideas came alive in a down to earth way. I think it is for this reason that Mattie's writing is easy to understand, as though she is reminding the reader of things she has always known, but never noticed.

Another aspect of Mattie's teaching was a conviction about the beauty of unfolding development. The drawing above her desk seemed to represent this – a flower with the mysterious face of a child in the heart of the blossom. Mattie was able to show, in the ordinary moments of a baby's life at home or in the confusion of the consulting room, how the Kleinian idea of the baby being object-seeking from the beginning unfolded in the context of relationships in the internal and external worlds. There was a kind of sturdiness in this, a lack of sentimentality that gave strength to the conviction that, given the fertile ground of the transference/countertransference relationship, development might find its path despite poor external conditions. We all saw so many children faced with appalling conditions in their external lives. Being part of the National Health Service meant that our psychoanalytic approach had a unique challenge and opportunity to become useful to children and families who would otherwise never encounter it. From this perspective, Mattie's conviction about the beauty of unfolding development also had a political dimension because it applied to all children, even those whose circumstances might otherwise thwart it.

A training culture is a complex and emotionally charged environment. There is comradeship mixed with rivalry; inspiration mixed with conformity; admiration mixed with idealization. Holding people together so they can realize their individual potential and their common purpose is difficult. I remember a moment when this challenge became apparent in something Mattie said. She told me that one of our tutors was having some difficulties, but that the best of her went into her work with patients. The problems of this tutor were evident to all her students and a cause of some disquiet. Mattie was asking us to place this in a larger context; to consider the complexity of a personality; to contemplate that there might be important things we could not see; and to demonstrate tolerance and compassion for difficulty. I remember feeling very moved by this, realizing that she was taking a risk by speaking to students in this way. It seemed to me that she was inviting us to expand our empathic imagination in the face of a real problem in our training community and thereby asking us to join this community as thinking adults.

CHAPTER TWENTY-EIGHT

Mattie's house: a memoir

Selina Sella Marsoni

I wish to begin my recollection of the person who was Martha Harris – Mattie for us, her pupils and friends, as for her next of kin – as I saw her the last time. She was sitting quietly in front of Don and me during the supervision of a clinical case, at Simsbury. It was Don Meltzer's wish that she should be present at the supervisions since he thought that the interrupted links of her brain could find alternative pathways (so, as a psychiatrist, he told me); and that exercising attention was a necessary requirement.

I can still see her making no movement but with her eyes and face listening very attentively to the dialogue between us; she had no speech, but through minimal hints she could show us assent or dissent to our comments on the material: her eyes were attentive and the spark of understanding showed the mind's unequivocal presence, even if the brain was damaged.

Then I saw her no more. However she reappeared again in a beautiful dream, sitting on a solid rock on the gently sloping shore of a river with her large gown extended on the gravel. It seems she was looking away from me, I couldn't see her face. Or was she perhaps turning towards me who was moving in her direction? I don't know. Leafy branches of trees reached out towards the ample river, reflected from the trembling water. Just like that. Dream, or memory of the dream perhaps.

Receiving from Meg the invitation to write a memoir on her mother, Martha Harris, for me my teacher of psychoanalysis, I felt from the very beginning that I would not speak of this science and method other than indirectly; that I couldn't speak any language other than that of describing the experience of my relationship to her, and that was what I had to do. It was about the responsibility to bear witness, trying to bring alive a person who deeply contributed to the building of a science, of a model of the mind, and whom I had the good luck to meet; I had had the great luck to spend almost two years in her house in Hampstead. "Why history?" Meltzer titled the first chapter of *The Kleinian Development* on Freud and gave his reasons: basically, that Freud's discoveries developed in an intertwined way with his personal life and time, connected in an evolving process.

I had written a first account, but I was not happy with it and didn't know why. I had to understand better and have experience of my own remembering; this started to happen through concentrated reading of the last talks given by Meg during her last visits to us in Biella, and through rereading other writings of Mattie, republished in *The Tavistock Model* (2011) besides other more recent volumes. I had to see something more, perhaps myself traverse a "growing point" as Martha describes it in one of her articles, reported here by Meg:

> It is a point at which different influences converge, meet, and create another shoot (a new idea or "baby"), and there is of course an implication of inevitable "growing pains". (See this volume, "Growing points", p. 75).

Concepts like "growing points" and "third eye" (this last meant particularly as a look free from moralistic connotations) threw light on my memories. It is quite an odd thing to re-live 40 years later, in the process of remembering, an experience lived intensely in its time, yes, but without truly realizing its significance. Strange but insightful too and disturbing. It reminds me of the renewed approaching of the threshold of the depressive position as Meltzer describes it in his review of his book *The Psychoanalytic Process,* when he suggests that later in life the need may make itself felt to face again the threshold of the depressive position, possibly "without retreating from looking down, towards the abyss", as he said about a patient of mine who in a dream had to walk through a suspended bridge across a deep space.

These last readings and reflections enabled me to look again from my suspended bridge into those years from a new perspective and to recognize better the great gift that it had been to live under the same roof with such special a person and be contained in those green days for so long. A perspective throwing light on the learning that came from the person herself, beyond her supervisions, seminars, lectures – completing them within a more integrated meaning, as I would like to evoke. Such is my wish now. However I did not in the end alter my first draft, I only added some comments on the way, and will at the end recount a few significant moments from which I learned fundamental aspects of our psychoanalytical profession and deontology, and also a new vision of the world and human relationships, in the company of the particular person who was Martha Harris.

Coming closer

Different circumstances led me to London to meet Martha Harris; a series of events, like stages or stations along the journey towards psychoanalysis, sent me in that direction. I realize that it is necessary for me to resume the path of that first linear track, like a guide helping through an account of external circumstances to recognize meanings of more internal nature. The inevitable autobiographical aspect brings difficulties. My account of the first year of coming closer to her began like this:

On a spring day of 1969 I arrived for the first time at the gate of number 4 Ferncroft Avenue, Hampstead, in London, to meet Martha Harris and bring her material from my work as an unqualified child psychotherapist for supervision. She herself had requested this when I wrote to her explaining who I was and what I was doing at the Centro Medico Pedagogico in Novara where I had been working for five years. The service was directed by Marcella Balconi, my first teacher and supervisor, who had generously (being an Anna Freud follower) agreed that I should turn for further learning to a person who was a living representative of the Kleinian school of thought: Martha Harris. I had also been directed to her by Lina Clements Generali whom I had asked for Kleinian supervision but who had declined my request. Lina however understood my fervour and said that she would rather send me to a person who could better help me; she told me about the Children and Parents Department of the Tavistock of which Martha was principal, and described its spirit at the heart of Kleinian child-psychotherapy, founded by Esther Bick together with John Bowlby. Lina was one of the "stations", together with five years' analysis with Franco Fornari, the weekly supervisions from Balconi and meetings of the staff, the Diploma of Psychology at the Cattolica University in Milan, the encouraging support of Elide Ravizzotti (co-worker with Balconi), ending with the reading of Mrs Klein's book *The Psycho-Analysis of Children*, a present received from Renata Li Causi. With Renata, who worked with me at the *Centro* in Novara, I shared a deep interest in Klein.

On the side of the gate before the house sat a big black cat. As a cat lover I felt this as a good omen. The cat turned out to belong to Monica, a Portuguese woman helping with domestic work in the house. I am pleased to remember her with all her rough temperament since, as I learned later, she was a substantial presence in the household – Mattie's household as I came to call it – to which I gradually and in a simple way received lucky access.

What I also wish to remember and try to evoke, beside the fundamental encounter with the person Martha Harris that was a turning point in my life (a real "growing point"), is the *atmosphere* of the big beautiful house with its two gardens. A short path led to the main door and here I was met by Mrs Harris herself, smiling and welcoming. It was immediately clear that a language of gestures and smiles and of the music of the voice could sustain a language of limited words, as we saw afterwards during the supervision. Not many preambles were needed; certainly I was offered coffee, I can't remember whether already in the spacious kitchen, about which more needs to be said – it too was a growing point for human relationships.

I was then introduced into a large bright room with windows on many sides and a bay window arching towards the front garden. The first thing that struck me and remained in my memory (even if my attention was not focused on the ambience at the time) was the floral atmosphere, with plants and flowers on the window sills and in vases even if they were on the point of withering, as if not to worry too much about the exterior aspect – accepting rather that flowers die and don't get thrown away immediately in order to hide their sight; this however is hindsight and my imagination. The room advanced towards the garden as if to allow it to enter and be part of the room, or viceversa, and this was the room's atmosphere, the atmosphere of a garden. Two things I noticed, dear to me: a grand piano with music scores open on the stand, which signified that it was being played, and a couch with an armchair positioned where the analyst sits. It was a room of thought, of aesthetic thinking. Only some time later could I recognize the true sense of one of Mattie's affirmations regarding the analytic setting: *The setting is first in the analyst's mind*. No rules about simple furnishing and a space free from personal traces of the analyst are sufficient (though truly containing a grain of truth) if the analyst's mind is not properly furnished.

With some apprehension I displayed the material, drawings and notes, and at Mattie's nod I started reading. I remember that I had chosen the difficult case of a severely disturbed little girl whom I saw three times a week; Marcella Balconi trusted my analysis with Fornari as a safeguard against my inexperience. (Those were hard times for child psychotherapy in Italy; and she, Marcella, the psychoanalyst in charge of the psychiatric department of the hospital in Novara, had been a valuable pioneer and follower of the Anna Freud inheritance.)

I proceeded as well as I could, reading an already translated text and underlining with gestures and face grimaces the story and events of the session. Immediately my impression was that Mattie understood, and when she started talking I too understood the meaning of what she was communicating to me, looking at me directly in the eyes, with those extraordinary eyes of hers, inspiring concentration. It pains me to have completely forgotten the material and its sense: but I do remember that *it had sense* and that now I could see a meaning unknown before. Reading Mattie's biography by Meg, I read of her accurate examination of the session's events, an experience reported by many of her supervisees, and this too made a deep impression on me from that very first moment and ever since, expanding the possibility of a more open and articulated focus on the material.

Already during that first supervision I told myself *this is the language I wish to learn,* and I never forgot that self-acknowledgment, which became a firm point in my professional life from then on. I can't refrain here from finding confirmation in what I heard Donald Meltzer say (actually what Don told me himself) that nothing was more interesting for him than the human mind – nothing that he was more passionately interested *to explore*. Obviously the "language" was that of psychoanalysis, which from then became closely linked for me with the English language: also later through the long and fundamental analysis with Mrs E. O'Shaughnessy. Gradually in the years to come this also became linked with its literature, of which I preserved some traces from the time when I was studying German Language and Literature at Ca' Foscari in Venice (which unfortunately I didn't complete).

Resuming the narrative of those years, it seems right to remember that Mattie had organized for me two more supervision experiences and had actually asked me to bring three clinical cases. Frances Tustin arrived the following hour, such different temperament but equally welcoming, making me feel at ease and facilitating communication; she too was of great importance in my further training just as was Isca Wittenberg, to whom I was sent the following day at her home in Hampstead Garden Suburb. I am happy to remember them here, these two dear competent persons to whom both I owe much for my training.

These facts tell by themselves Martha Harris' care and responsibility for the development of those who came to her showing interest and a firm intention to proceed along the road of psychoanalytical psychotherapy – which I had probably communicated unawares. A parental responsibility, I would say, besides a didactic one. In order to gain wider access to the landscape of my memory I find helpful to note a few irrelevant little facts from that early period of 1969-70. On the occasion of my first visit I had booked an hotel near Kensington Garden, the famous gardens, and from those whereabouts had taken a bus that brought me circling through many curves up to Hampstead; I remember quite well my impression of that springtime London, so different from the Dickensian England which I had imagined, dark and closed up – a real pre-formed transference one could jokingly say. Perhaps flowers and spring expressed the hope and expectations that I carried with me too.

After that first time which was so positive, it was decided that I would come to London once a month bringing three case materials to my three teachers (*maestre*) and so it happened. After the second visit Mrs Harris offered me to stay overnight at her home. What doesn't this say – thinking of it now – of her generosity and attention. Only now do I realize its full meaning; but Mattie saw *then* that I was really passionate and determined. She observed people with the "third eye", benevolent and scrutinizing at the same time, whose inner thinking was not always apparent, but a space was created within which one could feel at ease and think for oneself. Meltzer wrote in memory of her that she always *meant* what she said, even if she might not say all that she thought. This is a theme amply described in his paper on "*Sincerity*".

I remember few details of those monthly visits with my bag with the Novara cases, the content of which seems to have disappeared from my awareness. Yet they were useful in their transitional way, and I understood better what I was doing. At the end of those travels, before the summer of 1970, I "officially" asked Martha Harris for advice about my intention to follow a full training at the Tavistock, and for this purpose I went to see her in her room at the Clinic.

Decision taken

This was the necessary conclusion of the sequential visits and what I had gradually learned from Mattie, Frances and Isca – "began to learn" would be more appropriate to say, as the logical consequence of those first intense supervisions could only be a serious preamble to a proper integrated training. On the other side the dilemma presented itself of definitely leaving my family life, which still stood, albeit in a disrupted way after many changes of residence since the beginning in Venice. The necessary length of the training left no doubts about the time span: the move to London made a definitive cleavage evident; and the burden is even more clear to me now with which I made this decision, and was then received by Martha with her capacity of containment, not trying to stop a drive which she evidently perceived as authentic and presided over according to her principles. More, reading of her life through Meg's words, it is possible to find a connection between those principles and her own determination to initiate radical changes when she was sure of her insight. It coheres with her not giving conventional suggestions (which, it occurs to me now, may be what is meant by what Meg has called a "soft-humanist" mentality). In truth, in such cases she wouldn't give any kind of advice: she would simply expose the facts and leave freedom of decision.

This was a deep fracture in the life of a family. Now, thanks to this effort of remembering Mattie, as though she possessed an evocative power in the direction of the search for truth, I know why I remember so little of the events: the turbulence of the emotions surrounding this decision with its different proliferations (*ramificazioni*) let an horizontal curtain drop down. Why horizontal? It just came to mind, as a veil that covers the landscape of an entire event. I know it is a funereal image, it is death to the condition before and it takes time to traverse it; but all this goes back to other factors – here I am remembering Mattie. Yet I think of the cathartic quality of the psychoanalytic autobiography of which Meg spoke to our group in one of her talks in Biella; it was inevitable that the intertwining of events in my life took on a particular new direction from the exact moment of intersection with Mattie. Could it be what Meltzer calls "aesthetic reciprocity": the revelation that ensues from thinking closely of a significant person in one's life?

Thinking of turbulence, I am reminded of another concept expressed by Meltzer in relation to adolescence: he contradicts the common view that sexuality is at the core of adolescent preoccupations, and maintains that it is rather the search for knowledge, for the *episteme,* that drives the adolescent forwards – sexuality being a cover. He founds this conviction on the discoveries and conclusions of Melanie Klein: she observed the intense inquisitive activity in children and their search inside empty spaces or three-dimensional objects and the psycho-therapist's own body, projecting parts of the self – this being the "meaning" of the session. I am not here to make too many Kleinian references, I wish only to recall the fact that Mrs Klein postulated an "epistemophilic instinct" in human nature, which through Bion became the K link. Linking this acknowledgement of infantile states of mind with their intensified reappearance in adolescence, Meltzer postulated that this stance was the more active, connecting the possession of knowledge with the power of the adult which is what the adolescent mostly aspires to. Unfortunately I can't remember the text where he stated this. He said too, revisiting his book *The Psychoanalytical Process,* that in adulthood the need can present itself, even in analysed people, to face again the threshold of the depressive position, as it becomes necessary to look better at what there was to be seen, and what may not have been properly observed.

I do remember my interview with Mattie to examine my intention to start the training. It happened in her room in the Children and Parents Department. I didn't understand all she was saying to me; I was still in a phase of a very limited knowledge of the English language and I didn't understand well the difference between the status of "associate" and that of "trainee" – to which she told me I couldn't aspire, having only a diploma in psychology and not an honours degree as required by the rules. Optimistically encouraging me with the sound of her voice, however, she told me I could follow exactly the same curriculum of studies. "*Exactly the same*" she underlined clearly, and this sentence I remember quite well. I didn't understand the dilemma properly, or the difficulty that this might present for my professional future. She certainly did know, but didn't give excessive importance to this, and it was not discussed in detail, nor the pros and cons delineated. Martha Harris didn't give much importance to the matter of my institutional position, neither did I think it could be a serious problem, especially since she stressed the unaltered validity of the curriculum. The accent was all on the importance of pursuing the study and the experience in itself: this is how she spoke about it. So different from what Professor Gaddini, then president of the Italian Psychoanalytic Society, said to me some time later when I met him socially at a party at Susan Isaacs'. He was surprised and alarmed for me and urged me to first take an honours degree in psychology, the newly established faculty. I answered that I absolutely couldn't divert my energies from the training which I was already following full time, that Martha Harris had advised me so. I was about 15 years late already in starting the training and couldn't waste time. And her attitude was discrepant too from that of my former analyst Professor Fornari, whom I had previously asked for an opinion on my intention: he had stressed the real problem of family disruption and of intimate affects and the need to ponder carefully. A difference between three perspectives (vertices): institutional, affective and "indescribable".

These facts speak clearly about Mattie's mentality, which actually married – and it is not a joke – with Don Meltzer's; this mentality I had the opportunity of gradually experience and learn with the passing of time: a clear privileging of the substance and the passion in pursuing a chosen road, and this even if it meant the loss of institutional advantages that might have followed more convenient choices but that distracted from the chosen direction. Which considerations, what vision of the world was subject to this way of evaluating choices? Reliving the supervisions and open discussions within the atmosphere we breathed in Mattie's circle – which soon became Mattie and Don's circle – it was clear that it was a vision of the world open to knowledge as an innate drive to be cultivated without too much preoccupation with status and appearance and belonging, with advantages and disadvantages. Certainly Mattie was well aware of external reality and of the need to survive materially in the world and earn one's living; perhaps my case as a "motivated" person (as they say) even to the extent of being ready to leave behind a world of comfort, made preoccupation with survival less significant. Mattie knew that after proper training and work experience I could later be regularly accepted by the Association of Child Psychotherapists (as did happen), where competence and professionality were acknowledged to the aim of membership. Not so in Italy.

A fifteen years' stay in London

So it happened that on the 7th of September 1970, together with my son Alvise, aged 14, I arrived in London with my car and with our more necessary personal belongings. He was due to go to a boarding school in Dartington and he was invited to stay with us the few days before his school started. So began a lifelong friendship between him and Mattie's daughters, particularly Morag, closer in age to Alvise. It pains me to remember her, who died prematurely leaving three children, after so much dedication to important literary studies and teaching at the university in Bologna, and her writings on Schiller and Emily Dickinson, published by the Roland Harris Trust. We arrived for a long stay, while I undertook the training at the Tavistock; it resulted a definitive residence for study and work and family life for Alvise, who later married Alessandra, who trained at the Tavistock and still works there! Links between all of us were never severed, but kept alive in all dimensions, family, friendship, psychoanalytical deep interests and projects.

Here I am rethinking myself as a dweller in Mattie's home: she offered to rent me the same beautiful room that I knew well from the monthly visits of 1969-70. How to describe my relief and joy – and I wish to report that the rent was light; had she asked twice as much I would have accepted and she certainly knew it. Why do I set down this small, insignificant, even awkward detail? Because it is part of the spirit that inhabited her, always in harmony and in keeping with a sobriety of thinking, of living, free from opportunism and preoccupation with convenience. Again it brings to mind that clarity in keeping inwardly separate the boundaries of different spaces, never contaminating one another, within the concrete circumstances of the moment. *The setting of the mind.*

The beautiful house received us, the people and the spacious room that had been Roland's, as I already knew. With Alvise I went for a few days to Dartington, where he would study. So began my fifteen-year journey of learning and practising, under the guidance of Martha and of the other teachers Frances and Isca – and after some time, for my training with adults at the BAP, with Meltzer, Money-Kyrle and Hyatt Williams – the principles and method of psychoanalysis according to a model of exploration of the mind, of the inner world, already solid and congruent but open to evolution, growing upon itself. Such was my intuition then, and now, my major conviction.

In my room an ample window overlooked the rear garden. Gradually I learned of Roland's high human quality, as a father, as a teacher, and especially as a poet; often Meg interpolated her texts with poems by her father, of exceptional sensitivity but still unpublished. From Lina Clements and a few more intimate friends I learned of his premature death – he was only 50 years old. Mattie almost died herself from grief and for a week was in hospital between life and death herself; she was saved by expert care and a dream which she herself related in which Roland said that "she still had many things to do". She gradually resumed her activity, her clinical work as analyst with patients, the direction of the department in the Tavistock, the seminars, and eventually she lived again a new season in life, through sharing the psychoanalytical thinking with Donald Meltzer, who had been an intimate friend of Roland. The natural outcome of this closeness was their marriage and the long season of teaching, including abroad, mainly in Italy, often in Novara invited by Balconi, and even in our small provincial town of Biella.

From this point onward the story would be long to tell, I have to abandon the more linear narrative, in order to locate Mattie in my mind's memory through the daily life in the Hampstead house. Trying to evoke the rhythm of life through its inhabitants does perhaps allow one to capture a reflection of her personality, since she ran the culture of her home in the same way that she was running the culture of the Children and Parents Department. It was a good culture, where relations were governed by the respect due to experience, age, "temperature and distance", and not by institutional hierarchy. Yet at the Tavistock Mattie had to deal with the external local authorities as well, which meant confronting institutional mentality, and she managed it. I remember a description by Don, after her death: she could contain inwards her group, led in her way, and at the same time face and struggle with the public mentality outside in order to protect the internal space. Like a strong vase containing and protecting a precious element.

   I am not sure of being able to find the right words to describe the house in Ferncroft Avenue. It contained the meaningful life of a few persons, each with their individual personality, independence and activity. Initially it was composed of Mattie and her daughters Meg and Morag; then there was Monica, daily help, and up in the self-contained top floor apartment lived Mr X, who could be occasionally seen walking up and down the painted wooden stairs, where the mezzanine housed a bookcase with classic Penguin books and made a restful consultation place. A democratic freedom reigned, with use of the communal areas such kitchen, bathroom, living room with TV, and garden – not the analytic consulting room of course, which was sacred, just as personal room spaces were absolutely intimate. As in a respected democracy, some rules governed time and relationships, not laid down but learned through experience or trial and error, and gradually introjected by a new comer like myself, especially in relation to the kitchen, a most important station.

   We all converged at different times, casually or often contemporaneously. Its use was governed by discretion, intuition, cooking times for foods. Each of us had our own time, but in the sense of the necessary moment; the house had no fixed times apart from those of hunger and thirst, so the kitchen was the natural meeting place and could become an opportunity for longer conversation; yet what I wish to stress is the spontaneity of these encounters. The space in the fridge too had its natural internal division as each of us, Monica and myself, had a separate little space, respectful of the important purchases of Mattie, the joints of good meat which she would then cook – since yes, Mattie cooked, especially on Saturdays or Sundays for Mersea or Buttermilk, the country houses with friends, colleagues and relatives, where I too was often invited.

The rear garden, larger than the front one, with a central space of green lawn and flowers and flowers around and shrubs, all freely planted without a particular order but a spontaneous one, was a kind of mirror of the interior of the house: though carefully weeded, an open space inspiring freedom and concentration, not constriction, even with its configuration as an *hortus conclusus* – a container, not a claustrum. All around, outside the enclosure, trees from the space beyond seemed to be facing and sort of leaning inwards – at least this is how my memory or desire remembers it. This was the stage, the landscape in front of my eyes that I could observe sitting at the large desk placed right in front of the large window. Studying and writing at this table, occasionally looking out, and in the *belle stagioni*, a recurring figure of a girl appeared and would lay down on the lawn; leaning on her elbows she would read for hours, concentrating. Till this day I remember marvelling at observing such persistency and concentration in a girl who was not 19 years old, her dedication. It was Meg.

Special moments

In order to conclude this partial visit to Mattie's house, I would now like to relate a few episodes from those years. Simple episodes, that however evoke aspects of her person and spirit. So it seems to me. Catching them as flashes presenting themselves to memory, still alive today. Fixed in the mind and source of learning, showing how fundamental principles in human relations are linked up. They came from a person whose authority was due to experience, who never wasted words; rather, when they were uttered, they were bright symbols which could continue generating light.

On the occasion of a supervision on one of my cases of child psychotherapy at the Child Guidance in Barnet where I worked, a comment of hers remained engraved in my mind and guided me in all my psychoanalytic activity; I now think it has a far more universal character than one applying to only that particular situation. I had left open the small locker of the child previously seen, and naturally, the child coming next played in a way that showed the meaning of his reaction. I was then at the beginning of my Kleinian apprenticeship, and in the process of acquiring the psychoanalytic "language" I had come to London to learn. I began to read out my interpretation of the material of my small patient, but Mattie stopped me: "First you put things right, then you go on talking", she said, and I immediately understood. Those same words have stayed in my mind for 40 years. It was an important lesson for me: not that it had been imposed as such, I mean, but in the ampler and not moralistic sense that the word "lesson" has as *vision*, as a new thought imposing itself and impressing the mind. Always, since then, I first remedy any situation in which I might have made a breach of technique, acknowledging my omission or fault before searching for any interpretation. Anything I could have said would have been undermined by a spurious setting of relationships, based as these are on the reciprocal agreement of the setting as a private space. The patient *may* breach it, the analyst *must* not. I fear it sounds extreme, yet I do feel so.

Any acting-out of the analyst, by introducing concrete elements, diverts the analytical work from the exploration of the inner world, based as it is on the dialogue between the internal objects of patient and analyst contained within a *well defined setting*, by moving it outside. This I learned, even if at the time I would not have been able to articulate my understanding theoretically. I wish also to add, in remembering Mattie, that she spoke those words in a particular voice, which I had the opportunity to experience a few more times: a voice only slightly over its usual volume, but firm and definitive in tone, not admitting any useless discussion, yet at the same time not sounding authoritarian. Authoritative, yes. It came from a rooted internal conviction, it facilitated the introjection to the other, allowing the student to learn from experience through both the case material and the teacher's voice in the same moment of its happening.

The theme which to my mind links to the supervision is this: I was not ethically authorized to interpret the child's play, since I had myself broken the setting's regulations which commanded the privacy of any patient in respect to the other, and this was the reason why we wouldn't display drawings or works of other children and instead kept the room in a condition of spartan austerity, free to the externalizations of phantasy of the child in treatment at that moment. The respect for the privacy of the child patient extended itself also to the parents, to whom it was often quite difficult to explain it: giving them news only of their child's analytic progress, while stressing that the treatment was not in competition with the parents. Much depended on the sensitivity and intuition of the parents, in understanding this. The impasse presenting itself if these conventions are broken is that not only is the meaning of the material altered, following the acting out of the therapist (as happened with my forgetting and even more with carrying on as nothing happened), but the *trust* is broken and all the consequent meaning of the material is polluted and not authentic; it is *insincere*.

A minor event, nevertheless with its own significance, occurred at the very beginning of my living in Mattie's house when I was feeling disturbed owing to the splitting of my life between the new one and the old left behind. In one way or another I conveyed my state of mind to her. I didn't get soothing speeches taking me away from reality, but a gentle almost joking suggestion: "Have a warm bath!" Again I remember the precise words she uttered. I followed the recommendation. The bathroom in Ferncroft was beautiful. I remember its pink antique-rose colour; lying in the bath tub one could see an hollybush outlined against the sky. It seems somehow silly to report a small thing like this, yet it reveals the mental dimension of a person holding on her shoulder a model which recognizes psychological trouble, suggests a pause and a rest from conflicts and anxiety in order to restore a more balanced state of mind, but concedes nothing by way of a misleading offer of confused soothing mental paracetamol. This clarity in the definition of the inner borders between states of mind was reinforced by living in the atmosphere of Mattie's home. It is the basic principle for the separateness from private life in our psychoanalytical psychotherapeutic profession at the moment of immersion in that function, so different from an unconscious *splitting*.

This memory evokes another one, still connected with the turbulent states of that period. I made endless vociferous telephone calls to Italy, and once it so happened that I disturbed too much the adjacent analytic consulting room. Like lightning Mattie materialized out of the door, appearing higher in stature, as it is said the Greek gods – Minerva or Phoebus – used to appear to mortals, and she "spoke". What an experience of the paternal type "Now stop" on that occasion! (When I worked in my own studio in Biella and my neighbours made frightful noises, I appeared and tried to impress them, but to no avail. Perhaps there was insufficient "reciprocity" in the receivers who had no idea of what I was doing for hours in my room, far away from any psychoanalytical aura in the town.) And on this theme of "apprehended" lessons and their associations – I already said what I mean by "lesson", nothing moralistic – I shall remember how at a later time, with Mattie and Don driving from Lucca towards their house in Gromignana, after I had qualified with the BAP (perhaps just qualified), I made a comment which must have had all the traits of narcissistic complacency. With well chosen words I was informed about the professional dangers I would have encountered had I persevered. Don who was driving said nothing, but silently approved. Mattie had made me sit in the front of the car. I can't give the gist of the humour of the conversation, and I retain a mixed feeling about it – a bit of shame, a bit of relief that things could be said as they were thought, a bit of the beautiful landscape we were driving through. It was an example, as when reading recently about the concept of a "third eye", of how this really can exist even outside the consulting room or the observation setting, allowing space for thinking for oneself.

I have a few more things I could report, but I will mention only two. My analyst had said to me: "A psychotic child is not a training case." I hesitated to say a word about this, aware that the content of a session is private. However the reiterated statement, linked with some associations, eventually made me mention it to Mattie who was my main tutor. She became alarmed (some other tutor had given me that case) and she stressed the importance of what my analyst had said and which I should have immediately communicated. I became vividly aware that I had not understood the difference between an *interpretation* of meaning and the *information* relevant for the quality of my training. Immediately Martha took charge of the situation and provided me with a suitable case. The extraordinary fact is that she herself came to my house to discuss the matter and give details about the case I would soon start. This fact makes me think now about its reason, its "*raison d'etre*": also because there had been another occasion when she came to my house in Asmuns Hill (and I don't mean social occasions like a party given for friends, as also happened during those years). On that other specific occasion, she came when I had completed my training, having seen for the necessary number of years my three training cases, under supervision from different tutors, and attended the relevant seminars, according to the curriculum and much more that she had taught me. We sat in the living room, and Mattie then said to me: "You can consider yourself qualified." It was a private ceremony, almost the laying of a sword on my shoulder like a knighting by the Queen, drinking a cup of tea and much simple emotion, if one can match these together. Her words fell on my heart, and there stayed for ever. Thinking about it again, I believe that Mattie meant to imprint on my heart-mind the *identity* of my profession for my internal awareness, which the Tavistock as an institution would have given in the form of a certificate.

All this is not about myself and these minor circumstances; it is about a person who knew the difference between internal and external values: the difficulties, the confusions, in short the aspects of life, both as a member of a community and as an individual. When I showed complacency in the episode of the car, she made me aware, most of all, that ours is a service profession, a humble one and always in a state of evolution, as is the adult mind also. All this reminds me too of the question that was put to Dr Bion at one of his extraordinary plenary seminars at the

Tavistock about which was more valuable the external label or the internal? I don't remember Bion's answer, if any – perhaps he said something about "la réponse est le malheur de la question."

Finally, amongst the many various moments, I would like to remember the parties. Mattie put on huge parties that were special and colourful, for their bringing together of friends, colleagues, students, boyfriends and girlfriends, and for the variety of food, mostly cooked and prepared by herself, partly brought by others as their contribution, in a variety of free initiatives, like the flowers of her garden. No more psychoanalysis, only cheerfulness and the pleasure of meeting on the level of friendship. Unforgettable were those organized at Buttermilk, in the country not far from Oxford, or at Mersea in the summer, on the east coast estuary. I think they had in themselves an unpremeditated function, a coming together as a community, a community of friends. Yes, as a community of individual people going together in the same direction, as told in the words of a poem by Roland: the subject was the tacit harmony of two lovers who simply joined their hands as they recognized that they were going in the same direction, and of course, the poem is about individuals and intimacy, but a veil of analogy still persists, being the direction towards truth and beauty [*see endnote*]. And psychoanalysis has something to do with them.

Last reflections

I am well aware of how often I have mentioned Don Meltzer, intertwining his thoughts with those of Mattie. The fact is that it was really so, to a point. Their combined thinking began with their union or vice-versa, and travelling and visiting study centres interested in their thinking, amongst which Novara was an important one; they spread seeds in many parts of the world, generating knowledge and work groups. Italy owes much to their constant and regular commitment and regular visits to so many towns. If the voice of dissemination was mainly Don's, Mattie was the great motor of the internal dialogue between them, linked with symbol formation as an ongoing process. Don himself acknowledged his debt to her for completing his own thought. And it was infant observation regularly carried on in the places visited by Mattie, that threw new perspectives and light on their combined thinking, enlarging his vision, also bringing observation to a central position in analytic work and in line with what Bion himself maintained as fundamental – namely internal observation of one's own mind as filter, not only observation of external facts. It was a true "meeting of true minds" as the beautiful sonnet by Shakespeare says, with a dialogue not depleted by conflicts. Still, much has to be rediscovered about Martha Harris' own contribution to psychoanalysis, which the new editions of Mattie's publications can help us to realize.

I would also like to recall the extraordinary crowded seminars that Dr Bion gave at the Tavistock which were introduced by Mattie; I remember well both of them sitting on a platform in one of the three intercommunicating rooms, whilst all along the large parallel corridor was full of people, many sitting on the floor and following Bion's talks through television circuits, so strong was Bion's power of attraction. The image that came to me, idiosyncratic as it may be, was of the spirit of the great cathedrals of Europe in medieval times, when crowds swarmed after walking for hundreds of miles to listen to preachers such as Abelard. The spirit was religious, but not that of an ideology, I felt; it was the spirit of individual people who had come together to listen to a voice I would dare to say is prophetic, at that particular moment of the history of psychoanalysis.

Back to my country

Following Meg's suggestion to speak of my work once back in my country, I realized with dismay that I had not said a word about the 27 years that have passed since my return in 1985! Around 1984 the time had come for a decision: would I settle in England for good, or would I go back to Italy? Oddly enough a tale from *One Thousand and One Nights* came to my aid: about a king who had set out to explore his kingdom and rode for miles with his knights towards its borders, but he went too far, and wouldn't have sufficient life time left to ever ride back to his capital. I thought it was a useful admonition, considering that "life time" for me meant enough time to establish a clinical practice. I had come to London at 44 , I was now 58, and a year was needed to take leave from my patients.

So in July 1985 I drove back to Biella, my native town: a small provincial town whose culture was based on its past history of a successful textile industry, not given to be interested in less tangible inner worlds. People knew a lot about each other, so keeping a psychoanalytical setting separate and secluded wasn't easy, and demanded constant attention and interpretation. Such was Biella.

Why Biella rather than Venice where I had lived my own family life, or beautiful Genoa where I had taken seminars for five years travelling from London, or even Palermo in beloved Sicily? My grownup children by now lived in London and in the States. Perhaps I was influenced by the saga of the eels, that I had learned from my father Massimo Sella (1886/1959) who was a scientist and a marine biologist, but also a humanist, a musician and a photographer. Before the war, there was a need to map the yet-uncharted course of the many subterranean rivers which flow below the Carso plateau into the Adriatic Sea, along the upper Dalmatian coastline all the way to Istria. In order to do so my father, coupling science and imagination, and a certain sense of adventure, used the innate drive of the eels to swim from whatever part of the globe they live in towards their 'home', the Sargasso Sea – the place where they were born, reproduce, and eventually die. The eels were tagged and dropped into various watery sink holes high on the Carso plateau, whence they promptly swam down to the Adriatic Sea. There, waiting fishing crews caught them and, because of the tags, were able to pinpoint the location of the underwater outlet of the rivers as well as the approximate courses back to their inland sources. This association reminded me of both the archaic innate objects and the introjected ones and their propelling force.

I organized a consulting room for adult patients and another one for child psychotherapy and in September '85 I "opened shop". Balconi was helpful in referring patients to me, and some moved from London in order to continue treatment. From the very beginning, again with the help of Balconi and Meltzer who both introduced me to interested people, I was able to organize seminars. Apart from leading a two-year Observation Course in an institutional setting in Torino, my teaching work was done privately: first conducting a full Observation Course on my own at home, and later inviting Kenneth Sanders and Ross Lazar to take seminars for my small organization. In all I set up five complete Observation Courses, all well-attended, by psychologists and child psychiatrists from Biella, Ivrea, Vercelli, Borgosesia. At the same time we held clinical seminars and offered private supervision to people interested in the Tavistock model (the developmental model following the line of Freud, Abraham, Klein, Money-Kyrle, Bion, Harris, Meltzer), strongly supported by Meltzer himself who came often to teach in Biella. Unforgettable – many have told me – were the large meetings in the monastery of San Gerolamo with its 16th Century cloister.

What did I take back from London, and what could I do in Italy that I could not have done had I stayed in the UK? are questions I have been asked, and ask myself.

I found that after a while, a small core group (*drapello*) of truly interested and passionate psychoanalytical psychotherapists kept returning, for clinical presentations and supervision, and gradually assumed a clear identity of its own, even though the professional experience of the various members was very varied – prison work, neuropsychiatry, psychology, teaching, etc. We met weekly for many years; meanwhile more members joined and now share responsibility for furthering the work in all aspects of its organization – from the practical and business to the content of seminars and supervisions. The analogy comes to mind of how in relay races the torch-baton is not handed over abruptly, but the two people run for a while together before passing it from one to another.

A problem had posed itself from the very beginning in relation to the lack of a more formal training system: how to introduce new concepts and advanced ideas without the benefit of the organized structure of a school, especially in the context of supervision. I found myself often referring to my teachers when describing clinical situations, and what came to my aid was the fact that this "teachers' model" has a strong internal congruence;

it is not just an assemblage of concepts but has a logical integrity of its own, so that eventually, as in a puzzle, links could be made by all the members, and meaning gained strength.

Through the words of Mattie and Don, spoken, written, interchanged, remembered, what gradually emerged was a picture of how the mind manifests itself according to its innate nature, if presided over by a more mature mind. Starting with pre-conceptions (Bion) and freed from intrusive identifications (Meltzer), it encounters the beautiful "realization" of the mother-world in a space of reciprocal wonder and recognition where it can evaluate external as well as internal reality in a truthful way; always in terms of that individual child, and that individual mother (Harris). It involves suffering and undergoing catastrophic changes, but as Dr Johnson said (in a passage that Bion refers to): "Whether to see life as it is, will give us much consolation, I know not; but the consolation which is drawn from truth, if any there be, is solid and durable." Then the baby's growing pains are transformed from persecuting ghosts into "ancestors" (Williams) to whom we can be grateful. "You must pay for your milk", Kenneth Sanders said once in a seminar, leaving everybody astonished – all had believed that the "milk" was free.

Lately Meg has been exposing the fine detail (*filigrana*) and also the depth of Martha Harris' contribution. Not only as muse for thought as Meltzer valued her, but more forcibly, as the originator of the foundational awareness of how infant observation interacts with the transference-countertransference experience to comprehend the unique individuality of each mother-and-baby, patient-and-analyst. This is the contrappunto that makes the thinking process possible, and which comes into being first in an exchange between two minds, and then between the self and its internalized object.

Only in the course of writing these lines, and reaching the final investigation and description of my own memory of facts, did some sort of meaning emerge about what I may have brought back to my country, to those friends who for their own reasons stayed with me for so long.

Was it the effort of bringing to life and transmitting my experience of people and situations that enabled a link with their personal experience, through a relationship that lasted a sufficient time to deepen and evolve, allowing concepts and new ideas to take root? Is it this why I too, in the effort of transmitting my experience, relived it and learned a lot?

A sentence by Don Meltzer during a supervision comes to my mind, underlining his view that a little improvement was taking place in the course of the analysis: "It takes time at the breast, it takes time ...". Learning really happens through introjection facilitated by the experience of a true relationship within, which gives formal theoretical information a proper context.

Endnote: extract from a poem by Roland Harris

> We are of those blessed lovers
>   Who loved before they knew,
> Without pursuit or fleeing;
>   And met as pilgrims do.
>
> Whose eyes, bent on the going,
>   Turn once to ask the day
> And find their end's companion
>   Travelling that same way.

CHAPTER TWENTY-NINE

A tribute to Mattie

Patricia Kenwood

On reflection, I would say that Mattie gave me the core experience of my whole psychoanalytic training, although there were many other excellent, valued teachers. My experience with Mattie was over a period of almost eight years (1966-73) during the child psychotherapy course and subsequently. I was privileged to have weekly personal supervision with Mattie over this time, in addition to the weekly infant observation and clinical seminars, case conferences and unit meetings. Also, before I returned to Australia, she gave me a wealth of experience and supervision in crisis work, couples and family work, individual adult psychoanalytic psychotherapy, teaching infant observation and tutoring and mentoring.

I think the main thrust of Mattie's contribution in shaping me as a child psychotherapist (and later as an adult psychotherapist and psychoanalyst) was in allowing me to grow and develop from within, with my own capacities, drive and interests. She provided an environment in which she was always remarkably receptive and thoughtful, supportive and accepting, and she also contributed a wealth of richness in her perspective and capacity to think. In my supervisions, for example, my experience was at times like climbing a mountain and suddenly coming upon a vista that opened up before me, stretching to a distant horizon, with so much to see in front of me. In seminars, I always admired – and tried to emulate – her capacity to wait to hear what each member contributed before she would add her own thoughts and perspectives. She had the patience and confidence in her students to allow them to take in and learn as much as they were able to, day by day, year-in and year-out, without ever criticizing or negating their experience or efforts. She always responded to questions or requests for clarification without ever making anyone feel small or stupid. We were treated with respect at all times, and she always related to our most adult selves. She never trod on the toes of the analyst, for example, always keeping a clear distinction between what she was doing and what was to be left to the student's personal analysis. She could also be most helpful in personal and sometimes practical matters, and always related to us as herself.

In seminars and supervisions Mattie took very detailed notes as students presented material (linking all the words together in her characteristic way of writing). She would discuss the details in the sequence of each session. I know she discarded her notes afterwards as I once asked her for some detail of some material I had presented, since I was then writing a paper on that patient, and she told me that she didn't keep her notes. In the same way I have no longer kept any of my notes. However it makes me think that it was the ongoing process of thinking about the material and the experience with the patient at the time that provided the learning experience over a long and continuous period of time.

In those years to use Klein/Bick/Bion in a containing way as she did – a way that encouraged psychic growth rather than a sense of failure and persecution – was a real art. I think Donald Meltzer and Herbert Rosenfeld had it too.

Mattie was a very astute judge of character and was very clear about who was suitable or unsuitable for the training and for the work. She especially valued honesty and integrity, and she had no doubt about or hesitation in excluding or dismissing anyone who did not regard such qualities as of the utmost importance. When I look back, I realize how much she trusted us, very young as we were, with grave responsibility in the work, because she knew she could. I think all this helped us to grow psychically. The learning was through experience, and it never felt didactic. She inspired our great interest, motivation and passion for our work. Her warmth and genuine interest in our progress were always present.

Her generous hospitality was legendary, so much given with such apparent ease and largesse. And I was always made to feel most welcome by Mattie and Don whenever I returned to visit the UK.

Having been asked to write something for this book, four of us sat around a table over a lovely dinner and shared our recollections. It reminded me of how deep and lasting some of our friendships have been from doing this course together. I think not only because of the shared experience at the Tavistock with Mattie, but also because she knew how to choose her students. We can communicate with one another in a deep and meaningful way, which I think comes from a shared, and then from an absorbed common experience over a number of years, which has lasted and continues to develop inside us to this day – in our case, for more than 38 years since we left the Tavistock. We go on sharing with and nurturing each other. Mattie remains very much alive and enriching within each of us.

I realize that Mattie's enormous contribution, which I have so introjected, has enabled me to use the most valuable tool in my work, which is myself, the person I am, the person I have become and go on becoming. I am aware now how much faith she had in my potential, which she nurtured all those years – of which I, starting out at 24, had no idea.

With her passing, Mattie left an unfilled hole in the psychoanalytic world. She was unique, and I was fortunate to have had the experience that I did with her.

Thank you, Mattie. With love.

POSTSCRIPT

Among schoolchildren

Meg Harris Williams

It is not always remembered that Martha Harris was a schoolteacher before she was a psychoanalyst, and taught in a Froebel teacher-training college.[1] When she inherited Esther Bick's Child Psychotherapy training course in 1960, she brought to it a wealth of educational experience that would lie behind her radical restructuring of the course. It was not just her own direct experience but also that of her husband Roland, who taught for many years in secondary schools in disadvantaged areas of London. How to disseminate psychoanalytic knowledge in the wider community and help children who had no access to individual psychotherapy even if they might benefit from it, was a constant preoccupation. They both believed that emotional learning (learning from experience) and vocational learning (learning about) were interdependent; the key to child development lay in the relation between these two. A good school environment could offer opportunities for widening the perspective of any child's internal, core family values.

---

1 Friedrich Froebel established the first kindergartens in 1882, using play methods and materials to develop a holistic approach to very young children's education. His teachings are still used in modern practice.

These principles were translated from the schoolroom into the new model for the Child Psychotherapy training.

My mother was very much a realist, as her writings bear out. She stressed the fact that needy children (and adults) exist everywhere, not just in our capital cities, and her papers offer frequent examples of cases where some alternative to traditional psychotherapy has had to be sought, and where the struggle to provide may even have brought to light some unexpected advantages in terms of linking with the wider world. Some of these examples occur in her books for parents on child personality development (1969). Others occur in her papers "Consultation project in a comprehensive school" (1968b) and "Teacher, counsellor, therapist: towards a definition of the roles" (1972). The "consultation project" – the pilot for what later became the Schools Counsellors' course at the Tavistock – was carried out at my father's school, Woodberry Down Comprehensive, a flagship school that fostered much educational innovation at that time (the 1960s). My father was deputy head there for five years, at the same time as a very enlightened and dynamic headmistress, Mrs H. R. Chetwynd. When she retired he too left the school. The origins of the school's counselling service are described by Jack Whitehead in his history of the school:

> Over the years children came from all over the Commonwealth and we took in refugees from every war zone, so that the school became a complete melting pot. This has been the story of all London schools and has been for years, but I was able to watch the change from close up…
>
> For me the House system was a completely new and exhilarating experience. Instead of teaching a subject, we were getting to know the pupils, their brothers and sisters and the parents, over a period of years. We interviewed them at eleven and stayed with them until either they left, or we did. Officially their work was not our concern. We could always talk to the subject teachers when things went wrong and perhaps have a word with the child. We were often buffers between conflicting interests and could help smooth things out. Often all that was necessary was a period of closer observation and supervision.

> Sometimes things were more complicated that that. Some behaviour seemed inexplicable to me. A highly intelligent child could go off the boil. There could be a sudden change of attitude. A previously happy child could withdraw. There was no end of puzzling questions. I travelled into school every day with Roland (Doc) Harris, the deputy head, and one of the most perceptive people I have ever met. Amongst other things, I discussed some of my problems with him, bouncing off his brains. Mattie Harris, his wife, was a psychotherapist at the Tavistock Clinic, in Swiss Cottage. Roland told her about my problems and she came in to my houseroom at lunch time every Thursday for about a year. I interviewed my problem cases and she observed and gently joined in. Her help was invaluable, but there became more to it than that.
>
> The following year Mattie Harris opened a class for Counselling at the Tavistock, with Doc Harris in the chair. By this time he was at Brunel University, organizing work experience in industry for the students. Each week a group of about twenty teachers and social workers met for a lecture and a group discussion and at the end of the year we were all a lot wiser than when we started. Over the years hundreds must have attended these classes and become counsellors. Shirley Hase and I were among the first batch of Tavistock counsellors. And this all started in Doc Harris's van on the way to school. Very sadly Doc Harris had a serious stroke and died during the course of that year. A great loss, felt by everyone. Travelling each day in his van was a liberal education in itself.
>
> (Whitehead, 2009; internet citation)

We see how the Course had its roots in the mid-60s in conversations about individual children who posed "inexplicable" problems, which could be helped by the psychotherapist acting as "consultant to the counsellor" (as Martha Harris put it), whilst being present at the time. Mr Whitehead (personal communication, 2012) has described how in these consultations she would quickly pinpoint the psychological problem behind the learning or behavioural difficulty, and work out a means of trying to deal with it – generally within the school setting, either because this was sufficient, or because there was no realistic option of psychotherapy. He further writes, on reading "Consultation project" many years after it was written:

> I am fascinated to realize how carefully and discretely Roland and Mattie carried out their analysis of the school, looking at it from so many different directions, and how carefully they developed what was to become the Tavistock Counselling Course. What Roland and Mattie did was to examine the typical problems common to all large schools and so created the Counselling Course around familiar themes. As I read Mattie's words a new picture of the school emerges. So far as I knew, Mattie came in to see me interview my problem children. This was extremely helpful to me but at the same time she was quietly talking to other people and other children in other settings. Nobody knew about the other work she was doing and there was no discussion between us. Roland never discussed with me what Mattie was doing in our many journeys to and from school. Mattie was like a fish in the water, ever present, silent and alert. The resulting writing is like no picture of a school I have ever read. It is nearer to a piece of atmospheric music - a nocturne of some sort. Themes come and go, return in another key, and new themes appear seamlessly. (Whitehead, 2012, personal communication)

At the same time my mother saw a training opportunity for her students, interdigitating school and clinic work. Through Roland she was in contact with many of the heads of London schools and brought in many external lecturers to the Tavistock. In addition to the official counselling course, Mattie arranged for some of her students (as mentioned by several in the present volume) to do therapeutic consultations in schools; these provided special or protected time for problem pupils, or pupils with problems. It was an extension of the pastoral care which has always to some degree been a tradition in British schools – owing in part to the boarding school system, later complemented by the need for parenting in schools with more evidently disadvantaged children. She saw the potential for expanding psychoanalytic resources in schools, and at the same time, expanding students' knowledge of human development and dynamics. Doing this through Work

Discussion groups increased the acquisition of knowledge exponentially in both directions and amongst a greater number of trainees.[2] Her overriding goal was to serve "the child", finding a place in the world for her workers; and as Donald Meltzer has written, the administrative skills that she had to acquire and tailor to this task did not come naturally to her: "Mattie worked out her method for meeting the requirements of the Establishment without sacrificing the ethos of the learning work-group. But it cost her a lot, which only the support of Roland made it possible for her to sustain" (see Appendix).

In the two counselling papers, a great variety of experimental modes of interaction are catalogued, exploring "the dynamics of interpersonal relationships between individuals and groups, children and adults, both parents and teachers, and in personality development" (Harris, 1968b, p. 343). My mother's approach to enabling therapeutic consultations within the school environment was firstly, to make sharp and precise distinctions, clarifying the pros and cons of different settings (as in the "Teacher, counsellor, therapist" paper), but then to ensure the boundaries could be merged at points if it was necessary – depending on the realities of the situation. This, she says, is what happens in real life anyway, whether we like it or not. But it can only be done effectively if there is full self-awareness on the part of the worker: hence the necessity both to make distinctions, and to practice constant self-scrutiny – another of her favourite maxims. With her own students, as evidenced by many accounts in this book, she preferred to stress the growth of wisdom than to insist on rules of technique.

The work in schools, when combined with that with children and families in the clinic, led to the categorization of six different modes of learning, later written up with Donald Meltzer as "A psychoanalytical model of the child-in-the-family-in-the-community" (1976). The idea underlying all my mother's educational projects was the same as that in psychotherapy

---

2 A book about Work Discussion has been edited by Margaret Rustin and Jonathan Bradley (2008), and Gianna Williams is currently editing a book about Special Time with individual children (a concept that has been further codified, particularly in Italy).

itself: essentially, how to restore the natural processes of a child's impaired development – impaired for whatever reason, personal or environmental. She tried to keep opportunities for help flexible, without rigid boundaries, knowing that these would result in exclusions. In the school environment, the worker needed to be prepared momentarily to switch roles. For example, she might be leading a group session in which one child might show signs of making revelations too intimate for the context – in which case, she says, they should be stopped and asked to come and see her afterwards on their own. Conversely, in a more intimate group, but whose members' main problem is illiteracy, the worker should be prepared to fulfil a teaching role and allow reading and writing to be part of the communication. As Shakespeare said, we all play many roles – some of them simultaneously. Teachers and general practitioners, amongst others, have long known (though maybe not in these terms) that features of the infantile transference in an ongoing consultation process are not confined to official psychotherapy sessions. Bion's dictum, which my mother was fond of quoting, applies in all such situations: it is not necessary to be possessed of extraordinary intelligence, but such intelligence as one does have, needs to be available for use "under fire".

Following on from Jack Whitehead's historical picture, I would like to delve further back in time, and also in terms of the natural history of an idea, to pinpoint the emotional origins of the school therapeutic consultation: in particular to see what generated the cross-fertilization of the traditional teacher-as-pastoral carer, with the specialist understanding of the psychotherapist. One of my father's poems, written in his twenties (the late 1940s), records the origins of this new idea – which like all ideas, is really an old idea, experienced on the pulses and ready to take root in a new context. The poem was among those selected by my mother for publication after his death in 1969, and has no title, though it may be seen as a response to Yeats's *Among Schoolchildren* and to other poems by Yeats about introjection and projection (especially his "swan" poems). I quote the poem in full here, and will then say a few words about how it works:

The schoolroom empties; down stone steps tumble
a babble of children's voices; straight-backed desks
look upright and surprised; learning humble
as litter lies in wastepaper arabesques.
The sun clings quiet on the distempered wall
in tall oblongs flawed by the window glass.
The master closes a book, and breathes contented,
with the inward smile of one who has seen swans pass
morning time under old elms in the park,
on the tree-dark lake breasting dust from the water;
a vision of swans into October work.

The book closes, but questions one to ten
recur unanswered. It is difficult for a man
to enter the minds of children like a swan;
or to close the book on them, for they return
for something they have forgotten, or some whim,
when he is quiet as milk, inch deep in cream,
with their rough tongues they lap at him;
and when he sleeps, they stir him with a dream.
Most often he is wakened by one vague child,
high-bridged, streak-toothed, distemper faced, with spoiled
slum eyes unwinking, wide and wild.

This hair-fallen-forward wrapped-in-self wax idiot,
light-of-life flawed by window of man and wife
faulty or cheap glass, comes in like a cheat
and picks the mind's pocket of all other thought;
runs off and buys himself a gimcrack mirror;
sees ever no world new, nor other self
such as, head down through legs, a boy sees clear
with supernatural creative error;
but least like children, as from growth most far;
nor in one plane, the present, like them all,
but in one place of it, himself, lives caged and small.

Between fulfilment and its prophecy
we live, between worlds unborn and dead;
growth is the principle of our beauty,
striving to speak the inward sense of things:
not learnt-by-heart, nor shop-bought rootless flower,

> nor million dead perfections of newsprint,
> nor ordered anarchy of absolute political power;
> nor holy Aquinas even, scholared saint, in the Vatican,
> save as he is both after and before:
> one with the tangled childish script, and
> with long roots like a prophet's beard and hair.
>
> But not so complex is the idiot present,
> made of a past identical and empty,
> and futured so to no development.
> Cracked in the fit's heat, Dostoevsky's held
> All in the fragile vase; but this child ill
> with emptiness is dropsy-full of wind.
> The master thinks: an outworn style in masonry,
> eventually too the poetry is still;
> growth moves, and beauty, like a vision of swans.
> His peace the idiot pierces to the centre,
> child who in enters, whom he cannot enter.
>
> The outworn school dark prison high and fast;
> the cast-off socks of learning, like waste paper,
> are not the tragic buskin of plays past.
> It would be well, he thinks, losing his swans,
> to hold the wall as effortless as the sun
> brightens the steep, drab, school partition,
> in centuries of flame quiet as a nun;
> which rises, as on seamen long adrift,
> first warm from night (stirring the swans at home);
> then high and fierce its terrible gaze does loom
> over their vacant faces, grazed by the sheetless boom.
>
> (Harris, R.J., 1970, pp. 14-15)

The poem opens with the everyday world, as children's voices go like a babbling brook down stone steps and fade away. The classroom is now quiet and so is the mind of the teacher. When he closes his book, he can breathe contented, conscious of the beauty that infuses his everyday work, as figured in the vision of swans beneath the trees – the mellow autumnal phase of his "October work". The swans "breast the dust", cleansing the water of the mind's lake, which is rippled but serene. The children's formal learning lies in wastepaper arabesques, picturesque but discarded. But they return, as in a dream, finding some pretext to lap at the milk of that other knowledge which they believe is contained in his head. The dream carries their real, unformulable, questions: questions about their growth and development. How can such questions be received and answered in the context of ordinary lessons? "It is difficult to enter the minds of children like a swan." So, reciprocally, the teacher finds he cannot "close the book" on them; they find a way into his mind and stir its contents. Somehow, introjection and projection take place; they are "learning", and so is he.

But there is one "vague" child who, "caged and small", returns in a different, more disturbing, insistent way. He returns not because he has questions but because he has none, neither conscious nor unconscious. He does not swim in the stream of that growth which "is the principle of our beauty". To understand the use of the term "idiot" (which would be replaced by other more technical terms these days) we need to ask: in what does the ugliness of this child consist? At first it appears to be an ugliness of the physical, everyday world, conveyed by the clumsy, unmellifluous (consonant-blocked), unrhythmical lines "high-bridged, streak-toothed, distemper faced, with spoiled/ slum eyes" and "This hair-fallen-forward wrapped-in-self wax idiot".

This external ugliness is then translated into the possibility of broken, mismatched, or poorly endowed internal parents. How can he enter the "vacancy" within this child's mind? Vacancy seems one with impenetrability – a faulty container. Running through the poem is a metaphysical-style conceit of a glass or mirror through which the child sees himself, in relation to the light of his objects. The "window of man and wife" that engendered him was perhaps made of cheap glass that has resulted in a "flaw" in his life-light. This goes back to the first stanza where there was a naturalistic description of the sunlit patterns on the wall, broken by shadows from the window-bars. The external world now becomes dream-image; the words "distemper" and "flaw" take on psychical connotations, no longer referring merely to the material reality of paint and patterning, but to the psychological reality of splitting and disintegration. This "caged" child has no window of imagination such as that with which the normal child can experimentally reverse the perspective of his vision "with supernatural creative error", and foresee his potentialities.

The vacancy of the idiot child indicates a deficient life-force, and reminds the teacher of "cast-off socks of learning" that have been consigned to the bin or that can turn the schoolroom into a "prison", "an outworn style in masonry", all external shell with no inward light. The deprived child has no voice in his head that can "speak the inward sense of things", no vision of white paper arabesques turning into swans. The concept of mental rubbish expands through the teacher's meditation into more sophisticated versions, such as may be found in the "perfections of newsprint" or the "ordered anarchy of political power". Even the brilliant Aquinas is pictured as truly alive mentally only when an old man and a child, "after and before" but not during his enshrinement in the Vatican. In between "fulfilment and its prophecy" perhaps he too was a deprived child.

The teacher returns in his reflections to the idiot child, who is "less complex" in himself, yet more complex in the problems that he raises about the failure of the poetic principle in life: "ill with emptiness", he is "dropsy-full of wind". If he remains outside the stream of life, not part of its overall picture, then "eventually too the poetry is still". The opposite end of the spectrum is Dostoevsky's famous *Idiot* who, "cracked in the fit's heat… held all in the fragile vase" – the ultimate poetic container, that (in the ancient Chinese definition) encloses "heaven and earth in the cage of form". Thus two kinds of idiot are compared and contrasted, two kinds of constricted mental space: the claustrophobic, and the highly condensed; the empty, and the full to bursting. In one the container is flawed by too little poetic sensibility; in the other, by too much.

In the final stanza of the poem a strange change is heralded. The teacher has been unable to close the book on the idiot child. As in Yeats' *The Second Coming* ("the centre cannot hold"), he is "pierced to the centre" by the child who enters his mind and yet "whom he cannot enter". Forced to receive projections that do not even have the quality of a cry for help, so cannot be digested and returned, the teacher finds his own mind is on the point of undergoing some catastrophic transformation. He takes another look at the blocks of sunlight on the schoolroom wall with the cracks traced across them. They no longer bring to mind tranquil swan-thoughts – those are "lost". Now they are re-structured, through the faces of the entire group of children, who are no longer a babbling brook or a rippled lake: they are at sea, adrift, with "vacant faces" like the idiot child. The swans become huge sails; the window-bars that cross the light with shadows, turn into the "sheetless boom" that warns the ship is beyond the sailors' control. A warmth is engendered by the sunlight that "stirs the swans at home" – new shapes, new thoughts are born.

In the gradual crescendo of the last five lines of the poem, the quiet, secluded, nun-like flame expands with a rhythmic inevitability, growing into the "terrible gaze" of the noonday sun, "high and fierce" like Coleridge's "hot and copper sun". The onward sweep culminates in the deep resonance of the final triplet's rhyme, "home-loom-boom". The boom heralds the blow that will deliver the new knowledge and change the teacher's mind for ever, setting him on a new course that must somehow find a way of communicating with the nongrowing idiot child that exists in every classroom, every mind. The ends of the spectrum – the two types of idiot – are brought into contact. The "terrible gaze" of the new sun will "graze" those vacant faces – but not destroy them utterly. As Yeats put it, "a terrible beauty is born" (*Easter 1916*).

In this case, the new idea is that the idiot child is an aspect of ourselves, representing what Martha Harris referred to as "lacunae", unreachable parts of the mind. These are parts that cannot engage with growth in themselves, yet without which the whole personality cannot progress or be "born". "What rough beast/Slouches towards Bethlehem to be born?" asked Yeats. What catastrophic change is required of the personality for such elements to be acknowledged, empathized with, and enticed into the turbulent waters of life – the growth that is the principle of our beauty? The true poetic mind was defined by Keats as one for whom "the miseries of the world/ Are misery, and will not let them rest" (*Fall of Hyperion*, I.158-9).

The teacher's mind, coalescing with that of the poet, requires some psychoanalytic insight and methodology to include the parts which cannot keep up with the Pied Piper of the developmental process – or which result in "inexplicable behaviour" (Whitehead). The hope for humanity lies in the recognition that the "idiot child" is internal and universal. This recognition makes communication possible, available for use in transference situations. As was later stressed in *A Psychoanalytical Model of the Child-in-the-Family-in-the-Community* (Harris and Meltzer, 1976), in the "couple family" it is not enough to help *most* of the children develop – only the growth of *all* members is sufficient to maintain a "sense of security". An inacccessible tragic part of the personality, or non-developing child, means tragedy for all and is the source of human misery in the wider world. This was the perceptual basis on which Martha and Roland Harris worked out their marriage of educational and psychoanalytic principles, amongst the schoolchildren.

APPENDIX

Portrait of Mattie[1]

Donald Meltzer

She was tall and strongly built, even slightly masculine, if you didn't look at those arresting eyes. Heavy-lidded and deep-set, almost sleepy and yet penetratingly attentive, with a soft blue grey, "the hills in my eyes" she would say. The strong facial bone structure of her father rather overshadowed the aspects of delicate beauty from her mother ("What wonderful big hats she wore", Mattie would say longingly). Her gait in latter years was a bit stiff in the lower back which emphasized the fine, broad thorax. She looked particularly splendid in royal blue and purple and would have worn floral gowns for ever. Fine materials were a passion, and she could rapidly run up a dress, though never with the skill and patience of her mother. She always had too many irons in the fire, so that meals, lectures, the garden, sewing and reading tended to go on simultaneously in some mysterious economy. For days before giving a party for the students at the Old Rectory at Mersea, the shopping and cooking would go on in the interstices of the

---

1 Written in 1987 as a preface to *Collected Papers of Martha Harris and Esther Bick* (Perthshire: Clunie Press).

day and night. And on the day, amazing amounts in amazing varieties of meats and salads and sweets would emerge as if from nowhere.

She had a particular way of talking that often seemed at first a stutter but was in fact a complicated process of accommodation between the complexity of her thought and the minute responses of her audience. A typescript from a tape looked terrible, but the effect on a listener was like standing well back from the brushstrokes of a Van Dyke, amazed to see that the mass of wiggly lines suddenly fused into silk and lace and jewels. The slight soft Scottish furriness of her voice tempered her vehemence in debate, and her laugh chimed out in a most infectious way. While easily entertained by wit, she was not witty or entertaining herself, but her gaiety could fill a room and encourage the sallies of others, keen for her admiration.

Her hands were strong and later on slightly gnarled, death to weeds and dexterous with needles. When the film was being made in India in the hysterical atmosphere of too little time and money and a plethora of prima donnas,[2] Mattie's quiet and attentive knitting away soothed everyone, as a fascinating diagonal patterned pullover gradually emerged. She did not write easily but had to revise and revise. Her handwriting was the opposite of her mode of speech, for it looked lovely from a distance but was almost unreadable because she never took the pen from the paper. Everything was fused together, like Mrs Bick's description of "looping".

Animals did not attract or interest her much, despite her childhood on the farm, but the beauty of the landscape ravished her. The works of man made perhaps less impact, with the exception of literature, and there her knowledge and memory and comprehension often astonished. She read voluminously, but only very unwillingly of the psychoanalytic literature. Even Bion, whose supervision had been her great inspiration after

---

2 A film of Bion's *A Memoir of the Future* was started but never finished – owing partly to running out of money but primarily to Martha Harris's car accident in France in summer 1984, that resulted in her death in 1987. Several wellknown actors were involved in the film. For a verse narrative based on the story of the film see M. H. Williams (2005), pp. 221-40.

Mrs Klein's, she read half-heartedly. Though she'd been keen on sports in her youth (the broken front teeth came from the hockey field), games of any sort bored her. One couldn't imagine Mattie playing cards or chess, though Roland had been an enthusiast of the latter. But Scottish dancing – that was another matter. No reel was long enough for her.

She was devoted to children, but I never saw her dote on a child, or talk over his head, or violate his privacy. Her warm reserve was almost paradoxical, charming without effort, generous without being indulgent. She seemed always to mean what she said, but never said all she meant, and when something hurtful had to be spoken, she could "tell the truth, but tell it slant", as Emily Dickinson would say.

Martha Harris and the Tavistock course[3]

By both background and inclination, Mattie was a scholar of English literature and a teacher. Nothing was more foreign to her nature than the administrative requirements that eventually devolved upon her at the Tavistock. If ever anyone had "greatness thrust upon them", it was the reluctant Mattie at the time when Mrs Bick left the Clinic and it was up to Mattie to either take over to or let the infant child psychotherapy course fade away.

The way in which she came to terms with this crisis in her life—and here Roland's encouragement and help was essential—was by framing a radical pedagogical method. Many of the central ideas came from Roland, who was at that time deputy headmaster of a large comprehensive school in London, prior to his going to the Ministry of Education and later to Brunel University. The central conviction, later hallowed in Bion's concept of "learning from experience", was that the kind of learning which transformed a person into a professional worker had to be rooted in the intimate relations with inspired teachers, living and dead, present and in books. Roland himself, as poet and scholar, was an inspired teacher and the many textbooks he

---

3 This section was also printed as an appendix to *The Tavistock Model* (ed. M. H. Williams, 2011).

wrote concentrated on the development in the student of the capacity to read in both a comprehensive and a penetrating way.

The second central thesis was that learning takes place in a group context and that the management of the atmosphere was an essential task of the teachers. The prevention of elitism, the avoidance of competitiveness, and the replacement of selection by self-selection through hard work-tasks were the essential components of this task. But Mattie's experience as a teacher, during the war years and after, before she trained as a child psychotherapist and psychoanalyst, had taught her the importance of meeting the formal requirements of the Establishment if there was to be established a profession of child psychotherapy with positions in clinics and schools for the graduates of the course. Here again Roland's extensive administrative knowledge was an invaluable aid to Mattie, not naturally given to orderliness, let alone to giving orders. Eventually she became an impressive negotiator and even, some claimed, politician in the interests of the course and of the Association that was later formed in conjunction with the Hampstead Clinic and the Margaret Lowenfeld group.

Here again Bion's teaching about groups, and later about the structure of the personality, with its endoskeletal structure and its social exoskeletal carapace, played a central role in her thinking. In keeping with the differentiation between Christ and Caesar, Mattie worked out her method for meeting the requirements of the Establishment without sacrificing the ethos of the learning work-group. But it cost her a lot, which only the support of Roland made it possible for her to sustain. When he died suddenly in 1969 of a ruptured cerebral aneurism, she developed an acute aplastic anaemia from whose fatal consequences she was saved by timely diagnosis, medication with cortisone, and a dream in which Roland told her she still had work to do for the family and the Course.

REFERENCES

Alvarez, A. (1998). Failures to link: attacks or defects? Some questions concerning the thinkability of Oedipal and pre-Oedipal thoughts. *Journal of Child Psychotherapy* 24 (2): 213-231.

Baron-Cohen, S., et al. (1996). Psychological markers in the detection of autism in infancy in a large population. *British Journal of Psychiatry* 168: 158 – 63.

Bhownagary, A. (1983). Individual work in a young family care centre. *Journal of Child Psychotherapy* 9 (2): 161- 19.

Bick, Esther. (1964). Notes on infant observation in psychoanalytic training. In: *The Tavistock Model*, ed. M. H. Williams, pp. 97-116. Harris Meltzer Trust, 2011. First published in *IJPA* 54: 558-66 (1964).

Bick, Esther. (1968). The experience of the skin in early object relations. In: *The Tavistock Model*, ed. M. H. Williams, pp. 133-38. Harris Meltzer Trust, 2011. First published in *IJPA* 49: 484-86.

Bion, F. (1985). Envoi. In: W. R. Bion, *All My Sins Remembered*. Reprinted London: Karnac, 1991.

Bion, W. R. (1961). *Experiences in Groups*. London: Tavistock.

Bion, W. R. (1962). *Learning from Experience*. London: Heinemann.

Bion, W. R. (1970). *Attention and Interpretation.* London: Tavistock.

Bion, W. R. (1973). *Brazilian Lectures.* Vol. 1. Rio de Janiero: Imago.

Bion, W. R. (2005). *The Tavistock Seminars.* London: Karnac.

Bobath, B. (1979). Unpublished paper. London: The Bobath Centre.

Britton, R. (1989) The missing link: Parental sexuality in the Oedipus complex. In: J. Steiner (ed.), *The Oedipus Complex Today,* London: Karnac.

Brutti, C. and Parlani, R. (Eds.) (1989). *Quaderni di Psicoterapia Infantile* no. 18. Rome: Borla.

Brutti, C. and Parlani, R. (1990). Stereotipie: prime note con riferimento all"autismo. In *Quaderni di Psicoterapia Infantile* no. 22, pp. 183-92. Rome: Borla.

Brutti, C. and Parlani, R. (1996). Uso e abuso dell'osservazione. *Quaderni di Psicoterapia Infantile* 33: 5-18. Rome: Borla.

Brutti, C. and Parlani, R. (2003). Introduction to Chiozza, L., *Psicoanalisi dei disturbi epatici.* Perugia: Eidon.

Brutti, C. and Parlani, R. (2010). *Scrutatori d'Anime.* Roma: Asino.

Cebon, A. (2007). Supervision with Esther Bick 1973-74. Journal of Child Psychotherapy 33 (2), 221-238. Reprinted in *The Tavistock Model,* ed. M. H. Williams, pp. 347-73. London: Harris Meltzer Trust, 2011.

Chiozza, L. (2005). La coscienza. In: *La Psicoanalisi che Viene* no.2: *Coscienza e Affetto.* ed. C. and R. Brutti. Perugia: Eidon.

Chiozza, L. (2007). *Le Cose della Vita.* Troiona: Citta Aperta.

Datler, W., Lazar, R.A. & Trunkenpolz, K. (2009). An exploration of the quality of life in nursing homes: the use of single case and organisational observation in a research project. *Journal of Infant Observation*, 12 (1): 63-82.

Devereux, G. (1998). *De l'angoisse a la methode dans les sciences du comportement.* Paris: Aubier.

Eliot, G. *Middlemarch.* (1985 [1872]). Harmondsworth: Penguin.

Haag, G., et al. (2005). Psychodynamic assessment of changes in children with autism under psychoanalytic treatment. *International Journal of Psychoanalysis* 86: 335 – 52.

Harris, M. G. (1966). Therapeutic consultations. In: *The Tavistock Model,* ed. M. H. Williams, pp. 289-304. London: Harris Meltzer

Trust, 2011. Part of a paper written jointly with Helen Carr, *Journal of Child Psychotherapy* 1 (4): 13-19 (1966).

Harris, M. G. (1968a). The therapeutic process in the psychoanalytic treatment of the child. In: *The Tavistock Model*, ed. M. H. Williams, pp. 219-34. London: Harris Meltzer Trust, 2011. First published in *Collected Papers of Martha Harris and Esther Bick*, ed. M. H. Williams (Clunie Press, 1987).

Harris, M. G. (1968b). Consultation project in a comprehensive school. In: *The Tavistock Model*, ed. M. H. Williams, pp. 317-44. London: Harris Meltzer Trust, 2011. First published in *Collected Papers of Martha Harris and Esther Bick*, ed. M. H. Williams (Clunie Press, 1987).

Harris, M. G. (1972). Teacher, counsellor, therapist: towards a definition of the roles. In: *The Tavistock Model*, ed. M. H. Williams, pp. 305-16. London: Harris Meltzer Trust, 2011. First published in *Collected Papers of Martha Harris and Esther Bick*, ed. M. H. Williams (Clunie Press, 1987).

Harris, M. G. (1975a). *Thinking about Infants and Young Children*. New edition, London: Harris Meltzer Trust, 2011.

Harris, M. G. (1975b). Some notes on maternal containment in "good enough" mothering. In: *The Tavistock Model*, ed. M. H. Williams, pp. 139-62. London: Harris Meltzer Trust, 2011. First published in *Journal of Child Psychotherapy* 4 (1): 35-51 (1975).

Harris, M. G. (1975c). The early basis of adult female sexuality and motherliness. In: *The Tavistock Model*, ed. M. H. Williams, pp.189-206. London: Harris Meltzer Trust, 2011. First published in *Collected Papers of Martha Harris and Esther Bick*, ed. M. H. Williams (Clunie Press, 1987).

Harris, M. G. (1976). The contribution of observation of mother-infant interaction and development to the equipment of a psychoanalyst or psychoanalytic psychotherapist. In: *The Tavistock Model*, ed. M. H. Williams, pp. 117-32. London: Harris Meltzer Trust, 2011. First published in *Collected Papers of Martha Harris and Esther Bick*, ed. M. H. Williams (Clunie Press, 1987).

Harris, M. G. (1977). The Tavistock training and philosophy. In: *The Tavistock Model*, ed. M. H. Williams, pp. 1-24. London: Harris Meltzer Trust, 2011. First published in *The Child Psychotherapist*, ed. D. Daws and M. Boston (London: Wildwood House,1977).

Harris, M. G. (1978a). Towards learning from experience in infancy and childhood. In: *The Tavistock Model*, ed. M. H. Williams, pp. 171-88. London: Harris Meltzer Trust, 2011. First published in *Collected Papers of Martha Harris and Esther Bick,* ed. M. H. Williams (Clunie Press, 1987).

Harris, M. G. (1978b). The individual in the group: on learning to work with the psychoanalytical method. In: *The Tavistock Model*, ed. M. H. Williams, pp. 25-44. London: Harris Meltzer Trust, 2011. First published in J. Grotstein (ed.), *Do I Dare Disturb the Universe?* (Beverly Hills: Caesura, 1978). Translated into Italian as "L'individuo nel gruppo apprehendere a lavorare con il metodo psicoanalitico" (1981).

Harris, M. G. (1979). Training in observation and application of psychoanalytical concepts to personality development and interaction. London: *The Tavistock Gazette,* pp. 10-16. Available online at http://www.harris-meltzer-trust.org.uk/pdfs/MHtraining.pdf.

Harris, M. G. (1980a). A baby observation: the absent object. In: *The Tavistock Model*, ed. M. H. Williams, pp. 163-70. London: Harris Meltzer Trust, 2011. First published in *Collected Papers of Martha Harris and Esther Bick*, ed. M. H. Williams (Clunie Press, 1987).

Harris, M. G. (1980b). Bion's conception of a psychoanalytical attitude. In: *The Tavistock Model*, ed. M. H. Williams, pp. 45-50. London: Harris Meltzer Trust, 2011. First published in *Collected Papers of Martha Harris and Esther Bick*, ed. M. H. Williams (Clunie Press, 1987).

Harris, M. G. (1982). Growing points in psychoanalysis inspired by the work of Melanie Klein. In: *The Tavistock Model*, ed. M. H. Williams, pp. 65-92. London: Harris Meltzer Trust, 2011. First published in *Journal of Child Psychotherapy,* 8 (2): 165-84 (1982).

Harris, M. G. (2007). *Your Teenager*. London: Harris Meltzer Trust. Single-volume new edition of three books: *Your Eleven Year Old, Your Twelve to Fourteen Year Old,* and *Your Teenager* (Corgi Books, 1969).

Harris, M. G. and Meltzer, D. (1976). A psychoanalytical model of the child-in-the-family-in-the-community. In *Sincerity and Other Works: Collected Papers of Donald Meltzer,* ed. A. Hahn, pp. 387-454. London: Karnac, 1994.

Harris, R. J. (1970). *Selected Poems.* http://www.harris-meltzer-trust.org.uk/pdfs/HarrisPoems1970.pdf

Houzel, D. (1999). A therapeutic application of infant observation in child psychiatry. *International Journal of Infant Observation and its Applications* 2: 42–53.

Houzel, D. (2001) Bisexual qualities of the psychic envelope. In: *Being Alive: Building on the Work of Anne Alvarez,* ed. J. Edwards. London: Routledge.

Hoxter, S. (1981). La vecchia signora che viveva in una scarpa (The old lady who lived in a shoe). In: *Il Progetto Chance: Seminari Psicologici,* ed. S. M. G. Adamo. Naples, 2003.

Klein, M. (1921). The development of a child. Reprinted in *The Writings of Melanie Klein*, vol. 1, 1975. London: Hogarth.

Lechevalier, B. (2004). *Traitement Psychanalytique Mère-Enfant: Une Approche au Long Cours des Psychoses de l'Enfant.* Paris: in press.

Magagna, J. (1987). Three years of infant observation with Mrs Bick. *Journal of Child Psychotherapy*, 13 (1): 19-39.

Meltzer, D. (1960). Lectures and seminars in Kleinian child psychiatry. In: *Sincerity and Other Works: Collected Papers of Donald Meltzer,* ed. A. Hahn, pp. 53-89. London: Karnac, 1994.

Meltzer, D. (1975). The psychology of autistic states and of post-autistic mentality. In: Meltzer, D. et al, *Explorations in Autism,* pp. 6-32. Perthshire: Clunie Press. Reprinted Harris Meltzer Trust, 2008.

Meltzer, D. (1978). *The Kleinian Development.* Reprinted Harris Meltzer Trust, 2008.

Meltzer, D. (1981). Does Money-Kyrle's concept of misconception have any unique descriptive power? In: *Sincerity and Other Works: Collected Papers of Donald Meltzer,* ed. A. Hahn, pp. 496-513. London: Karnac.

Meltzer, D. (1988). Martha Harris and the Tavistock course. In: *The Tavistock Model,* ed. M. H. Williams, pp. 345-46. London: Harris Meltzer Trust, 2011.

Negri, N. (1989). La fiaba della nascita del fratello nello sviluppo emotive. *Quaderni Psicoterapia Infantile* 18: 45-75. Rome: Borla.

Negri, N. (1994). *The Newborn in the Intensive Care Unit: a Neuropsychiatric Prevention Model.* Perthshire: Clunie Press.

Negri, N. & Harris, M. (2007). *The Story of Infant Development: Observational Work with Martha Harris.* Harris Meltzer Trust. Published in Italian as *Andare Osservando un Bambino: La Lezione di Martha Harris.* Rome: Borla, 2008.

Noziglia, M., Olivetti Manoukian, F., & Vallino, D. (1997). *Nel Castello c'è Spazio per Giocare: Formazione e Organizzazione nei Servizi Educativi per L'infancia. Un Progetto Psicoanalitico.* Bergamo: Junior.

Panikkar, R. (1990). Amicizia ed ermeneutica. Reprinted in Rossi, A., *Pluralismo e Armonia,* pp. 7-14. Assisi: Cittadella, 2011.

Phillips, A. (1999). *Saying No – Why it's Important for You and Your Child.* London: Faber.

Piontelli, A. (1992). *From Fetus to Child.* London & New York: Tavistock/ Routledge.

Racker, H. (1961). *Psychoanalysis and Ethics.* Translated in Italian by C. and R. Brutti (unpublished).

Rhode, M. (2007) Helping toddlers to communicate: infant observation as an early intervention. In *Signs of Autism in Infants: Recognition and Early Intervention,* ed. S. Acquarone. London: Karnac Books.

Rustin, M. (2008). Work discussion: some historical and theoretical observations. In: *Work Discussion Seminars,* ed. M. Rustin & J. Bradley, pp. 3-21. London: Karnac.

Rustin, M. and Bradley, J. (Eds.). (2008). *Work Discussion Seminars: Learning from Reflective Practice in Work with Children and Families.* London: Karnac.

Schulman, M. (2002). *Vauvahavainnointioppia Observoimalla .* Helsinki: Therapeia Foundation.

Schulman, M. (2011). Infant observation as part of training and clinical work with infants and parents. In: *Varhaiset tunnesiteet ja niiden suojeleminen,* ed. J. Sinkkonen and M. Kalland, pp. 125-46. Helsinki: WSOY.

Stern, D. (1985). *The Interpersonal World of the Infant.* New York: Basic Books.

Stern, D. (1995). *The Motherhood Constellation.* New York: Basic Books.

Sternberg, J. (2005). *Infant Observation at the Heart of Training.* London: Karnac.

Tustin, F. (1972) *Autism and Childhood Psychosis*. London: Hogarth Press.

Tustin, F. (1980) Autistic objects. In: F. Tustin, *Autistic States in Children*. London: Routledge. Second revised edition, 1992.

Vallino, D. (1995). Il gioco di immaginazione dei bambini con l'educatrice che osserva, ascolta e aiuta. In: *Giocare e Pensare* ed. M. Noziglia, pp. 29-49. Milano: Guerini.

Vallino, D. (2009). *Fare Psicoanalisi con Genitori e Bambini*. Rome: Borla.

Waddell, M. (2006). Integration, unintegration, disintegration: an introduction. *Journal of Child Psychotherapy* 32: 148-52.

Whitehead, J. (2009). A history of Woodberry Down School. http://www.locallocalhistory.co.uk/schools/woodberry/index.htm

Winkler, Reiner (1997) States of mind and mind of states: infant observation, the fall of the wall and German unification. *Journal of Infant Observation* 1 (1), 111-39.

Williams, G. P. (1989). Mattie al lavoro (Mattie at work). *Quaderni di Psicoterapia Infantile*. Vol. 18, pp. 31-44. Rome: Borla. Revised and translated in this volume, Chapter 1.

Williams, G. P. (2008). Work discussion seminars with the staff of a children's home for street children in Puebla, Mexico. In *Work Discussion Seminars,* ed. M. Rustin & J. Bradley, pp. 253-66. London: Karnac.

Williams, M. H. (Ed.) (1987). *Collected Papers of Martha Harris and Esther Bick.*. Perthshire: Clunie Press. New edition in 2 vols, (1) *The Tavistock Model: Papers on Child Development and Psychoanalytic Training by Martha Harris and Esther Bick,* ed. M. H. Williams (Harris Meltzer Trust, 2011); (2) *Adolescence: Talks and Papers by Donald Meltzer and Martha Harris* ed. M. H. Williams (Harris Meltzer Trust, 2011).

Williams, M. H. (1989). A biography of Martha Harris. Revised 2011, available online at http://www.harris-meltzer-trust.org.uk/pdfs/MHbiography.pdf. In Italian in Quaderni di Psicoterapie Infantile, vol. 18, pp. 12-30. Rome: Borla, 1989.

Williams, M. H. (2005). Confessions of an emmature superego, or the ayah's lament. In *The Vale of Soulmaking: the Post-Kleinian Model of the Mind,* pp. 221-240. London: Karnac.

Williams, M. H. (Ed.) (2011). *The Tavistock Model: Papers on Child Development and Psychoanalytic Training by Martha Harris and Esther Bick*. London: Harris Meltzer Trust.

Winnicott. D. W. (1960). Ego distortion in terms of true and false self. In: *Maturational Processes and the Facilitating Environment*, 1965. London: Hogarth. Reprinted London: Karnac, 1990.

Wittenberg, I. (1970). *Psychoanalytic Insight and Relationships: a Kleinian Approach*. London: Routledge.

INDEX

NAME INDEX

Aberastury Institute, Italy 48
Alvarez, A. 72
Armitage, S. E. 117
Arnold, K. 185
Association of Child Psychotherapists (ACP) 63, 64, 74, 239, 269, 295
Balconi, M. xii, 110, 288, 296
Bandra Clinic, Bombay 65
Begoin, J. 33, 41
Bergonzi, F. 100
Bick, E. 58, 59, 71ff, 164, 259, 272-73, 288, 326
 and Martha Harris' teaching 1, 12, 23, 34ff, 40ff, 78ff, 104, 159, 210, 219, 220, 249, 250, 251, 310, 313
Bion, W. R. xxv, 8, 37, 40, 41, 69, 77ff, 159, 221, 238, 241, 247, 269, 283, 293, 304, 306, 326
 and Martha Harris' teaching 5, 7, 15, 17, 31, 50, 51, 61, 71, 78, 83, 86, 93, 102, 142, 158, 220, 224, 251, 252, 259, 262, 267, 274, 282, 302, 310, 318, 327
 Tavistock lectures 210, 221, 225, 263, 265, 278, 298
Bobath, B. 116
Bowlby, J. 34, 100, 231, 232, 236, 266, 288
Bridger, H. xv, 205
British Institute of Psychoanalysis ix, 41, 219, 224, 225, 232
Britton, R. 201
Carpelan, H. 69
Cassel Hospital xiv, 69
Centro Medico Pedagogico, Novara 288
Centri Studi Martha Harris (CSMH) xiii, xvi, 9, 38
Chatellier, A. M. 41

Chetwynd, H. R. 314
children/ patients
    Alex 88ff
    Andrew 205ff
    Anthea 251ff
    Baby A 275ff
    Charles 103ff, 251ff
    Federico 111ff
    Isabel 202f
    Joseph 244ff
    Lara 250
    Laura 197ff
    Liara 92ff
    Lucia 153
    Peter 142ff
    Serena 125ff
    Shelly 263
    Simone 27
    Stefano 110
    Susie 259
    Thomas 165ff
    Willie 199
Chiozza, L. xii, 51
Clements, L. G. 153, 288, 296
Coleridge, S. T. 323
Datler, W. 59
Descartes, R. 39
Devereux, G. 38
Diem-Wille, G. 59
Dostoevesky, F. 320, 322
Education, Department of 22
EFPP (European Federation for Psychoanalytic Psychotherapy) xvi, 37, 38
Eliot, G. 266, 268
Freud, A. 68, 225, 232, 236, 250, 280, 288, 289
Froebel, F. ix, 297
Garcia, M. 71
Gaveriaux, O. 38
GERPEN, France xiii, 11, 33ff, 39ff, 77, 163, 164, 197

Gill, H. 68
Gosling, R. 8
Gromignana 140
Guignard, F. 41
Haag, G. 33, 41, 42, 68, 164, 199, 209
Harris, M. G., writings
    "A baby observation: the absent object" (1980) 26
    "Bion's conception of a psychoanalytical attitude" (1980) 86
    "Consultation project in a comprehensive school" (1968) 13, 261, 314, 317
    "The contribution of observation of mother-infant interaction" (1976) 25, 26, 27, 30, 82
    "The early basis of adult female sexuality" (1975) 198
    "The individual in the group" (1978) 50, 51, 61, 83, 84, 159, 262
    "Growing points in psychoanalysis" (1982) 77ff, 151
    "A psychoanalytical model of the child" (1976) 206, 317
    "Some notes on maternal containment" (1975) 26, 80, 82, 103, 250, 252
    "The Tavistock training and philosophy "(1977) 26, 28, 29, 55, 62, 79, 83, 245, 246, 247
    "Teacher, counsellor, therapist" (1972) 314
    "Therapeutic consultations" (1966) 38, 199
    "The therapeutic process" (1968) 26
    Thinking about Infants and Young Children (1975) 75, 246

"Towards learning from experience" (1978) xxiii, 30, 32, 82, 158
"Training in observation" (1979) 2
Harris, R. ix, xxi, 22, 40, 229, 295, 296, 303, 308, 315, 316ff
Haugsgjerd, S. 228
Horniman Therapy Centre, Mumbai 65
Hoxter, S. 73, 217
Isaacs-Elmhirst, S. 196, 294
Israel, A. 58
Johnson, S. 291
Keats, J. 15, 31, 65, 81, 84, 86, 267
Kestenberg, J. 55
Klein, M. 12, 61, 236, 246, 293, 327
    and Martha Harris' teaching 20, 77-78, 81, 83-84, 219, 224, 246, 252, 269, 274, 282-83, 286, 288, 310
    and Meltzer's teaching 41, 68, 286, 293, 306
    supervision with 39-41
Lechevalier, B. 37, 199
Lowenfeld, M. 280, 328
Mahler, M. 55
Magagna, J. 71
Meltzer, D. 35, 40, 61, 68, 69, 78, 80, 82, 151, 164, 199, 206, 208, 220, 249, 251, 271, 286, 290, 305, 306, 308
    teaching with Martha Harris 27, 33ff, 39, 46, 50-52, 60, 125ff, 141, 153, 163, 173ff, 224, 226, 237, 238, 285, 291, 293, 294, 303, 307
Mentalhygienisk Rådgivningskontor, Oslo, 41

Mersea, the Old Rectory 74, 107, 228, 238, 256, 298, 303, 325
Miller, L. 239
Money-Kyrle, R. 296, 306
Norwegian Psychoanalytic Society 228
Noziglia, M. 160, 161
O'Shaughnessy, E. 290
Panikkar, R. 45, 47
Perugia 210
Racker, H. 47, 51
Reid, S. 230, 234, 239
Renton, M. I. 72
Rosenfeld, H. ix, 163, 164, 310
Shakespeare, W. 25, 80, 82, 213, 250, 304, 318
Stern, D. 200, 208
Stork, J. 53
Tavistock Gazette 2, 235
Therapeia Foundation, Helsinki xiv, 75
Thomas, D. 77
Thomas, D. M. 236
Thorner, H. 42
Treviglio Hospital, Bergamo 110-11
Turku University, Finland 76
Tustin, F. xiv, xviii, 41, 199, 202, 221, 290
Tuters, E. 218
VAKJP, Germany (Society for Child and Adolescent Psychotherapy) 60
Walker, D. W. 167
Weddell, D. 141
Whitehead, J. 314-16
William Tyndale School 100
Williams, A. H. xix, 224, 296
Winkelmann, A. 57
Winkler, R. 58
Winnicott, D. W. 80, 82, 102, 224, 232, 250, 252

Wittenberg, I. 69, 101, 235, 290
Woodberry Down School 314
Wordsworth, W. 270
Yeats, W. B. 318, 322, 323

SUBJECT INDEX

aesthetic conflict 82
aesthetic reciprocity/ beauty 225, 289, 293, 321
analytic setting 289, 296, 299, 301
anxieties 16, 38, 54, 81, 143, 159, 300
   analyst's 30, 79
   catastrophic 74, 206
   claustrophobic 199, 238, 322
   contamination 114, 119
   about death 112ff
   maternal 29, 112ff, 176, 275
   separation 101, 173, 185
   shaken away 104
   students' 13-15, 72
art-science, psychotherapy as 55
Aspergers xvii, 88
autism 41, 54, 64, 71, 88, 197ff, 220-21
   "idiot" child 321
basic assumption group 3, 69, 83, 257, 262
becoming an analyst/ mother 26, 29, 49-50, 55, 57, 61, 80, 84, 102, 158, 215, 265ff, 293, 311
beta-elements 96, 102, 142
breast, *see* object
breastfeeding 117ff, 128ff, 165
catastrophic change 77, 307, 323
child psychotherapy training 3ff, 12ff, 20, 28, 31ff, 34ff, 48, 50ff, 55, 65, 68, 85, 100, 159, 219, 224, 225, 229, 229-30, 237, 242, 247, 261, 279, 294
   history 1ff, 12, 34, 40, 219
   and publishing 236
   top-up adult training 222
claustrum/ claustrophobia 97, 199, 238, 298, 322
committees, Martha Harris and 10
container/ containment 16, 29, 61, 71, 78-79, 81, 87, 166-67, 168, 171, 177, 182, 196, 199, 206, 209, 250-52, 253, 259, 297
   v. "shut in" 97
   see also object
co-operation
   in baby 171
   in couple 201, 233
counselling in schools ix, 101, 242, 314ff
countertransference 28, 101, 103, 106, 164, 198, 192, 221, 245, 274, 283
crèche/ nursery 35, 160, 166ff, 200, 209, 242
defences 25, 27, 31, 40, 51
depression, maternal 172ff, 251
depressive position 282-83, 289
development, *see* personality development
dissociation 237
epistemophilic instinct, *see* knowledge, search for
ethics of psychoanalysis 50, 51
existence, sense of 37, 158, 198, 200
family consultations 199ff
feeding difficulties 126ff
foetal personality/ development 112ff, 181

good enough mother 80, 102, 250ff
good grandmother transference 161
group, internal 78
group relations xiv, xv, 5, 7, 49, 55
hallucination
hospital assessment
identification xxv, 30, 35, 78, 114, 282
    adhesive 4, 10
    introjective 215, 252, 268, 297
    projective/ violent 10, 70, 82, 123, 158, 215
identity 46, 51, 78, 158, 302
infant observation 2, 12ff, 22, 25ff, 35, 55, 64, 67, 70, 79, 99, 115ff, 174, 186, 188, 216, 244, 250ff, 275, 306
    and analytic couple 29
    extension of 159
    therapeutic 201
intensive care, neonatal 160
interview technique xxv, 20, 68, 74, 99, 197, 211, 213, 214, 215, 220, 222, 234, 237, 242, 267, 181, 293
K link *see* knowledge, search for
knowledge, search for 41, 51, 81, 102, 278, 289
lacunae, mental 82, 323
learning, modes of 84, 313
    from experience xxiv-vi, 21, 62, 79, 97, 100, 214, 241, 279, 303, 308, 327
    from infant observation 35, 185
    and teaching (course) 3
    see also becoming an analyst
learning disability 237
negative capability 15, 31, 84, 86
non-verbal communication 144, 163, 226
not-knowing 86, 97, 215
object/ object relations xxiii, 27, 29, 58, 75, 78, 106, 156, 158, 166, 179, 194, 201, 215, 238, 252, 253, 293, 299, 321
    absent object xxiv, 26, 182, 259
    autistic object 202, 204
    from birth 250, 283, 305
    good object 86, 87, 91, 192, 198, 199, 206
    part-object 198, 208
    persecutory/ bad 149, 204, 246, 262
    psychoanalytic object (Bion) 156
    see also container
observation, participant 36
observation, psychoanalytic 35, 47ff, 78
observer, experience of 27ff, 36, 46ff, 69, 78-80, 103, 104, 159, 171, 201
    see also third eye
Oedipus complex 201, 204, 207-10
omnipotence 49, 123, 147, 212
personality development/ growth 11, 12, 46, 50, 78-80, 87, 103, 110, 146, 181, 200ff, 217, 241, 252, 279, 283, 313-14, 321
    growing point 77ff
    and introjection 158
    problems in 27, 71, 251, 323
    seminars in 85, 216, 217, 267-68
    the therapist's xxv, 13ff, 36, 64, 72, 220, 258, 262, 263, 268, 279, 287, 310, 317
play as symbol-formation 48, 97-98, 203, 207, 150, 244, 299

post-Kleinian thinking 54, 62, 82
prenatal life/ placenta 46, 111ff, 154-58, 181
primitive states 91, 96, 115, 166, 201, 209, 210, 219, 259
respectful experience 84
reverie 92, 106, 144, 161, 252, 259, 274
schools, working in 14, 22, 24, 49, 63, 66, 100, 160-61, 213, 229, 257ff, 313ff
   emotional aspects of learning and teaching (course) 3
   therapeutic groups in *see* special/ protected time
second skin 71, 74, 82, 104
separation 54, 93, 100, 101, 119, 122, 166, 183ff, 204, 155-57, 282
self-scrutiny 79, 84, 97, 333
self-selection, assisted xxv, 4, 10, 253, 271, 344
siblings 16, 272, 276
special/ protected time in schools 100-101, 259, 332-33
subjective/ objective 47, 188, 274
supervision technique 6, 14, 54, 64, 71, 74, 85ff, 104, 114ff, 142, 154ff, 171ff, 198, 201, 150-51, 218, 221, 227, 244-45, 274, 283, 289, 299, 310, 326
Tavistock model courses 9, 37, 58, 66, 75
theory, role of 1, 10, 19, 39, 48, 50, 79, 100, 104, 199, 218, 227, 251, 269
third eye/ third position 78, 103, 202, 286, 291, 301
   v. voyeuristic eye 79
two-dimensionality 27, 78, 82
unintegration 78, 87, 166

work discussion seminar 3-5, 10, 13, 29, 59, 79, 100, 159, 213, 237, 317
work group 17, 42, 60, 303, 317, 328
work with parents seminar 222, 244
young child observation 22, 59, 75, 244